THE TRANSFORMATIONAL LEADERSHIP COMPASS

THE TRANSFORMATIONAL LEADERSHIP COMPASS

A Dynamic Coaching System
for Creating Big Change

BENNY AUSMUS

THE TRANSFORMATIONAL LEADERSHIP COMPASS
A Dynamic Coaching System for Creating Big Change

ISBN 978-1-5445-1741-4 *Hardcover*
978-1-5445-1739-1 *Paperback*
978-1-5445-1740-7 *Ebook*

Dedicated to the good, the true, and the beautiful.

CONTENTS

SYLLABUS

Installation 1: **TLC**: Install the **TLC** system into your mind.

Installation 2: **Status Quo**: Map where you are and plan your next actions as you go.

Installation 3: **Leadership**: Define, declare, and develop your leadership.

Installation 4: **North Star**: Define and declare the direction of your company.

Installation 5: **Change Agents**: Select your change agents and create your charter.

Installation 6: **Culture**: Understand your culture and how to shape your new normal.

Installation 7: **Brand**: Refine and express your authentic brand to the market.

Installation 8: **Events:** Run a calendar of improvement workshop events.

Installation 9: **Assets:** Co-create clear plans and reference points for your transformation.

Installation 10: **Teams:** Build and develop highly effective teams.

Installation 11: **Games:** Design systems of effective management.

Installation 12: **Results:** Track the data and facts and collaborate on strategy.

Installation 13: **Player:** Attract, select, develop and retain your valuable players.

Installation 14: **Rhythm:** Embed a consistent rhythm of communication and practice.

INTRODUCTION

"To be honest, I want to change *everything*. For starters, I'm thinking of changing my job title from CEO to cat-herding firefighter. I can't leave for a holiday or even take a day off without worrying that it will all fall to pieces. And that's when things are going well."

John, the brilliant but battle-scarred CEO, took a long sip from his glass of red, furrowed his brow, and looked me straight in the eye. He continued, "Whenever we have a crisis, a disaster, bad news from the market, or COVID-19, we find ourselves in total chaos.

"I don't think we handle change well at all. We get by, but it always seems like we are operating in survival mode, swimming as hard as we can but staying in the same place, our heads bobbing just above the water. We try to put new strategies in place, commit to new ways of doing things to improve the way we work, but we always seem to go back to our old ways as soon as the pressure is on.

"When we do solve problems, it's like Whack-A-Mole.[1] We hit one and three more pop up in different areas. That's why I called you. They say you are good at seeing the whole picture, and that your approach goes beyond the surface-level problems.

"Look, I don't mean to paint a bleak picture. We have a very good company. I just wish people would take the initiative and responsibility to make it great and work together to make things better. I want to create a legacy here, something that keeps growing and stands the test of time. The problem is that no one steps up. It's like they don't even know where to start.

"Sometimes it seems like everybody here is out for themselves, moving in their own directions for their own careers, and doing their own things for their own agendas, their own little circles of friends and allies. They just do what they have to do to get through the day before they run off home to complain about it."

John took a deep breath. "The truth is, Benny, the whole thing is very complicated. I know we need to change; I'm just not sure where to start. Here. I made a list of what I think we need to get this company to where it needs to be." John

---

1 Whack-A-Mole is an arcade game from the '70s. The term is used to describe a systemic series of problems in computer programming, and debugging it refers to the act of fixing a bug that creates another bug needing to be fixed. Carl Brown, "Strategies for App Development Success: What Could Possibly Go Wrong?" InformIT, July 23, 2014, https://www.informit.com/articles/article.aspx?p=2235828&seqNum=14.

reached into his briefcase and pulled out a Moleskin notepad, and I read the first page.

We need to:

- *Remain profitable as we grow in size.*
- *Develop* **leadership** *capability in our people.*
- *Manage and improve the performance of our people.*
- *Build a strong* **culture** *that we can feel proud to be a part of.*
- *Build a* **brand** *people recognise and trust in the market.*
- *Develop the foresight and discipline to develop and execute our strategy.*
- *Find a better way of innovating, collaborating, and working together.*

John continued. "The truth is, I want to transform this company. I want a legacy that outlives my time here, something that keeps on going and growing long after I have hung up my boots."

I asked John what he had tried in the past. "We have tried all sorts of programs and trainings. Nothing has been effective long-term; it just does not seem to move the needle on our performance or our profits."

"I want a complete system of transformation. I'm sick of all of these ad-hoc trainings we do. I want something that brings it all together, something we can all wrap our heads around and make work."

I could see where John was coming from. I had spent the past two days getting to know the people at his company. I went to their meetings. I interviewed people from all roles at all levels.

I ate lunch with them, I asked a lot of questions, and over time, they began to open up to me to help me understand their world. As I got to know the people, they would tell me things like:

- "Everyone here is just out for themselves, trying to make a name for their career."
- "People don't really work together as a **team**."
- "It's all about getting one up and proving yourself over the next guy."
- "We are constantly reacting to the next problem and never getting to the real issues."
- "We have been so caught up in the fast demands of the business, we don't even know who we are as a company anymore."

I stood there looking at the old values posters plastered on the walls in their offices. Reflecting on words like "**team**work, collaboration, excellence, and communication." In reality, they were faded posters that seemed like ancient artefacts, remnants of a board room exercise that never went further than an offsite workshop.

It may seem strange, but in most of my talks with the staff, there was a strong but quiet desire to make things better, to improve the whole company and to transform the workplace. In all truth, this was not strange to me, because I saw elements of this in every company that I visited.

The people wanted change. They wanted to make the company better. They knew there was a better way, but they were stuck. So instead, they waited for something, going through the motions half-awake, occasionally dreaming of a new and better world but still waiting—waiting and wanting their **leaders** to tell them what would come next.

Now their new CEO, John, a legend in business, was waiting for me to tell him what would come next. "Benny, we need a way to get them all moving, working, and growing together as one company, not just a bunch of individuals. Can you help us make it happen?"

I knew I could. This was not my first rodeo, but I had problems of my own. I knew what to do next, the right questions to ask, and the right advice to give, all based on the studies and experiences I had received over the years. I knew how to transform a company's **culture**, to develop and shape leaders, and how to get the whole business moving together. My problem was that I was reaching capacity in my coaching and consulting practice. There are only so many hours in a day, and I wanted to help as many leaders as possible. We needed to teach this system to others. That's why I created this book.

TLC stands for **T**ransformational **L**eadership **C**ompass. This book captures the same methodology I have developed to help all of the leaders and companies I work with. It will help you improve every area of your business by developing **transformational leadership** capability in yourself and in your people.

WHO IS THIS BENNY AUSMUS GUY ANYWAY?

Fair Question. My name is Benny Ausmus, and I've spent the last ten years working closely with leaders to help them *transform* their companies. I am a trusted advisor, coach, facilitator, and *change agent* working to help these leaders create their *new normal.* This involves developing updated and upgraded

leadership and management practices embraced by all and aligned in harmony.

I've worked with yogurt factories, IT consultancies, telecommunications firms, tech businesses, flying trapeze schools (seriously), manufacturers, accounting firms, recruitment companies, web developers, real estate agencies, and just about every sort of business and industry you could imagine.

I live in Melbourne, Australia, with my amazing wife, Fernanda, and I'm lucky to have two wonderful kids, Tyler and Nile.

In all truth, I love the work that I do. I get out of bed each morning and find myself immersed in the challenging, difficult, and rewarding work of business transformation with leaders I respect and admire. I am not an academic. I am an autodidact, one who has learned by reading, applying, and reflecting. That said, the **TLC** is not something I just made up out of my own experiences and ideas. Rather, this methodology is an attempt to integrate hundreds of years of research, thinking, and theory developed by people far smarter than me across many disciplines. I have brought these methods together in the most teachable way I know possible.

Through reading, applying, reflecting, and documenting what works best in making a company-wide transformation successful, I have developed the **TLC**. It draws from and attempts to bring together theories and research in the areas of:

- **Leadership** development
- Management theory
- Systems thinking
- Integral theory

- Developmental psychology
- Organisational development
- Change management
- Organisational culture change
- Agile project management
- Coaching
- Facilitation
- Strategy and execution
- Business intelligence
- **Brand** development

The saying "standing on the shoulders of giants" certainly holds some truth here. However, I must add a caveat that although the **TLC** references draw from hundreds of theories and years of research, it is not at all perfect. It does not claim to seamlessly integrate all of these bodies of knowledge. If I have, in my haste to get this out, misquoted or failed to reference any of the many geniuses who unknowingly contributed to my thinking, I offer my sincerest apologies.

To be clear, the **TLC** is not a simple model, and transforming a company is not a simple process. It requires a dynamic understanding of many elements to successfully transform. The **TLC** system is complete in the sense that it covers all of the elements required to transform the living system that is your company. The **TLC** system itself is always evolving and improving based on the latest tools to serve the transformational **leader** in their work.[2]

---

2 Upgrades will be made available online at our website at *bigchangeagency.com* as plug-ins to each element of the system.

My commitment to you, dear reader, is that I will do my very best to impart the things I have learnt from my work in a way that is as clear, inspiring, and practical as possible.

You can reach me directly with questions and feedback at *benny@bigchange.group*.

So how do we do it? How do we create BIG change in businesses, over and over?

I am going to give you my secret system. I am going to give you the **TLC**.

JOHN'S NEW NORMAL

Twelve months after our initial meeting, I sat with John at the same bar. This time, we enjoyed a much better bottle of red wine.

"When we started on this journey, Benny, I was worried about losing control of the company. Through this **TLC** journey, I have developed a lot more trust in those around me. It's a different world here now. People know how to take the lead and how to share information to make better decisions. They have the balance of freedom and responsibility to make the company better every single day."

I had to agree with John. There was a fresh buzz about the place. You could feel it, see it, and most importantly, you could measure it. Departments and **teams** huddled in their daily **rhythm** of stand-up meetings, in person and online. They discussed and shaped their **culture** as they shared their stories, marked up their **game** charts, met the day's challenges, and solved the latest problems together. All hands were in to help, and everybody had a voice in improving things each day. This was their **new normal**—a world of constant growth and improvement.

Communication was clear, visible, and consistent across the whole business, and leaders from every level of the company held conversations that shared and shaped beliefs about who they were and what was most important. They had won the hearts and minds of their people, and this enabled them to produce extraordinary **results**. Productivity and efficiency had gone up by over 45 percent and showed no signs of slowing down. Profits soared, and staff-engagement scores doubled.

The company won a "Best Place to Work" award and talent flocked to their recruitment department for a chance to be part of something they had heard was more than just another job. The company had gone from the old-world **status quo** of command and control to its **new normal** of trust and track, a world of continuous growth, and improvement. John looked like a different person, and he was even ready to take that holiday he had been dreaming of since he started in the role.

What happened here, and how was this all possible?

They learned how to use the ***TLC*** *system.*

WHY ARE YOU READING THIS BOOK?

This may seem presumptuous, but I am going to try and guess why you are here. It's the same fundamental reason all of my clients seek me out. Essentially, you are here because you want things to be better. Like John, you want things to improve. Maybe it is because of some crisis, and you have to improve or die, or maybe it's just that you want to make things better than they are right now.

Right? Good, I sincerely respect and admire you and your efforts. Transformation is tough and complex work.

WHO IS JOHN?

John is not a real person; he's a literary construct. I know many of my clients will wonder if they are John. Let me assure you; you are not John. John is a composite character made up of the many challenges my clients have faced. He is a blending of hundreds of leaders I have had the honour of facing challenges with. I have included John's story at the start of each installation to help paint a picture of the old-world **status quo** and the **new normal** to help you imagine and reflect upon what is possible in your company.

You may have all, some, or none of John's problems at your company. As you certainly know, there is always room for improvement. Truth be told, I like to think there is a bit of John in all of us.

THE POWER OF THE TLC

It is my conviction that the ultimate competitive advantage is a unified **culture**, expressed through an **authentic brand**, and bolstered by effective and efficient **leadership** systems of decision-making, feedback, and improvement. Competitors can copy your strategy, mimic your marketing, and steal your playbook, but they can never duplicate your **culture** and the living system that makes a truly great company what it is. The hard truth is that this is not easy, and you need some powerful tools to help you on your way. **TLC** is a dynamic coaching system designed to guide this transformation.

Management guru, Peter Drucker, once said, "Only three things happen naturally in organisations: Friction, confusion, and underperformance. Everything else requires **leadership**."[3] That's where you, the **TLC leader**, steps up and in.

You are going to need to push against the current **status quo** to bring calm and order to chaos and create your **new normal**. At times, the transformation journey will be tough and uncomfortable, and it will require a strong commitment from you to realise a better future. The truth is, most people would rather accept things the way they are and stick with the **status quo** for as long as possible. If you're happy with things the way they are, this book is not for you. I don't want to waste your time.

However, if you are ready to embark on a journey of transformation, experience personal and professional growth, take people on a journey with you, and truly lead in difficult times, then read on. I'm writing in earnest for you and your people.

This book is for existing and aspiring leaders of companies and organisations of all shapes and sizes. If you, like me, are open-minded and an evergreen learner who knows you don't know everything and are called to step up to the unending challenge of change and improvement every day, then the **TLC** will help you. I wrote this for those who value growth,

3 Peter Drucker, *The Essential Drucker: In One Volume the Best of Sixty Years of Peter Drucker's Essential Writings on Management* (New York: Harper Collins, 2001).

developing the potential of their people, and who see their own life and work as an ongoing path of growth and learning.

The **TLC** is best suited for those who:

- Have the humility to know that they don't have the answers and the courage to seek the truth through inquiry and reflection.
- Continue to develop self-awareness to search for their own blind spots, uncover their own areas for work, and face each challenge as an opportunity to grow.
- Those who value meaning, growth, and profits for the purpose of improving their lives and the lives of those around them.
- Those who want to thrive and help others thrive, to fight and drive to make tomorrow better than today.
- Those who courageously take thoughtful and decisive action and know small daily efforts lead to BIG changes in **results**.

Making BIG change happen is the brave work of the transformational **leader**. Yes, the work of transformational change can be difficult, and it often requires persistence, courage, and strength. The leaders who step up to this challenge will often find themselves in moments of doubt, confusion, and even chaos. This book is a guide to help lead you through these times. Herewith is a system of tools to make it all fit together, to make sense of an increasingly complex world, and to take the right action at the right time to develop your **leadership** capability. In doing so, you will also develop the world around you.

It is with the deepest respect for transformational and integrative **leadership** that I present the **TLC**.

THE PROMISE OF THIS BOOK

The **TLC** will assist you in creating transformational change in your company.

I assume you are a **leader** who does not have a huge amount of free time on their hands. Thousands of books about business and **leadership** are published every single year. We live in an age where information is available at our fingertips; however, we seldom have the time or attention to be able to organize this knowledge in a practical way. Although nothing as complex as transformation is ever simple, I have done my best to make this work as simple, sharable, and practical as possible.

The **TLC** will help you develop the thinking required to become a better **leader**. It will give you a simple language to teach others so you can be on the same page and move in the same direction toward a better future, a **new normal**.

The **TLC** is not a book. It is an operating system. You can think of the **TLC** like mental software.

Your success will be revealed in how you use this system to improve your world.

I am not here to tell you what to think; I wouldn't dream of that arrogance. I am here to help develop and enhance how you think about everything you decide to take responsibility for. There are so many geniuses in so many fields that no one can fathom all the wisdom and apply it all. However, I have done my best to save you time and to deliver this information in a way that is true, clear, and highly practical. I hope you enjoy the **TLC** like a fine wine, whiskey, tea, or whatever steadies your engine and floats your boat.

HOW TO APPROACH THE TLC

As you move through these passages, you will find questions and *reflection points*. Take these points as opportunities to write your own notes and your own application of this thinking in your own unique situation. You will also find that each chapter contains exercises. Make the time to work through these practical steps as you go through your transformation journey. At the end of this book, you will find a series of benchmarks presented as assessment questions. These are designed for you to assess whether you have successfully installed the complete dynamic **TLC** system into your company.

I invite you to invest the time to absorb, reflect on, and understand these principles. Then take the steps to apply this knowledge. If you do, I promise you will experience a true transformation within your company. That means better and more sustainable **results**.

Now buckle up, dear reader. We are about to install the Transformational **Leadership** Compass into your mind.

"LEARN HOW TO SEE. REALIZE THAT EVERYTHING CONNECTS TO EVERYTHING ELSE."

—LEONARDO DA VINCI

INSTALLATION 1

TLC

TRANSFORMATIONAL LEADERSHIP COMPASS

Before we begin the first installation of the **TLC**, it is necessary to get familiar with the simple language of the **TLC** system. You will find these terms throughout this book in **bold**, and as you read on, you will deepen your understanding of each term and how each term works together to make up this dynamic system of transformation.

I recommend you read the following definitions on this page three times over to embed this language in your memory and to set you up for a powerful **TLC** learning experience.

TLC LEXICON

- **Leadership.** The practice of taking responsibility in decision-making for all of the elements of the **TLC** (listed below).
- **North Star.** The guiding direction of the company consisting of the vision, mission, values, BIG goals, standards, and principles.
- **Status quo.** The current state of affairs in our life, company, and world.
- **New normal.** The improved and sustainable change that the **TLC leader** creates.
- **Culture.** The internal, deeply held and taken-for-granted beliefs and assumptions of a group or company of people who remain consistent over time.
- **Brand.** The external and expressed representation and promise of the company to the market and the world.
- **Events.** Planned, collaborative workshop sessions to change and improve the company.
- **Assets.** Documented outputs of **events** used as reference points for change.
- **Rhythm.** The habits and cycles of communication and practices of the individual **player**, **teams**, and the company.
- **Teams.** Groups of **players** that agree on and work toward a common goal or purpose.
- **Player.** An individual and unique person attracted, selected, and developed within the company.
- **Results.** Objective facts and data captured and used to inform and develop strategy.

- **Games.** The **TLC** system of management. **Games** is an acronym for goals, activities, measures, expectations, and support.
- **VUCA.** Volatile, Uncertain, Complex, Ambiguous environments and circumstances.

Make sure you read these definitions three times before we go deeper into their meaning and dynamics. It will serve you well. Finished? Great, now let's take another look at John's world.

JOHN'S OLD-WORLD STATUS QUO

It was yet another strategy session in John's boardroom. Coffee was pouring, yet eyes were rolling as the confusing and convoluted stream of jargon and management speak made an already complicated mess even more difficult for the **leadership team** to understand.

"Our OKRs and KRAs and KPIs need to be more agile so our systems can be lean and build our synergy by practising continuous improvement," said the head of strategy.[4]

Half the room had a look on their faces that seemed to say, "Wait, what? What do you mean?"

It seemed like every other quarter the company would introduce the next flavour of the month and another set of management fads and terms that served only to confuse the situation and bamboozle the workers with more and more

4 OKRs—Objectives and Key Results; KRAs—Key Result Areas; Agile—A system of project management based on fast iteration of testing ideas.

"management speak." All this noise and babbling on was enough to make the geekiest head spin.

While everyone was doing their best to demonstrate how clever they were, they had failed to engage their people in the journey. This problem was one of the many reasons why so many earlier transformation efforts had failed. In order to truly work together to build something greater, they needed to get a simple, clear language that would allow them to communicate, collaborate, and grow together.

The executives and the managers weren't the only ones who needed clarity. The entire company had to understand what was happening. They needed a shared and simple language that would help them navigate the necessary changes. After all, these days, we pay people to think and relate, not just to do simple tasks—that's what the robots are for. In order to get everyone working together in unity, we need to share and understand the basic language of what we are doing here. This allows the employees to help, be a part of the transformation, and be of value together in the company.

JOHN'S NEW NORMAL

We taught the **TLC** method. Soon after, the foundations were set. Every person in the company knew the simple and clear definitions of the **TLC**. They all understood clearly what great **leadership** meant at their company; it was defined and declared by John. They knew what we meant by **north star**, and they understood the direction the company was heading.

They knew what **culture** meant to the company: what we take for granted as deeply held beliefs. They could see that

brand is how our customers experience us through our interactions and our products. They knew that the **new normal** was the set of behaviours we made consistent, and that became the deeply held beliefs of our **culture**. They practiced their **rhythm** of communication in their daily huddles and project meetings and developed the consistent discipline of feedback and improvement day by day.

For the first time, employees were involved in **events** to work on improving the company from the ground up. They co-created **assets** to help shape the business in the future, and together they built their capability to change fast and deal with disruptions in the market and the economy. They knew how to have a **team** ethos conversation and to guide and shape common beliefs together and uphold them as a group. They felt productive and empowered in their **games** and enjoyed how the **games** worked to measure progress and found a productive flow in their work. They also knew that **games** are how they can plan and propose their actions to reach their BIG goals together.

They knew that **results** were the facts we collected to measure our progress and plan our next moves and strategies. They saw themselves and those around them as active **players** in making the change happen.

Some had a basic understanding of what each of these terms meant and were along for the ride. Others went deeper still, developing a rich understanding of each element of the **TLC** and how the elements affect each other.

We now had a very simple language that everyone could speak, and we used this framework of language to build a new world together, a **new normal.** The journey was well underway with everyone speaking the simple language of the **TLC.**

WHAT YOU'LL LEARN AND DO IN THIS INSTALLATION

In this installation, we take a quick look at each part of the TLC. By the end of this installation, you will have installed the TLC into your own thinking as a mental model. You will also be able to communicate it to your company to get everyone speaking the same clear, straightforward language, so you can bring them all along for the journey. After all, transformational leadership is about bringing your people with you.

It is important to note here that the TLC is an ongoing process and, as you will see, each element of the TLC affects every other element. It is dynamic and alive, just like your company and just like you. Each installation will more fully explain each of the elements of the TLC system to help you and your people on their journey of transformation. In the following pages, we take a helicopter ride over the TLC and deepen our understanding of each element and dynamic of the TLC system.

Ready?

VUCA

We live in an increasingly volatile, uncertain, complex, ambiguous (VUCA) world.

In very simple terms, VUCA[5] is:

5 This term first came to be in 1987 and was referred to in the leadership theories of Warren Bennis and Burt Nannus.

- **Volatility**—The ups and downs of changing situations.
- **Uncertainty**—The lack of predictable outcomes or **results**.
- **Complexity**—The problem of not knowing what action produced a **result** because there are so many interrelated things going on.
- **Ambiguity**—An unclear, foggy picture of the world, seen differently by different people leading to further confusion and more **VUCA**.

In our **VUCA** world, external and internal forces are constantly challenging us to grow and develop how we respond and adapt to change.

A market that keeps changing and shifting, surrounded by people with complex wants, needs and desires adrift a sea of competitors can only be described as **VUCA**. Similarly, COVID-19 placed the world in chaos and created a scary place where change is the only constant for all. These forces come through like waves and shake our company and **leadership**, demanding change and adaptation in exchange for survival and growth.

VUCA is not just in the external world, crashing our party and making things harder. It is also inside our company and inside each of us. The **TLC leader** is responsible for constantly winning the battle over **VUCA** and bringing order and calmness to the company. This is not set-and-forget, nor a one-time process. Although victory in battle over **VUCA** is sweet and valuable, it is a war that never ends. This is part of the ongoing practice of transformational **leadership**.

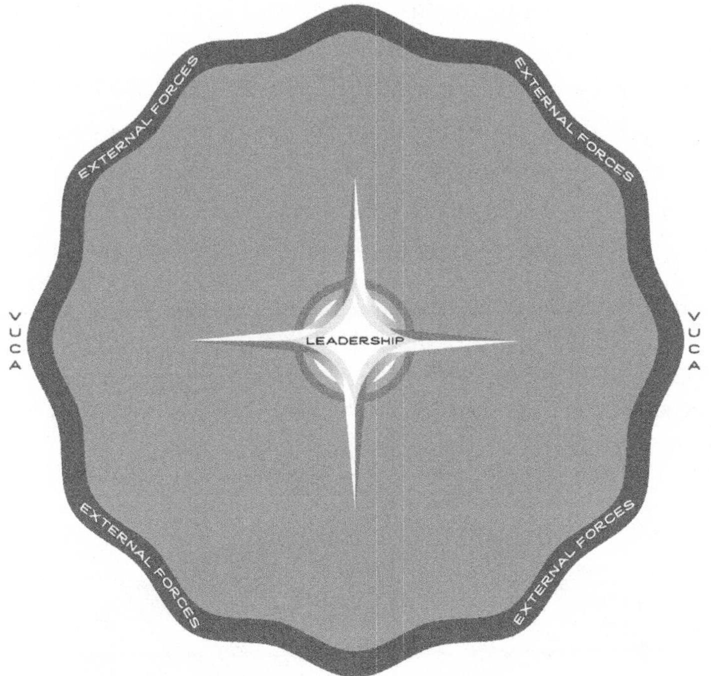

LEADERSHIP

In the midst of this **VUCA** world, we find ourselves probing, sensing, acting, thinking, and attempting to make effective decisions.

We ask ourselves questions such as:

- What do we do next?
- What is the most effective Strategy?
- Where do we go from here?
- How do we deal with this person, this problem, this pain?

The only certainty in the world of **VUCA** is there will be constant uncertainty. Your ability to bring certainty and consistency to situations as they emerge will be your strength as a transformational **leader**. In order to grow, we must embrace the change and brace for **VUCA**. We must become strong and flexible to not only remain relevant but also to grow and expand as times change.

In order to face changes and emerge with a larger sphere of influence and the required understanding of the situation, we need to shift and shape our thinking. In the middle of **VUCA**, we rely on our ability to navigate the waves of chaos, where **leadership** is most needed. The **TLC** helps you make the right decisions and have the right conversations at the right time to go from chaos to calmness, as illustrated below.

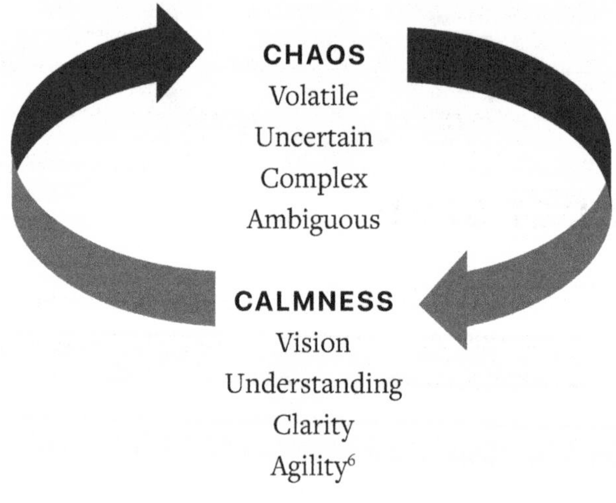

6 This VUCA model is called VUCA Prime and is borrowed and adapted respectfully from the great Bob Johansen.

The **TLC** is the compass to calmness, the instrument that the transformational leader uses to reach **VUCA** prime. Or, in the words of Bob Johansen, "Vision, Understanding, Clarity and Agility."

This is a constant dance. We don't move from **VUCA** chaos to total calmness where everything is fine and dandy with beer and Skittles forever. If that were the case, we would have no need for transformational **leadership**. Rather, there is a constant process of change, growth, and adaptation with **leadership** placed firmly in the centre to steer the ship. The **TLC** allows us to bring our people along for this ongoing journey and to work together to find new and better ways to grow.

When we do well using the **TLC**, we expand our **TLC** through our **culture** and **brand**. Then the **TLC** takes up more space. It brings consistency, certainty, simplicity, and clarity to more of the world, and we earn more customers, make more money, and grow our businesses to have a bigger impact and influence on the world around us.

Not only do we become better at adapting to change, we also become so strong and balanced that we benefit from changes around us while our competitors drown in an ocean of **VUCA**. We go deep into **leadership** in the installation titled, you guessed it: **leadership**.

NORTH STAR

Of course, we need direction.

The **north star** is the direction and desired destination; it's where **leadership** is taking us. It is the direction in which we define and use to guide and align every **leader, team, game, player**, and **result. North star** consists of the company's vision, mission, values statements, company-wide standards, BIG goals, and first principles. This is the BIG picture that unites everyone on the same journey. Without a strong **north star**, we are adrift in the ocean of **VUCA**, paddling for dear life, all in different directions.

Your **north star** will be defined very clearly and thoughtfully so that everyone in the company knows it and knows how to head towards it. When defined poorly, it lacks strategic thinking. It is hidden away, only known to a few. Decisions are not made based on it, and it amounts to just another shitty MBA exercise that's done for the sake of checking a box, and it tends not to affect any sort of positive change. Quite often, I see elements of a company's **north star** sitting on a plaque in a hallway or at the start or end of an induction manual that is glanced over once and forgotten about. This is one of the fatal errors of leaders using a textbook vision mission values statement instead of the **north star** and the **TLC** system.

Done well, on the other hand, **your north star** directs all strategy and behaviour. Everyone is on board, aligned, and engaged towards moving forward in the same direction. A **TLC north star** gives clarity and direction to every single person who works for you. Every other element of the **TLC** lines

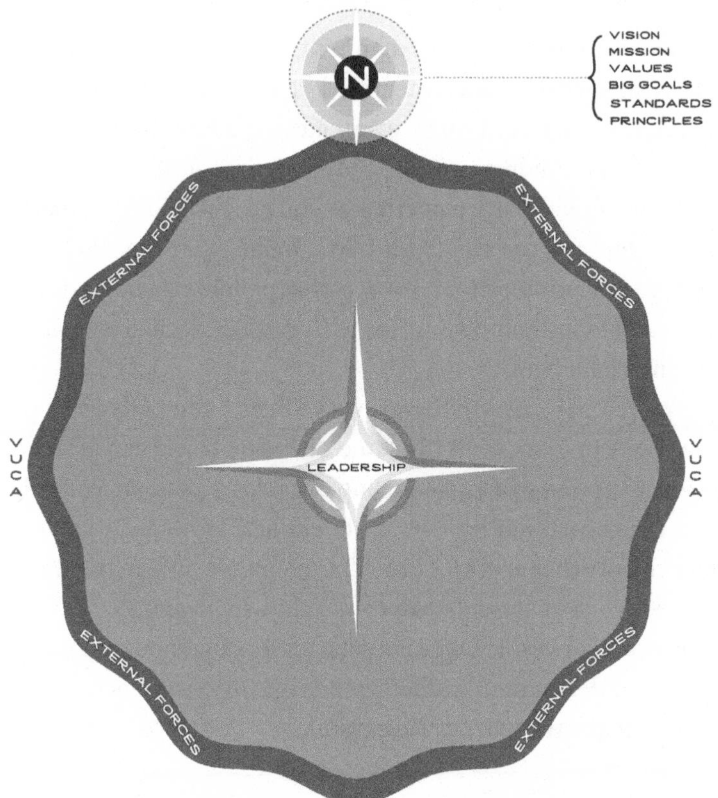

up to the **north star**. Therefore, it needs to be well-defined and communicated by **leadership** to frame the direction for every decision made within the company.

The exercises in this book will help you create a **north star** that inspires, impacts, and influences people to make better choices day to day. You will create (or work with the existing) vision for the business and the mission. The values we share can be articulated to help the organisation and individual calibrate their own compass to be able to move on this journey together. In the **north star** installation, we will look at how to establish our direction in a manner that's clear, concise, articulate, memorable, and integrated. Then, through the **TLC**, you can design and align everyone's thinking and journey towards this guiding light of focus and direction.

If you already have a **north star** you are thrilled with, that's great! You can use what you have already, and the **TLC** will help you communicate it in a way that people understand and can explain in their own terms with respect to their own ideals and challenges.

In creating the **north star**, we've begun the path of helping our people move in the same direction so we can achieve greater success as a unified company. As you read on, you will learn the **north star** by itself is not enough. However, when we pair the **north star** with other **TLC** elements and do the work to help each **team** and **player** develop their **games**, we not only get great **results**, we also get a group of people who share the same destination in their minds and know the actions to take to make the journey successful.

THE FOUR WINDOWS

The four windows are the elements of **TLC** thinking required to get the full picture and perspective of what's going on. In each of these installations, we will look at and through the windows in order to decide what to work on next and to determine where a challenge can be overcome. The four windows are as follows:

- **Results**: the facts and data
- **Games**: the systems of management

- **Player:** the individual person
- **Teams:** the group(s) of **players** working together

The four windows were inspired by Integral Theory philosopher Ken Wilber's Four Quadrants in his powerful and groundbreaking work.[7]

In order to develop a full perspective of anything, we need to look at it through these four windows.[8] As you look at and through these windows, recognise that each one affects and is affected by all of the others. This thinking is incredibly powerful in making effective decisions in the **VUCA** world. Now let's go a little deeper into each window.

---

7 Ken Wilber, *A Theory of Everything: An Integral Vision for Business, Politics, Science & Spirituality*. (US, Shambhala, 2001), and Ken Wilber, *Sex, Ecology, Spirituality: The Spirit of Evolution*, (Boulder, CO: Shambhala Publications, 2001).

8 In Ken's integral thinking, we look at the world through interior/exterior and individual/collective to get a more complete picture of the world around us.
- I—Individual Interior—Self, psychology, intentional, subjective, individual purpose, and values.
- WE—Group Interior—Worldview, meaning, and group values, intersubjective.
- IT—Objective Science, the facts, behaviour, empiricism.
- ITS—Systems, economics, and environment, inter-objective.

I have simplified these quadrants in **TLC** and also included **culture** as the larger **we**. This will make more sense as you read on.

RESULTS

Results are the facts, data, behavioural measures, accounting metrics, and performance figures. We can measure our **results** and use this information to help us create the right strategy to decide what to do next, to learn, and to grow. Yes, we are paid to achieve **results**. However, we cannot influence **results** directly. A **result** is just the facts and data. We can't just ask the **results** to change. We need to address it through the other windows and elements of the **TLC**.

We can, however, use **results** to inform our strategy, to see the patterns of what works and what doesn't, and decide what to do next. In order to improve our **results**, we need to create the right **games**, build the right **teams**, and develop and coach the individual **players** so we can achieve the outcomes we want and move towards our **north star**. We will go deeper into **results** and strategy in the installation titled **results**.[9]

9 Notice that the leader has waves rippling out from the centre into these four areas of focus. This is the power of the Transformational Leader's influence, sending waves of change and growth through the company and out into the world, rocking your competitors' boats and creating some made-at-home VUCA for your rivals.

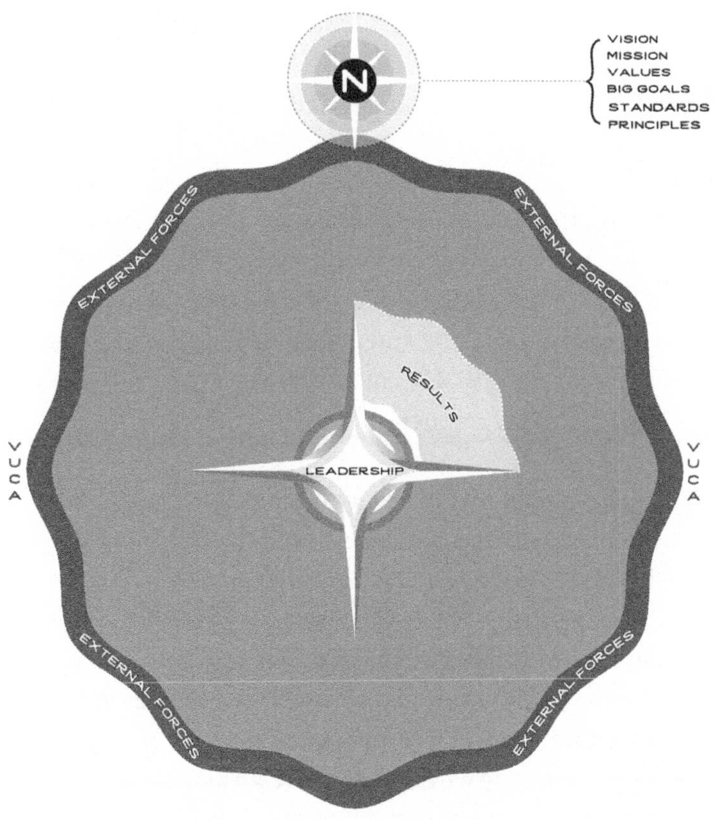
VISION
MISSION
VALUES
BIG GOALS
STANDARDS
PRINCIPLES
N
EXTERNAL FORCES
EXTERNAL FORCES
RESULTS
VUCA
LEADERSHIP
VUCA
EXTERNAL FORCES
EXTERNAL FORCES

GAMES

Games are the systems of management by which we achieve the **results** that guide our direction towards our **north star**. Whether we are playing to win or playing just to keep playing for the love of the **game**, we are playing **games. Games** are an effective way of engaging and managing people and progress in an ever-changing **VUCA** environment.

Games is a **TLC** acronym:

- Goals—What we are trying to achieve.
- Actions/Activities—What we need to do to make this happen effectively and efficiently.
- Measurements—How we measure and see our actions and progress clearly using scoreboards.
- Examples/Expectations—Examples of success and what we expect from each other as rules.
- Support—How we develop the **team** and **player** through the **games** and the feedback loop of **rhythm.**

Is it really that simple? No, there are simple, complicated, complex, and chaotic systems, and these systems can be made into **games**, and they each have a place within your **TLC.**[10]

In the **games** installation, I will clarify all of the above so you can learn to design and play good and even great **games.** Furthermore, we will learn how to give people an engaging

10 This thinking is inspired by David Snowden's Cynefin Framework created in 1999 as a "sense-making device."

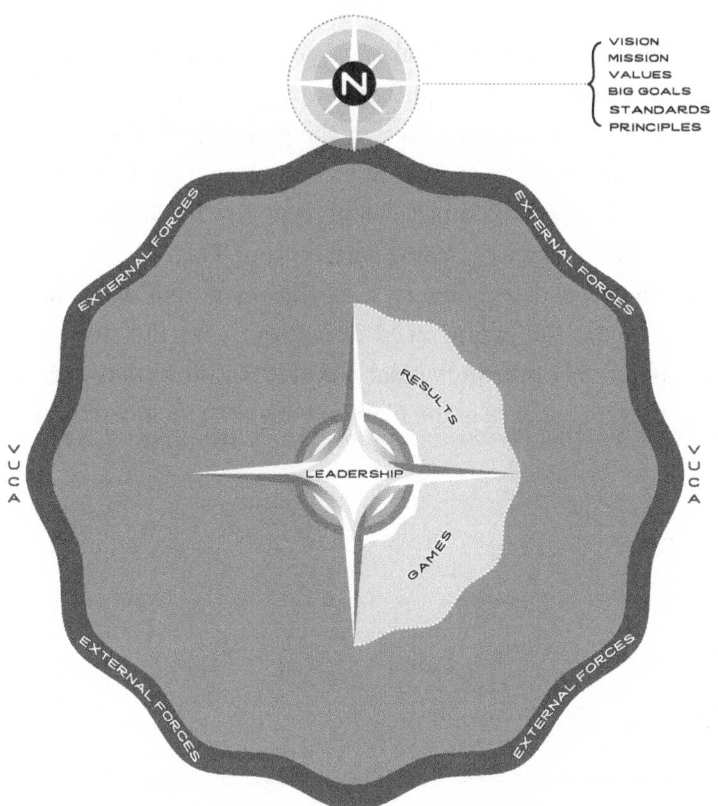

way to play the **games**. We design **games** with certain criteria in mind. Namely, where:

- We can make progress visible.
- We can see improvement.
- We have the fastest feedback possible to keep us engaged, on the hook, and continually on the edge of getting better.

We do this because it makes us more productive, and damn it, it makes work more fulfilling.

I encourage you to codesign the **games** with the **players and teams** through **events** and to do this often. Then, your **games** will develop, improve, and respond with flexible grace to the **VUCA** waves crashing hard on your **TLC**.

Games need to connect with the **team**, and also, most importantly, the **games** need to connect with the strengths and potential of the individual **player**. This allows every **team** and **player** to have a **game** plan that aligns to the **north star**.

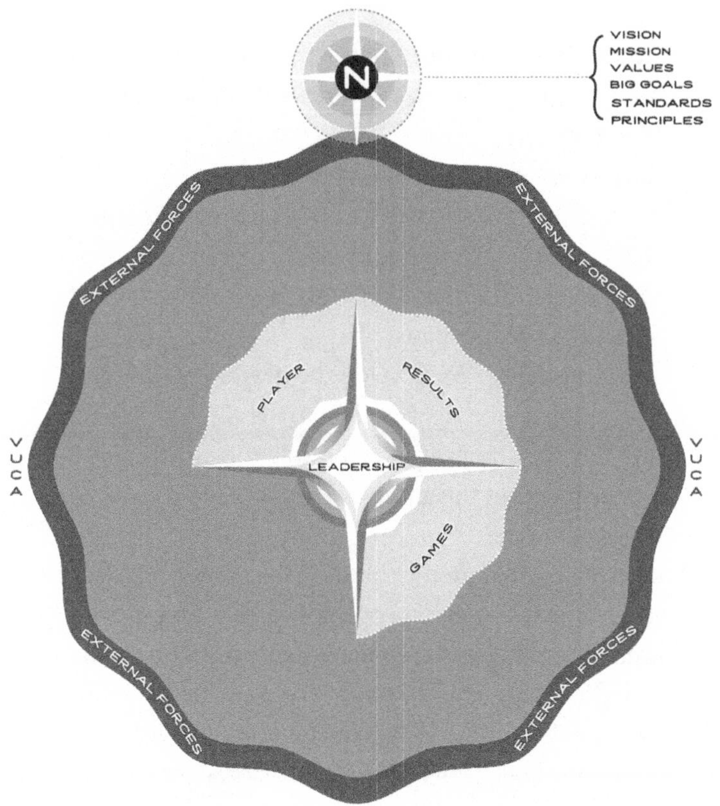

PLAYER

Players are your individual people, the unique and valuable humans who make up your company. Through the **players'** window, we assess attraction, selection, development, **results**, and retention of the individual **players** that we need to succeed.

- **Attraction**—We create the right **culture, brand, north star, teams**, and **games** to attract the best talent for your company.
- **Selection**—We assess if this person has the right personality and attitude for the **culture** and **team** ethos. Do they have the right skills and experience to match the **game**? Is their own **north star** in the same solar system as the company?
- **Development**—We develop the **players** we selected. They require the right coaching, the right assistance, and the right mentoring to be able to help them perform within the **games**.

We need a plan for doing this, and the **assets** of **players** are the maps we build to help people be better at the **games** and help them understand and connect with our **teams**. When we do this well, we are able to retain the right talent producing the right **results**. In the **player** installation, we learn how to effectively approach this with the **TLC** system.

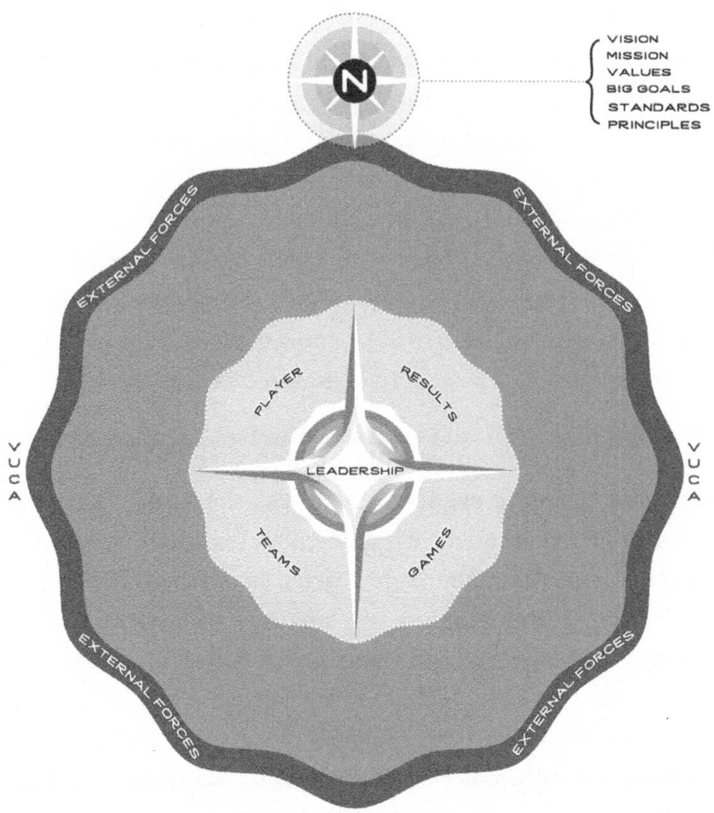

TEAMS

Teams are the groups of **players** working together to produce a **result** through a **game**.

Great **teams** share a collection of beliefs, understandings, and attitudes. They have a collective ethos that they work by, and it becomes who they are as a group. You can have your **north star**, the vision, the mission, the values of the company—everything necessary for the BIG picture—but unless your **teams** get it, understand it, and can articulate it in their own terms, it will mean nothing to them.

We define each **team's** own ethos at each level and align it to the direction of the **north star**. It's not sufficient to create a **north star** that engages everybody in a business with hundreds or thousands of staff. They will always feel left out of this process and disengage. In order to bring purpose, direction and transformation to life, people need to know why they are there as well as be able to communicate this in their own terms and understanding.

To use the power of our **players** and supercharge engagement, we facilitate **events** and express the **north star** with an **asset** of ethos and a clear **game** plan that our **teams** work together to create. Then we practice it in our **rhythm**.

Building **teams** requires the language of **leadership**, the language of **team** ethos, the language of belief. Have you ever seen somebody who is able to influence and move the people in a way that almost seems magical? Great leaders speak a language that paints a picture of change. In fact, brain research shows us that when we speak the language of possibility, belief, and, as Simon Sinek puts it, *why*, we engage the limbic brain and people are more likely to listen and participate.[11] You can think of your **teams** as smaller sub**culture**s within your company, each with their own nuances and purposes.

It is worth noting at this point that problems are rarely solved in the window that they appear. For example, a problem with a ***player*** *must be examined through the window and perspective of*

11 Simon Sinek, *Start with Why: How Great Leaders Inspire Everyone to Take Action*, (New York: Portfolio/Penguin, 2011).

*the **game** they are playing, the **results** they are producing, the **team** they are in, and more broadly, through the **culture** and **rhythm**.*

Now it's time to look at the bigger picture of our **culture**.

CULTURE

When we zoom out on the **TLC**, we encounter the nebulous blob called **culture**. You will notice that all the **TLC** content sits within the **culture** and, when shaped, aligned, and maintained, points towards your **north star. Your culture** can be made by accident, by putting people together, and by giving them objectives and seeing how they behave. Better yet, **culture** can be shaped purposefully through conscious and careful decisions and the inclusive facilitation of **events** led by transformational **leaders.**

Consider what **culture** is and what it is not. Let's use the example of Italy as a national **culture.** I want you to ask yourself, "What is the **culture** of Italy?"

You might think of many elements of this when thinking of Italian **culture.** It is about pasta, pizza, restaurants, a lifestyle of community and family, painting, opera, the romantic language, how people deal with each other, the attitudes, politics, history, the art, etc.

What do you notice here? **Culture** is everything we take for granted about the collective group. It's defined by the basic assumptions we hold together along with time-tested truths. The very word *culture* is said to be first used by the ancient Roman Orator Cicero where he described, using agricultural terms, the cultivation of the soul or cultura animi.[12]

It is deep, collective, and internal, made of shared norms and assumptions—poetically, it is the soul of the company.

---

12 Marcus Tullius Cicero, *Tusculane Disputationes Book II*, Cultura Animi Philosophia est. (Rome: 45 B.C.).

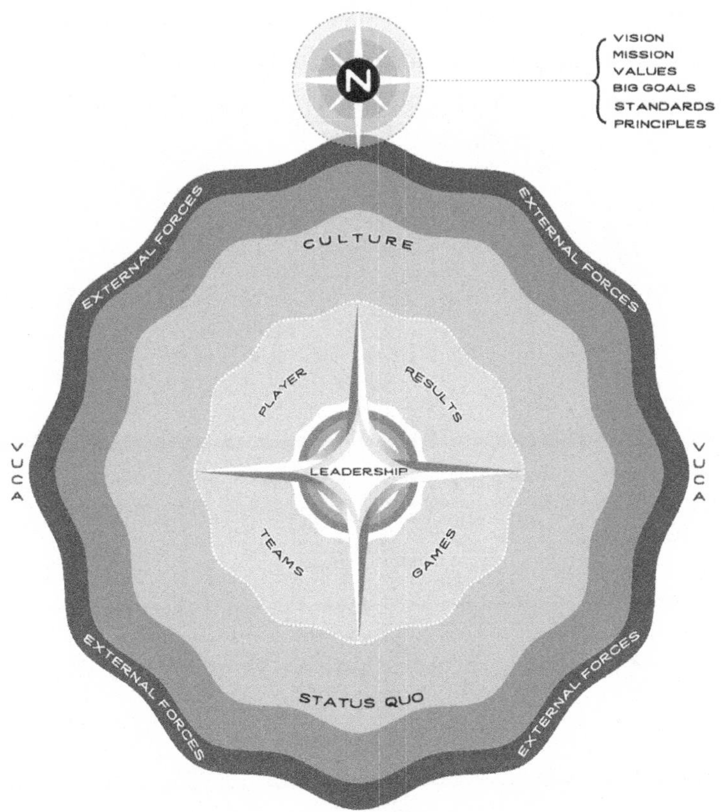

Culture is essence; everything inside the **TLC** that is stable and true. This also means, like **results**, that it can't be worked on directly. In order to transform **culture**, we have to look at all of the dynamic elements that give rise to it. When we look at it through the **TLC** windows, then we can shape and evolve this essence over time. In the **culture** installation, we will develop an understanding of what company **culture** is all about and share the thinking to help you create and evolve your **new normal**. You will also learn how to use the

TLC to shape your **culture** by helping your **players** shape their **teams, games**, and of course, the **results** you achieve through your **rhythm.**

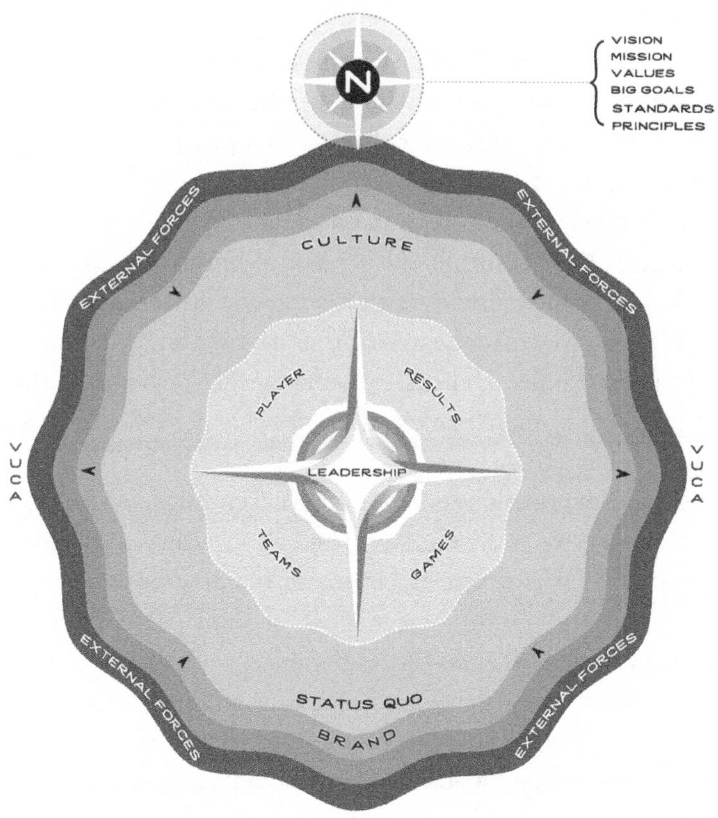

BRAND

Authentic **brand** in **TLC** language is an expression of your company **culture**.

The most authentic **brands** in the world are the **brands** that create a real sense of belonging around them. The purchases we make and the **brands** we choose to engage with and feel ownership around all share something in common. They represent a particular set of beliefs, a particular point of status, a special club, or community that people want to be a part of. Authentic **brand** is a reflection and expression of the company's internal **culture.** Authentic **brand** is about expressing what is true, good, and beautiful about who we are and what value we create in the world around us.

The **TLC** points from **culture** out to **brand** because true, authentic **brand** must be an expression of **culture**—an expansion of who we are to the world around us and an invitation to join as a customer or client. By using the **TLC**, we expand the **brand**, earning more market share, growing our influence and overcoming **VUCA.**

Brand evolves alongside your internal **culture** as an expression of who we really are, warts and all. It is an honest, true reflection of who we are as a business; not how we want to be perceived, and not the veneer, gloss, or shiny paint. Think of your customer. What do they experience when they deal with your **players**? How they experience your product or service is a **result** of how you're playing the **games**, as well as the quality of how the **players** work together in **teams** to create or provide value.

An authentic **brand** cannot be sustainable if the internal **culture** does not match the expression of **brand** that you promise to the marketplace. Sure, you might say, "We're X," and for a while, people might believe it. But if your people, processes, and their true beliefs and actions do not match what you're telling the market, then the invisible hand of the market will slap you right back into **VUCA.**

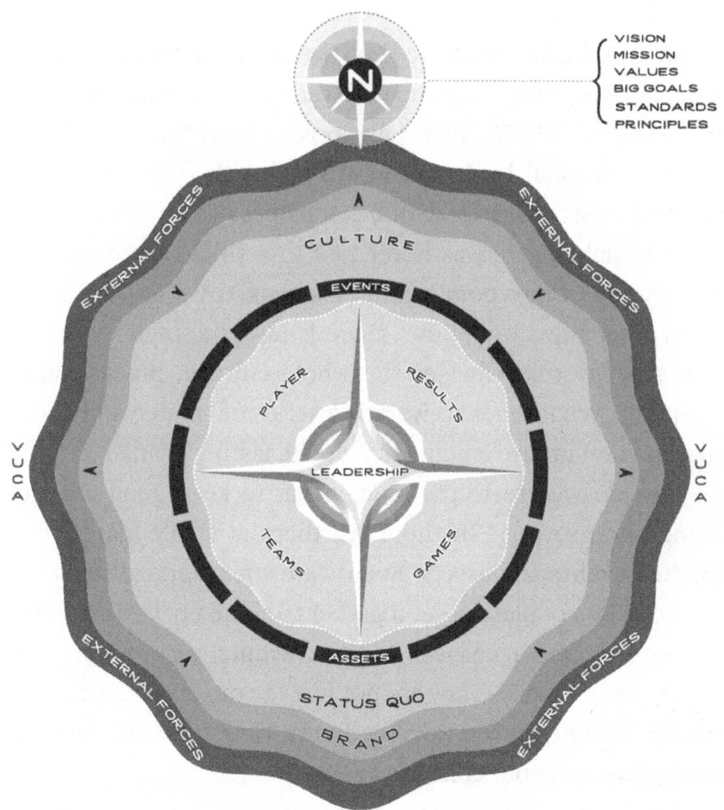

EVENTS AND ASSETS

You may be asking at this point, "How is all of this practical, Benny?" I'm glad you asked. The **leader** brings people together in an **event** and creates an **asset** that defines the company going forward for the foreseeable future.

An **event** is a facilitated session to work on improving the company.

An **asset** is the clearly documented output of the **event**.

We run regular **events** to keep the **assets** improving, evolving, engaging and to keep up with the ever-accelerating speed of change in **VUCA**. When we look at the literature where transformational **leaders** have worked with their people to create a massive change within companies, we find that transformational change was never tied to a single **event**, as the mighty Jim Collins points out in his book, *Great by Choice.*[13]

In great transformations, there is rarely a single **event** or one strategy that changes the whole **culture**, process, and company. What tends to work is a series of small **events** and incremental improvements that create lasting change.

How do we create the momentum to keep good change going and growing? In the **TLC**, there is a calendar wheel marked **events** and **assets**. **Events** are your planned sessions where **teams** of **players** get together to come up with an **asset** or improve existing **assets**. In these **events**, we work *on* and not *in* the company. They are not just for the executives; they are for anyone with a valuable brain. Hopefully, this means every **player** in your company.

Within the **TLC**, we set aside time for a series of **events** where we go through each element. We reflect, review, reset, redefine, and redesign at these **events**, and we involve everyone. In the process, we create **assets**.

An **asset** is the most powerful and simple representation of our next strategy, whether it is for the whole company, a department, a **team**, or an individual **player**. In the installation

13 Jim Collins and Morten T. Hansen, "Great by Choice: How to Manage through Chaos," *Fortune* (October 2011), https://www.jimcollins.com/article_topics/articles/how-to-manage-through-chaos.html.

on **events**, we build a calendar of sessions that occur throughout the year at regular intervals that allow us to continuously improve, evolve, and upgrade what we are doing and we learn how to set up an **event** for success as a facilitator.

The great and obvious secret here is that you need to involve your people in the process. The **TLC** is all about harnessing the collective power of people towards your **north star**.

Through **TLC events**, we learn to deal with great disruptions in **VUCA** by teaching our people to constantly adapt and adjust as we change and evolve together. Our goal is to create shifts towards company unity and ongoing improvement. We accomplish this through **assets** that our **players** create together. The purpose of these **events** is to harness the wisdom of the room and drive consensus to what needs to change. We also get commitment and accountability to fulfilling that change and a more powerful set of perspectives for better decision-making and strategy development.

Now, to make it all work together, we need to practice consistently and develop our company's collective discipline. As with any **asset**, the **assets** we create in our **events** appreciate or depreciate in value. **TLC assets** appreciate or depreciate in value based on how consistently they are practiced in the **rhythm** and appreciated by your **players**.

RHYTHM

Rhythm is the consistency of how we meet, communicate, and collaborate. It is the practice of what we say we will do, what we decide on and document as **assets** in our **events**, and how our behaviour reflects our promises and commitments to ourselves, our **team**, our **culture**, and our **brand**.

To make any change sustainable, we need the habit of **rhythm**.

Rhythm is our discipline of practice and communication. It is symbolised in the **TLC** as increments of time, like a clock.

I'll tell you right now; **rhythm** is usually the hardest thing to get right.

If **rhythm** is new to your company, it will need reinforcement by **leadership**. The great secret truth is that as **rhythm** becomes part of the **new normal** (the way we do things around here), it becomes self-managing. The group begins to coach, manage, and lead itself. Change comes through consistent focus. Focus becomes words, which become actions, which then become habits. Habits then become the **new normal**, our collective character and **culture**.

A **rhythm** of communication and an effective schedule of meetings and actions is required to make this happen in your company at every level, with every **team** and across **teams**.[14] You can think of **events** as a calendar and **rhythm** as a clock.[15]

Your communications **rhythm** is best served to happen every day for a short and highly valuable amount of time.

---

14 More on cross-functional teams in the teams installation.

15 This is conveniently displayed in the TLC image.

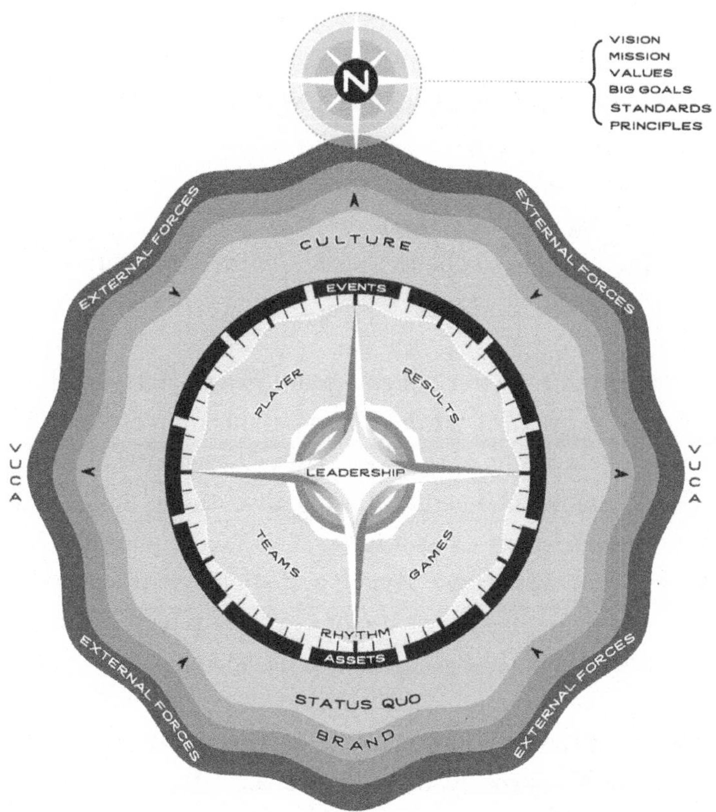

Eventually, this will be run and sustained by your **team**, and this is the early evidence that new **leadership** capability is emerging. You can see the **rhythm** in a daily stand-up meeting, or a huddle, or a project meeting, where **teams** get together consistently to work through the following:

- They realign to the **north star**.
- They share their stories that bolster the **team's** ethos and company **culture**.

- They discuss the **assets.**
- They look at the **games** and how they are doing through the scoreboards.
- They make commitments and adjustments about what is going to change today.
- Their behaviour changes a little bit every day in this **rhythm.**

The **rhythm** is your system of collective habits, and it is the most overlooked advantage an organization can have in achieving the vision of the **north star**. Consistently bringing people together at a certain time to discuss the things that matter most aligns us as a **team**. This is a requirement to be able to make change happen and stick. **Events** are necessary to figure out the next steps in the strategy, hypothesise where the map is going to take us, and align us to point in the same direction. The **rhythm** of communication is subsequently required to make these things habit, iron out the kinks along the road, and solve the many small problems that will come up in the day-to-day operations of the business—together.

Another reason many transformation initiatives fail is because of a lack of consistent and clear communication. Our competitive advantage as a species is our ability to change readily and collaborate effectively. We get better at this through practising a consistent **rhythm** of communication and a clear agenda where we discuss things we've committed to and map our progress together. By constantly gathering, we embed the changes.

Be warned—without the commitment from **leadership** to

develop consistency in your **rhythm**, nothing in this book will work for you.

However, the great reward is that in working through the **TLC** in the daily **rhythm**, we create the **new normal**.

NEW NORMAL

The **new normal** happens when something becomes the way we do things around here. It is a shift in **culture**, a transformation of what we hold true and believe deeply as a collective.

We begin by creating our **assets** of **teams**, **games**, and **players** through **events**. Then we make sure it is aligned to our **north star**, improve it, refine it, make it great, and of course, practice it through our **rhythm** to the point that it becomes second nature. Then, and only then, does it become our **new normal**. When something becomes the **new normal**, we can accept it as part of our **culture**, and we can confidently express it as our authentic **brand**.

Creating the **new normal** is a victory over the **status quo**, and the battle over **VUCA** is won—at least for now.

The **new normal** can and will always change and evolve, and it is the role of the **leader** to make this process effective. You can even think of this as the **next normal** because change is the only constant in a **VUCA** world.

The **TLC** is a living system. When the transformational **leader** understands all the elements of the **TLC** and the dynamics of how each element affects others, we are able to change our world and create the **new normal**.

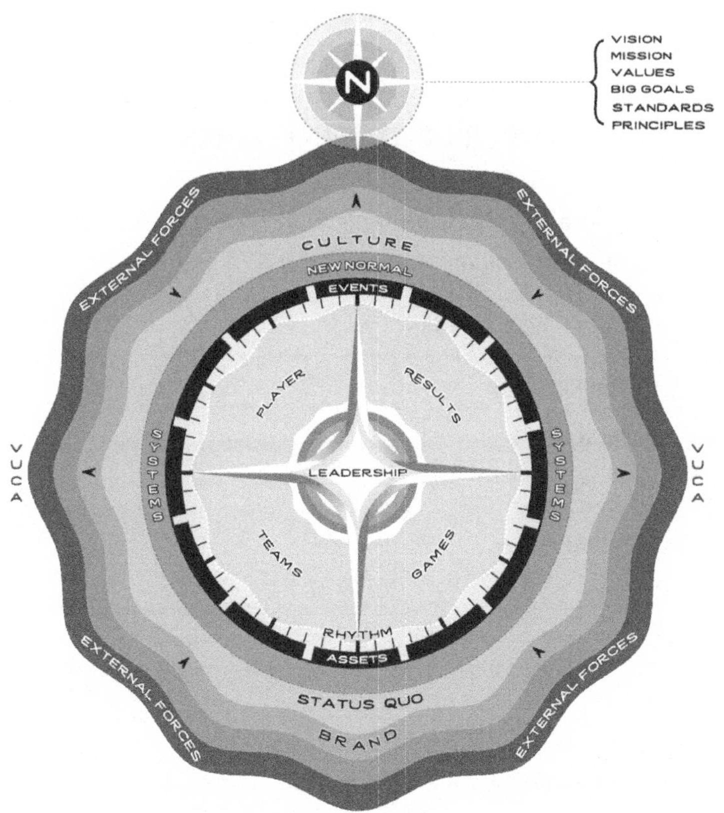
VISION
MISSION
VALUES
BIG GOALS
STANDARDS
PRINCIPLES
N
EXTERNAL FORCES
EXTERNAL FORCES
CULTURE
NEW NORMAL
EVENTS
PLAYER
RESULTS
VUCA
SYSTEMS
LEADERSHIP
SYSTEMS
VUCA
TEAMS
GAMES
RHYTHM
ASSETS
EXTERNAL FORCES
EXTERNAL FORCES
STATUS QUO
BRAND

EXERCISES AND APPLICATIONS

EXERCISE: TLC DEFINITIONS

Complete the following table with your understanding of the definition of each of the **TLC** elements.

Element	Definition
Leadership	
North Star	
Status quo	
New normal	
Culture	
Brand	
Events	
Assets	
Rhythm	
Teams	
Players	
Results	
Games	
VUCA	

Run an **event** session and teach the **TLC** language to one of your **teams**.

EXERCISES AND APPLICATIONS

EXERCISE: TLC DYNAMICS

This exercise is designed for you to consider how each element of the **TLC** affects every other element in the dynamic system.

For example, how does the **north star** affect:

- Leadership?
- Status quo?
- New normal?
- Culture?
- Brand?
- Events?
- Assets?
- Rhythm?
- Teams?
- Players?
- Results?
- Games?

The advanced exercise of the **TLC** dynamics template is available at *www.bigchange.group/Resources/TLC*.

In this **TLC** installation, we learned the elements and language of the **TLC** system and developed an understanding of the connectedness and dynamics of the system. This understanding will serve as the foundation for your transformation plan. Your knowledge will deepen as you go further into this book.

In the next installation, we will look at how to use this book to map out your **status quo** and develop your ongoing plan to purposefully create the **new normal.**

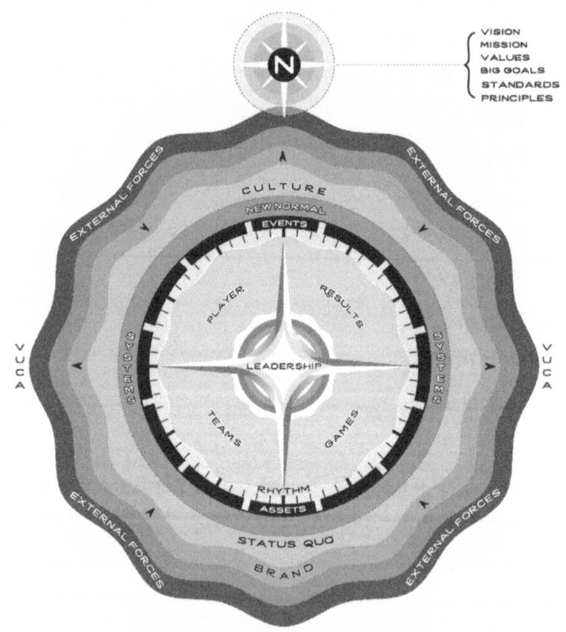

INSTALLATION 2

STATUS QUO

MAP WHERE YOU ARE AND PLAN YOUR NEXT ACTIONS AS YOU GO

JOHN'S OLD-WORLD STATUS QUO

"This is great, Benny, but where do we start? It seems that there are a thousand things to do now and although this is exciting, I can't see how we can bring it all together. Where do we even begin?"

John and his people had a good understanding of the elements and dynamics of the TLC, but I could sense John's obvious overwhelm. You, dear reader, might share this as well.

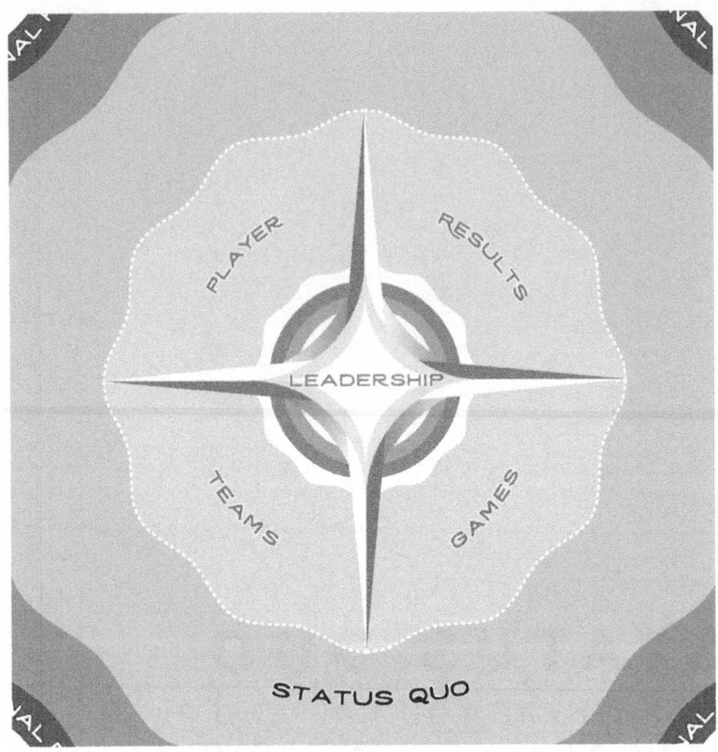

"Benny, can't we just dive in and make all the changes right away and send a list out to people about what is going to change?"

"Well, no," I said. "The power of transformational **leadership** is about involving people in the change. Yes, we need to think it through, be strategic, and to do this effectively, but we also need to take the time to challenge our own understanding of where we are on our journey, our **status quo**."

John nodded. He knew that past change efforts, the slapdash strategies that were "designed" to change the **status**

quo, seemed to default back to the old ways just months or even weeks after they were put in place.

"I want these changes to stick, Benny. I want to permanently shift the **status quo**. I want a new way of doing things around here. A new world, a **new normal.**"

And the journey of journaling, documenting, deciding, and mapping the **status quo** began.

JOHN'S NEW NORMAL

A few weeks later, John had decided on the next actions. He had worked through the **TLC** dynamic elements and the contents of this book. He had given considerable thought to where his company was and the next step to take.

John had used the **TLC** system to curiously inquire about and clearly see each element in his company to carefully consider and consciously decide on the next step to take. This was not a one-off practice. John regularly set aside time to work through the **TLC** system and give thoughtful consideration of where he was, where he was going, and what to do next while taking counsel and feedback from his **players**.

John now understood how to think about managing and leading change and no longer felt the overwhelm of a thousand small things because he could see the whole picture. With the **TLC** mental model in his head, the **status quo** journal in his hand was now the best map he had ever owned. This constantly evolving map allowed him to direct the **TLC** by working with what was already there and engaging with his **players** to make the changes work.

WHAT YOU WILL LEARN AND DO IN THIS INSTALLATION

In this installation, we get practical.

We will set you up to make this book work for you and get you ready to make notes and observations as you move through the rest of the installations in the **TLC**. We will arm you with the knowledge of a transformational **leader** and, in doing so, you will develop your own transformation map and a living plan for creating all the changes you want in your company.

Keep in mind that if you actively journal and map out your thinking as described in this installation, you will get the most out of this book. This installation is all about understanding how to constantly shift the **status quo** to the **new normal**. In order to create our **new normal**, we need to understand where we are, our **status quo**. This process is all about working through this book to develop your own ongoing and always improving transformation strategy for your own company.

The content of this book is as flexible as you are. I have included as much content as I could that would add value to your context. Everything included in this book can be applied to the **leader's** thinking to improve their **results**. However, this content is only valuable in its application.

As you move through the installations, take notes about what you see in your company and yourself. I encourage you to take something out of every section of every installation, write it in your journal, and go out there with an attitude of curiosity and experimentation to see what you can improve within your world. Take this content, plug it into your context, and document the **results**.

TWO TYPES OF NOTES

As you move through this book, there are two types of notes to take.

One set of notes is for your company. You will take notes of what you notice as the **status quo**, what you believe the next action should be, and you will also document things that become the **new normal**—more on that shortly. The second set of notes is your own journal experience day-to-day. Let's get started on both right now, starting with your **status quo** notes.

EXERCISES AND APPLICATIONS

EXERCISE: STATUS QUO NOTES

As you read through each installation, write your notes in the table below. Note the installation you are reading, reflect and write where you think you are currently, consider the next action to take, and document changes that become the **new normal** over time.

You can download this template at *www.bigchangeagency.com/TLCresources*.

Installation	Status quo	Next Action	New Normal

This is a very simple way of developing your own transformation plan and continuously improving and refining that plan as you go. The wisdom that emerges from this practice will be unique and valuable to your company.

- **Installation:** What element of the **TLC** am I considering?
- **Status quo**: What do I notice is going on now?

- **Next action**: What is the next small step to take or decision to make?
- **New normal**: Three months later, what change has become stable?

As the full picture of the **TLC** emerges, your thinking will be whole and powerful. I encourage you to do the exercises and document the changes as they occur.

At the end of this book, there is also a table of benchmark questions that map all the elements of the **TLC** to each other and provide the criteria for a complete **TLC** installation.

You cannot install the whole **TLC** into your entire company all at once. Work through the **status quo** exercise and reflect on the **TLC** benchmarks at the end of the book to track and qualify your transformation progress. An alternative to this is to just think about it and not write it down. Although this will still be valuable, in my experience, it is nowhere near as powerful. Of course, the choice is up to you.

EXERCISES AND APPLICATIONS

EXERCISE: YOUR OWN PROGRESS JOURNAL

The second recommendation is to journal your own personal **leadership** journey.

As you progress, keep a journal to record what you notice, what you experience, and how you are learning and growing. This can be as simple as a journal in bullet point format that lists wins for the day, the one thing you want to improve, things you are most grateful for, and the things you would like to set up tomorrow. Here is a simple formula for this that has been widely used in the micro journaling or bullet journaling community.

- Date:
- 3 x wins for the day
- 1 x improvement
- 3 x learnings and thank you statements
- 3 x next actions
- Notes...

You may also choose to take this further and have a journal where you empty your mind each day. This practice is recommended for several reasons:

- You'll sleep better. As the great David Allen taught us, our minds are great at coming up with ideas and solving problems but terrible for storing information.[16]

- A journal practice for the leader to empty their mind each day can improve overall well-being and assist them in increasing self-awareness. Remember, we're all on a journey here.
- Reflecting back is how our knowledge becomes our wisdom.
- Our wisdom only comes through the application of knowledge and the reflection of experience.

If you make this part of your daily practice, it will pay great dividends to you as you go through this process.

16 David Allen, *Getting Things Done: The Art of Stress-free Productivity* (New York: Penguin Books, 2015).

TAKE SPECIAL NOTE OF WHAT PISSES YOU OFF

Natural pearls form when an irritant, usually a parasite (not the proverbial grain of sand), finds its way into an annoyed oyster. As a defence mechanism, the oyster uses a fluid to coat the irritant and add layer upon layer of protective coating. Something beautiful and rare forms. This is a wonderful metaphor for wisdom—pearls of wisdom.

We develop wisdom not through reading passages in books but through application. When there is a problem that surfaces like an irritating parasite or grain of sand, something just itching for a remedy, we need to put knowledge into action. We reach into our resources and bring forth the best solution within our knowledge. When it works for us, we tend to apply it again and again. As we see this hardening of the pearl, we come to understand how this application of knowledge works. To gain wisdom is to create your own pearls. Everything you read here can be used to create a coating around your irritating problems. It's up to you to take action to make those pearls your own. Just don't cast them at swine!

In this installation, we set up a practice of journaling and documenting your transformation process and your **leadership** development insights. Take notes as you move through this content. Plan your transformation as the light bulb moments occur in each installation. You can find more inspiration for the longer-term process at the back of the book in the **TLC** assessment benchmarks section in the appendix.

Remember: small, well-considered, consistent changes create transformation and BIG change over time.

Now, pen and journal in hand, we are ready to go deeper into the concept of **TLC Leadership**. Let's go.

INSTALLATION 3

LEADERSHIP

JOHN'S OLD-WORLD STATUS QUO

"If everyone just did what they were supposed to do, this place would run perfectly!"

The words echoed in the halls of the offices of John's company.

"I'm fed up with this!" declared John.

"Why is the stuff that's so obvious to me overlooked by the people who are supposed to be leading this place?"

Talking to the managers, the same sentiments cascaded down through the ranks.

"We need people to take on the initiative. We have to find people capable of making this work," said the managers.

"I'm just trying to do my job. If management listened to us and made the right changes happen, life would be great around here," said the staff.

"Why don't they do what they promise?" asked the market. "I am leaving!" said the customers, as one by one, they began to shuffle off to the company's hungry competitors.

Everywhere we looked, we found blame and fear. Everyone seemed to be stuck, waiting, uncertain, and wondering. Everyone reacted to every bump in the road, and people were scared and overflowing with protective excuses. Every action was a Band-Aid to protect the safety of business as usual and keeping the old **status quo** world safe.

But safe was no longer good enough. We were on the edge of wanting to change because things could be better and needed to change. We might not survive if we didn't.

Putting on my most diplomatic of coach hats, I asked John, "Where is this coming from? Why do you think that people act this way? Why are they so protective, selfish, and unsure?"

The **culture** was one of mistrust and fear in a place where failure was fatal. Employees only achieved safety by making the next excuse to protect themselves from punishment. When we failed to deliver on a budget, goal or target, a flurry of excuses pointed a hundred hands in a thousand different directions like some broken wayfaring sign pointing everywhere but home. This was no place to call out the real problems, and there was no sense of safety for people to do so. Every piece of communication in the company was to protect the **status quo** as if pointing out the herd of elephants in the room would lead to a stampede of dire consequences.

John glanced around the empty boardroom until his eye caught the mirror in the corner. "It's me. I did this," he quietly stated.

John saw the **culture** he had created. The **culture** of hide it and sweep it under the rug, the **culture** of mistrust and protection, and the **culture** of blame the other guy.

"This has to change," John asserted. "If I want to change the **status quo**, I have to change the way I lead. I have to change the way I think, and the way I communicate with my people if I want them to change."

With this commitment, the world around John began to transform.

JOHN'S NEW NORMAL

A few months later, the concept and mindset of **leadership** had shifted in John's world. The business had set the foundation for a **new normal**.

Failure was no longer condemned, shunned, and feared. Rather, it was celebrated as new learning. Feedback was embraced and rewarded. People raced in, safe and open to claim ownership of each problem as it surfaced, and responsibility was claimed as an honour, not a terrible burden.

People worked together to get to the core of issues. They brought all the mess and ugliness to the surface to be dealt with and resolved. The truth was, all the problems they were facing were always there. We just made it okay for them to be openly solved. The danger of being "caught" and reprimanded for mistakes and missteps had vanished.

What was left as the dust settled was undoubtedly messy. The fog of fear had lifted to reveal the real work that had to be done to build the **new normal**, the new world. You could almost hear the **culture** breathing a sigh of relief through the halls as the people came to terms with the work that needed to be done to build a better future. It all started with John's commitment and a bold, clear message that made it okay to change.

John committed to the following:

Leadership *at our company will take 100 percent responsibility for our* ***culture****, our* ***results****, our* ***brand****, our* ***teams****,* *our* ***games****, and our change. The buck stops with me, and everything we do hereafter is my responsibility to improve. I am committed to demonstrating this in every action and communication to our people.*

John approached the meetings and memos with the same clear message:

The Message and Commitment from the CEO

We are here to change, to transform and to grow together.

To shape our ***culture*** *and create something bigger than ourselves, something we are proud of.*

This will not be easy, and our ***leadership*** *is committed to making these changes.*

I will now commit to and expect total responsibility at all times from myself and my ***leadership team.***

This means that we will be working on developing a new style of ***leadership.***

I know we have a lot of work to do in our ***culture*** *and company, and we need to make this work together.*

My decisions will be based on what is best for our ***culture*** *and our company.*

Over the next twelve months, we are going on a journey.

This will be the first of many messages from me, and we will be asking each and every one of you to contribute to making this work.

Yours in Service,
John, CEO

When the people read the message, they wondered how long it would last.

"Is this a fad?"

"What is he reading?"

"What is he on?!"

"When will things go back to normal?"

The business started to make change happen. As the **events** began running and the facilitation opened up, the people began to see this change was not going away. As the **results** improved and the **rhythm** got stronger, they knew one thing for sure—John was here to change things for good. The awakening of transformational **leadership** had begun, and nothing would ever be the same again.

WHAT YOU WILL LEARN AND DO IN THIS INSTALLATION

In this installation, we will develop a deeper understanding of effective **leadership**. Journeying through the evolution of **leadership** theory and research, we will draw on the most effective styles and practices of **leadership** as we step into the centre of the **TLC** and take responsibility for the elements in our company. We will tackle the wicked problem of teaching **leadership** and get to work raising our own levels of awareness. Finally, we will define the skillsets and practices required for transformational **leadership**, and you will get ready to make your own declaration of what **leadership** means in your company.

SCOPE OF LEADERSHIP

The transformational leader steps into the centre of the **TLC** and takes on the responsibility of the world around them. This is the **leader's** sphere of influence, and it will expand or contract based on the amount of responsibility and complexity that they are able to manage effectively. To expand the **TLC** means:

- To take on more space and territory.
- To increase the impact and influence on the world around us.
- To expand our **culture** through our **brand.**
- To bring more **players** into our world and along for the great journey ahead.

The actions you take and decisions you make will ripple out from the centre to the BIG wide world, and what you are capable of leading and taking responsibility for will grow. This is visualised in the **TLC** dynamic system.

Worlds are built on words. With every exercise and **event** that you create, you will expand your **TLC.** Every time you miss an element of the **TLC** in your communication and actions, the **TLC** shrinks and withers. Every time you let the standard rule of **north star** or let the **rhythm** miss a beat, the **TLC** will contract and shrivel, and your scope of influence and **leadership** will diminish.

When we forget to consider the individual **player,** neglect to set the **games,** miss an opportunity to strengthen and galvanise the **teams,** or fudge a **result,** the **VUCA** ripples inwards and it comes back as a meaner, wickeder, and more complex problem in your world. To build this into your mind, you can think of this as constantly expanding or contracting based on the little things you do each day. The small conversations that matter most in the long-term produce the largest **results.** Your responsibility, influence, and power can expand through using the methodology you will find in the **TLC.** This is an invitation to shape your thinking about **leadership** and, at the same time, document this in your **status quo** and **leadership** journal. Take action, run experiments, and find out what works for you as we earn and learn our own lessons and wisdom.

Now before we move ahead with defining and declaring what **leadership** means to you and your company, let's take a fast (and very incomplete) look back at the last 500 years of **leadership** thinking and reflect on how we got here. We do this because there is value and truth in all of these theories, and it will help us create our own **leadership** philosophy.

A FAST AND INCOMPLETE HISTORY OF LEADERSHIP THINKING

Now, let's get some perspective as to where all of this transformational **leadership** thinking comes from.[17] Sure, you can skip over this part if you like; however, I recommend reading through these pages to deepen your understanding of what it means to be a transformational leader.

17 This is an early attempt to integrate leadership thinking. This in itself is a momentous task and enquiries for collaboration on the second edition of this book are warmly welcomed.

There is a vast body of research spanning hundreds of years pursuing the quest for effective **leadership** methods. The **TLC** honours and builds upon this wealth of knowledge. As you move through these points, notice how each of these developments relate to your own ideas around what great **leadership** means to you and your company and take your own notes in your **leadership** and **status quo** journal.

Enter "The Prince," Niccolò Machiavelli.[18] The Mach[19] was one of the first writers of **leadership** philosophy and is considered by some to be the father of modern political science and philosophy. He believed in being feared but not hated, because fear created respect, and respect was far more important to being loved or even liked. The Mach believed in putting a perfect image forward and in showing himself as always being the embodiment of success. However, it is quite clear in his writing he did not believe anyone was capable of authentically being the ideal he represented.

Machiavelli believed the leader was to be a personification of the state. "The prince is the state, and the state is the prince." Or, in modern terms, "The leader is the company, and the company is the leader."

Mach believed that the vision and values he demonstrated would be what the crowd followed. He thought that whatever principles the leader held, the followers would take their cue and follow suit. He also believed that a leader must understand history and read and reflect on the deeds of

---

18 Nicolo Machiavelli, *The Prince*, trans. W. K. Marriott (Project Gutenberg, 2006), https://www.gutenberg.org/files/1232/1232-h/1232-h.htm.

19 Yes, I've decided to refer to him as the "The Mach."

outstanding people (kind of like what we are doing right now in this installation).

The Mach gets a bad rap, and many ineffective modern leaders are compared to him when they make unsupported moves or lead from a place of tyranny and control. He did, however, value collaboration and camaraderie and thought it necessary to utilise the strengths of those around him. In our **VUCA** world, we require ample flexibility and responsibility from our people in order to change fast and often. We find this commanding and controlling tyrannical style to be going the way of the dinosaurs. Nonetheless, there is partial truth and value in his philosophy, and many of his early sentiments carried through to the philosophies that followed.

In the 1800s, British historian, Thomas Carlyle,[20] believed the leaders of the time were iconic hero figures enamoured with the traits of courage, physical strength and charisma. They were the alpha personality figureheads who played the dominant role in shaping the **culture** at the time. Galton[21] and James strongly supported this notion and firmly believed leaders were born and not made. Rather, individuals were leaders by their very fixed traits and nature, and nothing could be done to teach **leadership** to those born without this gift.

Mining magnate and politician, Cecil Rhodes,[22] jumped into the conversation and asserted that **leadership** could be

---

20 Thomas Carlyle, *On Heroes, Hero-worship, & the Heroic in History: Six Lectures; Reported with Emendations and Additions* (New York: D. Appleton & Company, 1841).

21 Francis Galton, *Hereditary Genius* (London: Macmillan, 1869).

22 Cecil Rhodes, 1853–1902. This vision was the foundation for Rhodes Scholarships.

nurtured by working with young people with "moral force of character and instincts to lead" to develop their natural abilities further. By now the thinking was moving towards this new and somewhat radical idea that effective leaders were born that way and also could be made better through nurturing and development.

Flash forward to the 1940s and research leaders, Bird,[23] Stogdill,[24] and Mann[25] worked through approximately twenty-five years of available data and concluded that a person does not become an effective leader through a combination of traits. Instead, actions and the leader's behaviour were seen to play the biggest roles in whether a leader was effective or not. This behavioural theory became the most popular theory of the times and continued to be the major school of thought through the early 1970s.[26]

As the thinking shifted to behaviourism, the focus of the research moved to figuring out the most effective way to behave as leaders, and the studies focused on finding the best way to practice and teach **leadership**. As the geniuses of the time worked to decode and explain the most effective

23 Charles Bird, *Social Psychology* (New York: D. Appleton-Century Company, Incorporated, 1940).

24 Ralph M. Stogdill, "Personal Factors Associated with Leadership: A Survey of the Literature," *The Journal of Psychology* 25, no. 1 (January 1948): 35–71, https://doi.org/10.1080/00223980.1948.9917362.

25 Richard D. Mann, "A Review of the Relationships between Personality and Performance in Small Groups," *Psychological Bulletin* 56, no. 4 (1959): 241–70, https://doi.org/10.1037/h0044587.

26 Fred E. Fielder, "A Contingency Model of Leadership Effectiveness," *Advances in Experimental Social Psychology*, 149–90, Elsevier, https://doi.org/10.1016/s0065-2601(08)60051-9.

behaviour, they were also dealing with the increasing complexity of the world around them. In doing their best to map out influence and decision-making processes and behaviour, Fiedler's Contingency Theory came to light[27] in 1967. Fiedler's research thoroughly analysed the data and surveys, but try as they might, they could not find a single style of **leadership** that was universally effective. Thus, they concluded that there was no real correlation found between behavioural patterns of effective **leadership**, and unfortunately, there was no "one way" of effectively leading. The search for the ultimate **leadership** way seemed fruitless at this point.

Then, Vroom and his mates, Yetton and Jago[28] put forward something they called expectancy theory. "This theory emphasizes the needs for organizations to relate rewards directly to performance and ensure the rewards provided are those deserved and wanted by the recipients."[29] Expectancy theory provides a whole language around different situations and how effective **leadership** can motivate behaviour in each scenario. This took it to the next level as they were able to map the most effective behaviour to the circumstances. They showed there were indeed patterns we could learn in order to be better **leaders**, and there were rewards we could engineer to drive the behaviour of ourselves and others.

---

27 Ibid.

28 Victor H. Vroom and Philip W. Yetton, *Leadership and Decision-Making* (Pittsburgh, PA: University of Pittsburg Press, 1973).

29 Patrick J. Montana and Bruce H. Charnov, *Management*, 4th ed. (Hauppauge, NY: Barron's Educational Series, 2008).

This inspired and influenced Robert House to develop his Path-Goal Theory of **leadership** effectiveness.[30] House showed us that an effective **leader's** behaviour or style is what best fits the work environment. The **leader** can choose to behave in a way that is best suited to their employee's needs, strengths, and weaknesses, guide them along their path and help them obtain their goals. This was the birth of what we now call situational **leadership**, and it taught leaders that the best style of **leadership** depended on the situation. He identified five styles:

- **Autocratic 1:** The leader makes his own decision with current information.
- **Autocratic 2:** The leader collects information from followers and makes the decision alone.
- **Consultative 1:** The leader shares problems with relevant followers individually and seeks their opinions, but makes the decision alone.
- **Consultative 2:** The leader shares problems with a group and seeks their suggestions, but makes the decision alone.
- **Group-Based:** The leader discusses problems with the group, and the group makes a decision.

I'm sure you can see how this plugs into the ***TLC*** *system of* ***events*** *and* ***assets****. Yes, you will make some decisions alone in an*

30 Robert J. House, "A Path Goal Theory of Leader Effectiveness," *Administrative Science Quarterly* 16, no. 3 (September 1971): 321, https://doi.org/10.2307/2391905.

autocratic manner, but often you will build stronger engagement and attain greater perspective by employing a consultative and group-based approach through your **events,** *the creation of* **assets,** *and your* **rhythm.**

Then in 1977, Robert Greenleaf gave us Servant **Leadership,** a philosophy of putting the needs of employees first and leading from a place of service in order to help **players** grow and develop.[31] This can often **result** in better engagement and performance for the company as a whole, and has been adopted by many successful companies to this day.

In 1985, Daniel Goleman finally and thankfully gave us EQ or emotional intelligence. He recognised the capability of effective leaders to observe their own emotions and the emotions of others, label them appropriately, and use this information to guide their thinking and behaviour. This allowed them to adjust and manage emotions and adapt to changing environments, goals, and personalities.[32]

As the philosophy of EQ took hold firmly, we entered a new world of interpersonal **leadership,** and the whole curriculum changed for the better. Values, integrity, moral intention, role models and empowerment came to the forefront.

In 1985, presidential biographer James MacGregor Burns identified and presented a new and emerging style called transformational **leadership.**[33] Transformational **leader-**

---

31 Robert K. Greenleaf, *Servant Leadership: A Journey into the Nature of Legitimate Power and Greatness* (Mahwah, NJ: Paulist Press, 2002).

32 Daniel Goleman, *Emotional Intelligence: Why It Can Matter More than IQ* (London: Bloomsbury, 1996).

33 James Macgregor Burns, *Transforming Leadership, A New Pursuit of Happiness* (New York: Grove Press, 2004).

ship occurs when a leader works with a **team** of people to identify and define the changes required, create a vision to guide these changes, and then work with the people to make the changes or **new normal** happen. The overwhelmingly convincing amount of evidence from these studies showed that we can enhance the performance, motivation, and morale of a company through building the individual and collective identity.

Burns had identified four simple yet powerful attributes of transformational leaders.

1. Idealised Influence—A role model consistent in **north star**.
2. Inspirational motivation—Providing purpose and energy through an appealing **north star**.
3. Intellectual stimulation—Encouraging innovation, improvement, and challenging **games**.
4. Individual Consideration—Understanding individual **player's** needs, strengths, and concerns.

By now, I hope you can see how this can be brought to life in your company through the dynamic elements of the **TLC** *system.*

But is it practical to use this style all the time, or is there a better way?

In 1990, Bernard Bass and Bruce Avolio took the theory of transformational **leadership** further and brought us the Full Range **Leadership** Model. Through hundreds of company studies that examined the **results** and behaviour of leaders, they concluded that the least effective style of **leadership** was the most passive, and the most effective style was the most active.[34] In other words, the more active, transformational, and involved the leader was, the better the **results**.

They mapped a tonne of data around style and effectiveness to the following categories:

FULL RANGE LEADERSHIP

Laissez-faire. French for, do what you want, I don't give a shit.

This style abdicates responsibility and avoids making decisions. *It is the most passive and least effective.*

Transactional management by exception. This style actively looks for broken rules and standards and intervenes only when standards are not met. They look for problems and try to fix them.

Transactional goals and rewards. This style promises prizes for **results**, builds contracts of contingent rewards, and actively recognises people's work and accomplishments.

Transformational leadership. This style, as you know now, works with the **players** to improve the whole system through idealised influence, inspirational motivation, intellectual stimulation, and individual consideration. *This is the most effective style of* ***leadership*** *and also the most active style requiring the most effort, energy, aptitude, and ability.*

This Full Range model stands as one of the most well-researched and documented theories of **leadership** we have today and is an enormous inspiration for the **TLC** system.

---

34 Bruce J. Avolio and Bernard M. Bass, eds., *Developing Potential Across a Full Range of Leadership™: Cases on Transactional and Transformational Leadership* (London: Lawrence Erlbaum Associates, Publishers, 2001).

Let's go a little further into what this is all about. Transformational **leaders** specialise in the following:

- Working to change the system
- Solving challenges by finding experiences that show that old patterns do not fit or work
- Wanting to know what has to change
- Maximizing their **team's** capability and capacity

Transactional leaders do the following:

- Work within the existing system
- Start solving challenges by fitting experiences to a known pattern
- Want to know the step-by-step approach
- Minimize variation of the organization and protect the **status quo**

Another way to put it: Transactional is a "telling" style, while transformational is a "selling" style.

From 2010 forward, this has brought powerful developments in system **leadership** theory.

In his groundbreaking work, "The Fifth Discipline," Peter Senge[35] proposes system **leadership** and recognises that with the fast curve of development in technology, collaboration, and collective intelligence, it's essential to solve wicked problems. This is another huge inspiration for

35 Peter M. Senge, *The Fifth Discipline: The Art and Practice of the Learning Organization* (New York, Doubleday/Currency, 2006).

the **TLC** system in recognising the dynamic elements of transformation.

Now in 2020, a quick search on Amazon reveals over 90,000 books on **leadership**. Everyone and their dog seem to have an opinion. Some are based on rigorous research, but most are pure speculation. The **TLC** works to bring the most proven methods together in a practical and teachable system.

As we have learned from the research and literature, the most effective **leadership** style is transformation. This means it is active, involved, and yes, more time and effort are required. Transformation calls for more leaders at all levels of the company who can help lead transformational change.

The **TLC** provides a system for developing a full range **leadership** capability through the real-world activities of a company transformation. In short, you will develop more leaders using the **TLC** system. Not only will you transform to your **new normal**, you will also teach others to learn how to carry on this system through their own **leadership** development journeys.[36]

So how can we develop active leaders in your company? This indeed is a wicked problem.

---

36 I firmly believe that working towards a more complete and integrative definition and practice of leadership is one of the most important challenges the world faces. We are only just beginning to develop this definition, and TLC is an early contribution towards the practices required for this research.

YOU CANNOT TEACH LEADERSHIP

> *"Leadership, like swimming, cannot be learned by reading about it."*
>
> *—Henry Mintzberg*[37]

We cannot learn to swim by reading books. Although it is powerful to understand the techniques and develop our knowledge, we need to get in the water and risk drowning to turn knowledge into wisdom through our own experience. We must test each stroke, feel the water gliding past us, and the resistance of each pull. No programme, MBA course or book can teach **leadership** by telling you what to do next. Even if I could tell leaders what to do, they would just be following instructions, and of course, following instructions is not leading; it is following instructions.

Hmm...So, you see the problem here, you can't learn to lead in a step-by-step way. There are no modules to complete or tests to take except the modules of your next problem and the test of the latest challenge.

The **TLC** is not a step-by-step program, nor is it a straight path, and it is definitely not twelve easy hacks to becoming a better leader. Like you and your company, the **TLC** is a dynamic and living system. Each part affects every other part. There is no start or end. The only levels are the levels of capability the leaders have over their responsibilities. Like your mind, the **TLC** is an operating system that allows the leader

37 Henry Mintzberg, *The Nature of Managerial Work.* (New York: Harper Collins College Div, 1973).

to develop their ability to think and respond to the **VUCA** environment. When we use the **TLC** effectively, we do not teach people what to do. We teach them how to think about what to do to overcome **VUCA**.

The **TLC** provides a language leaders can use to make better decisions. When we share this language, we focus the power of our collective intelligence and experience growth as we move together in the same direction. Through this language, the **TLC** leader lifts the sights and actions of the people. They are conscious of how the living system of their company works. In leading, they raise the consciousness of everyone around them.

And what is consciousness? Read on.

CONSCIOUSNESS AS AWARENESS

When James MacGregor Burns first introduced the concept of transformational **leadership** in his 1978 book boldly titled ***Leadership***,[38] he defined it as a process where leaders and their followers raise one another to higher levels of morality and motivation.

It's one that lifts the level of consciousness of their followers. If this seems out there for you, bear with me.

What is consciousness? What does it mean to be conscious?

Okay, these questions have evaded philosophers and for the most part, have been avoided by scientists, so we are not going to get to the bottom of this here. One simple and practical answer that will suit us just fine for now is that

38 James MacGregor Burns, *Leadership* (New York, Harper & Row, 1978).

consciousness is the state of being aware of something and the sense of individual and collective identity.

It's to be awake and aware of what is going on around you and within you. To lift consciousness is to raise awareness of self and others to "higher levels of morality and motivation" and to work in developing our sense of identity as individuals and collectives.

Now, how do we go about raising awareness?

Well, we need to help people to "think different" as Steve Jobs would say as he inspired generations to buy his computers.[39] We need to be able to ask the right questions in order to build their awareness. Questions raise awareness and raise a question. When we help somebody think differently by asking a thoughtful question, they expand their awareness by seeking an answer. This is the very heart of coaching and **leadership** development. The thing is that in order to raise anyone else's awareness to help them grow and develop so they will grow and develop our company, we need to raise our own awareness.

SELF-AWARENESS

> *"Watch your thoughts; for they become words.*
> *Watch your words; for they become actions.*
> *Watch your actions; for they become habits.*
> *Watch your habits; for they become character.*
> *Watch your character for it will become your destiny."*
>
> *—Unknown*

39 Walter Isaacson, *Steve Jobs: The Exclusive Biography*, Reissue ed. (New York: Simon & Schuster, 2015).

This quote has been attributed to many different thinkers. Some say it was the great Taoist sage, Lao-Tzu. Some say it was Ralph Waldo Emerson. Some even say it was Margaret Thatcher's dad. Needless to say, there is great power in these words.

When we become aware of our own thinking patterns, it allows us to master communication.

When we master communication, we're able to act in a way that sets an example for those around us.

When we do this consistently, it becomes habit and these habits define us over time and lead us to our destiny.

There is a choice here to program yourself, to set your mind on purpose toward what you want to create and who you want around you. This begins with choosing the quality of our thoughts through awareness, contemplation, and practice. When we think in terms of the thoughts that we choose, we have a choice to either see them as imposed upon us, or something that we create and have a responsibility for.

In our **VUCA** world, we are constantly bombarded with noise from the world around us. It is the practice of a transformational **leader** to consciously choose the thoughts they think on a day-to-day basis and to look at each element of the **TLC** and examine the thinking that created it. This may seem elementary, however, since the vast majority of people in my experience see their thoughts as something that are completely outside of their control. There is an invitation here to consciously take stock of the way we think and choose to develop the thinking that allows the leader to take their followers where they need to go.

We can, as leaders, audit and edit our own thinking so we may emerge with a stronger understanding of a situation and a more complete map of the world around us. In order to be successful in this, we must challenge our own habits of thinking.

> *"Habits of thinking need not be forever. One of the most significant findings in psychology in the last twenty years is that individuals choose the way they think."*
>
> —*Martin Seligman*[40]

Let's think about that, or, more to the point, choose to think about that.

I believe one of the biggest problems in **leadership** is the problem of self-awareness, and the biggest problem of self-awareness is that people don't know if they don't have it. After all, how could someone possibly be aware of not being aware?

Transformational **leadership** requires us to take ownership of all the things we can control and accept the things we can't control. Developing self-awareness is an ongoing practice, and it is one that is best approached with a sense of curiosity and humility. It's like a muscle that you build within your day-to-day workings at your company through the practice of **leadership**.

The blind spots that we all have can be our greatest weakness and also our greatest area for improvement. These are areas we cannot see in ourselves but are important to those around us.

---

40 Martin E.P. Seligman, *Learned Optimism: How to Change Your Mind and Your Life* (PublisherNorth Sydney, Australia: Random House Australia, 2011).

To be aware of our blind spots can seem impossible. How could we possibly know? They are blind by definition. This is why it is useful to work with trusted advisors and coaches who ask challenging questions and help you discover the areas that you can't see.

There is a huge danger in declaring that you are completely aware of everything around you because at this point, the journey to remove blind spots and increase awareness comes to an end. A good coach will interrupt your thinking and challenge you to confront your blind spots while throwing salt in your sore spots. If they are really good, they will tell you what no one else will tell you. Until the leader decides to work through this process of self-examination, until we question our beliefs and our biases, until we confront our blind spots and heal our sore spots, and until we consciously examine who we are as leaders, a lot of things that occur in our world will seem outside of our control. Yes, it is true that many people would rather not do this work. If you have read this far, however, it is likely you are different.

Here lies an invitation to claim ownership of your self-**leadership** and preferably do this before we jump into the work of transforming your whole company. Here, we dig deep into what makes us tick and do our best to be open and flexible enough to adapt and change this to serve your people. The fastest way to do this is to look at what we take full responsibility for in our lives by defining what responsibility is and what it is not. For this, we will borrow the concept of above and below the line thinking.

Above the line and below the line thinking is one of the more useful concepts in personal and **leadership** development. It comes from the work of a great football coach named Urban Meyer[41] and is used by coaches around the world to help people recognise where their thinking and level of responsibility sits.

Above-the-line thinking is quite simply:

1. Above the line thinking owns the situation.
2. Taking responsibility, seeking feedback, the catch cry of the above the line thinker is: "If it is to be, it is up to me."
3. They believe that they cause and are 100 percent responsible for all of the **results** that they see in their life.
4. Above the line thinkers have the empowerment and the choice to take responsibility without fear of blame or fault.
5. Responsible thinking exists above the line.
6. When something happens, the above the line thinker will pause, reflect, adjust, and respond.

The opposite of this is below the line thinking.

Below the line thinking is when people put the **results** outside themselves. They blame others, they see the world has problems, they think the world happens to them, and they deny what's happening around them.

1. They have no responsible power in what they're doing.
2. They find fault.
3. They see obstacles.
4. They're stuck in a victim mentality.

---

41 Urban Meyer, *Above the Line: Lessons in Leadership and Life from a Championship Program* (New York: Penguin Books, 2017).

5. The world happens to them rather than them happening to the world.

Reactionary thinking tends to be below the line.

Something happens and stimulus occurs and reacts in a certain way—it pushes it away and avoids the pain. The below the line thinker sees the world as something that is happening to them, something outside of themselves, and something that is someone else's fault.

The truth is that we tend to act from above the line or below the line depending on where we are in our own development and the situation in which we find ourselves.

The question for the leader is: where do you spend most of your time?

This requires constant conscious awareness to decide to pause a thought or conversation. Between above and below the line, there is always space for a choice to be made. This pause allows us to lift our level of awareness and expand the choices we have in the behaviours that we act out in the world.

Viktor E. Frankl knew that the power to choose to be above the line, to take time and space to claim ownership and responsibility of any situation, no matter how bad or dire, was our ultimate freedom.

> *"Between stimulus and response there is a space. In that space is our power to choose our response. In our response lies our growth and our freedom."*
>
> —*Viktor E. Frankl*[42]

42 Viktor E Frankl, *Man's Search for Meaning*, trans. Ilse Lasch (Boston:...

This choice of response is a requirement for transformational **leadership**. Take responsibility in the moment.

When we think in terms of the thoughts that we choose, we have a choice to either see them as imposed upon us or something we create and have a responsibility for. The wisdom is in creating the space for careful thought and conscious consideration between something that happens and our response to it. The very idea of taking responsibility means slowing down the reactionary process to consider all options in order to produce a better response.

The quality of the leader's thinking is the quality of the thinking that occurs between a stimulus and a response. The leader's responsibility is simply their *ability to respond* effectively.

It is useful to consider and journal all the things you tend to react to, and all the things you have put on autopilot, and notice what brings up reactionary emotions within you. Notice what stirs up anger, frustration, irritation, or sadness, and then the exercise is to sit with this and consider what might be a more conscious alternative to the knee-jerk reaction.

> *"The amygdala in the emotional centre sees and hears everything that occurs to us instantaneously and is the trigger point for the fight-or-flight response."*
>
> —*Daniel Goleman*[43]

...Beacon Press, 1959).

43 Daniel Goleman, *Working with Emotional Intelligence* (London: Bloomsbury Publishing, 1999).

The implication is that every trigger that happens gets passed through the amygdala first. This is the ancient part of our brain that exists to see things as a threat. What this means is if we don't teach ourselves and others to pause before we react, to take a breath and think and *then* respond, we will continually have patterns of knee-jerk reactions that cause conflict and can sabotage our transformation work.

The power in this simple model is that you can teach it to a group and then use it as a reference to notice when people are deferring ownership or responsibility and gently help them lift their awareness and thinking above the line. You can use above and below the line thinking to name and change **leadership** behaviour through practice. To use this model, it is simple to define, draw, and teach, but its implications are profound when we use this as part of the **TLC** to drive conversations to better outcomes.

When we teach leaders to pause, take a breath, think, and then respond, over time, the thinking, talking, acting, and habits will bring about the character and virtues of transformational **leadership**. Of course, we also need to develop the right skillsets and practices to be effective in making our transformation happen.

SKILLSETS AND PRACTICES OF LEADERSHIP

The practices and skillsets of the **leader** are exactly that—practices and skillsets. They go on and on, and we only get better as our knowledge and experience develops. There is a tonne of carefully researched frameworks for **leadership** practices. The **TLC** borrows from the Leaderplex Model from

Denison, Hooijberg and Quinn.[44] We will work to define each of these skillsets and practices in the following page and then apply them in the following installations.

The transformational **leader** develops these skillsets by using the **TLC system:**

INNOVATOR

The skill of the innovator is built through solving problems and creating valuable **assets by** working through the elements of the **TLC** and running **events** that encourage collaboration and the testing of ideas.

BROKER

The skill of the broker is developed using **results** (facts) **and games** (plans) to acquire new resources from "upstairs" and/ or external customers and investors to gain worthy investments in time and money.

PRODUCER

The skill of the producer is developed as the leader works through the **rhythm** and helps close off tasks to produce the desired **results.**

DIRECTOR

The skill of the director is developed in aligning **TLC results** and strategy towards the **north star** by codesigning **games**

44 Robert Hooijberg, James G. (Jerry) Hunt, and George E Dodge, "Leadership Complexity and Development of the Leaderplex Model," *Journal of Management* 23, no. 3 (June 1997): 375–408, https://doi.org/10.1177/014920639702300305.

that set the goals, activities, measures, expectations/examples, and support.

COORDINATOR

The skill of the coordinator is developed in keeping the **rhythm** and **events** consistent and making sure they happen in an organised and coordinated manner and through building and resourcing **teams** that play to the strengths of each individual **player**.

MONITOR

The skill of the monitor is developed in being aware across the development of all the elements of the **TLC** and by learning to measure what matters most, share this information, and act on changes in a timely manner.

FACILITATOR

The skill of the facilitator is developed through **events**, the creation of **assets**, and the practice of **rhythm**. In an **event**, facilitators learn to harness the wisdom of the room and converge on an outcome and consensus, which then becomes an **asset**. A skilled facilitator can drive and guide a conversation in order to be able to take the knowledge of the people in your company and make better decisions.

MENTOR

The leader develops the skillset of a mentor by working with and listening actively to individual **players**. Over time, they become able to present themselves as an example to others and can provide advice on the path they have walked. By honing these skills as a mentor, they are able to develop other leaders to be able to carry on the work long after they have gone.

COACH

On top of the Leaderplex Model, I have added coach. Different from mentor, the coach's skillset is to ask questions that develop the thinking of the **player**.

The coaching skill is developed by working with the **players** on the **teams** through the **game**. Great coaches ask great questions to be able to help somebody else develop their line of thinking. Asking the right question at the right time is another practice you will develop over time through experience and conscious effort.

These practices of **leadership** development are never-ending. **Leadership** is an infinite **game**. You play to keep playing, learning, and helping others do the same.

EXERCISES AND APPLICATIONS

EXERCISE: DEFINE AND DECLARE YOUR LEADERSHIP MESSAGE

In this exercise, you are to define what **leadership** means at your company, your philosophy of what good **leadership** looks like, and declare it to your company.

Read John's declaration at the beginning of this installation, reflect on what you have learned, write your message, and share it with the people at your company.

Feel free to share it with me as well by sending it to: *benny@bigchange.group*.

EXERCISES AND APPLICATIONS

EXERCISE: BUILD YOUR OWN PERSONAL TLC

The advanced exercise for this chapter is to build your own personal **TLC** that maps the elements of the system to your personal and professional life. The complete exercise can be found in the appendix at the back of this book.

In this installation, we took a journey through the history of **leadership**, discovered the power of transformational **leadership**, deepened our self-awareness, widened our scope of responsibility, identified the skillsets we will develop, and declared our **leadership** philosophy to the world around us. In the next installation, we will get to work creating our **north star**, so we bring direction to our transformation.

INSTALLATION 4

NORTH STAR

JOHN'S OLD-WORLD STATUS QUO

I stood in front of a room full of senior leaders at John's company. I drew a picture on the board of arrows in every direction and asked the room, "What word comes to mind when we see this picture?"

"Chaos," said the operations director.

"Explosion," Sue from marketing commented.

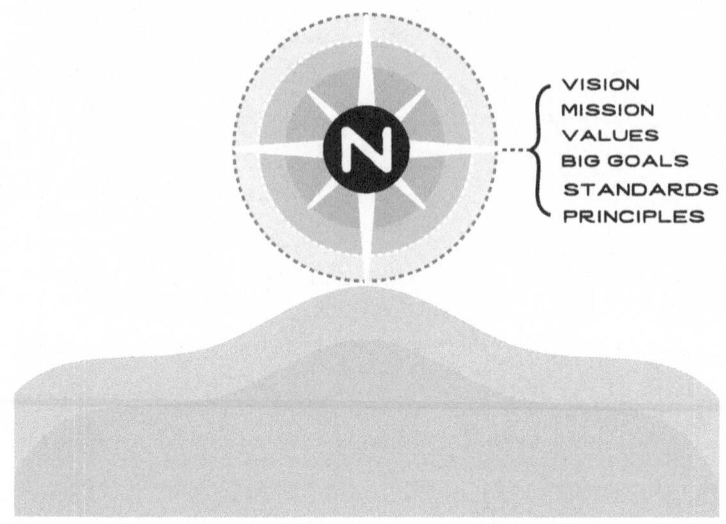

"The Big Bang," quipped the head of engineering.

"Our company," said John.

"A broken compass," Shane from IT remarked.

I like that—a broken compass.

"More like 1,000 broken compasses," the operations manager added.

I prodded him to develop this. "And what do all working compasses point to?"

"North," the room responded.

"If we keep following a working compass north, where do we end up?" I asked.

"Top of the world, baby!" Jane yelled with unbridled enthusiasm that was met with much laughter from the room.

You're damn right, Jane. It leads to our destination and our vision. And where are we leading these people to? Where are we going? Is it somewhere we have been before? *No!*

It's a new path. Uncharted, unknown, and floating in an ocean of **VUCA**. So how do we get there? Do we even know where it is? What is our reference point? How do we know we are moving towards it? And, most importantly, what is it? So many questions needed to be answered.

"There are two things we need to figure out together today," I said. "First, we need to know where we are taking the company. Second, we need to know how to bring our valuable people with us on the journey."

"Let's look at the arrows again. What does *one* company with everyone *moving* in the same direction look like? What would it look like if we are all pulling in the same direction, towards the same goals, on the same mission, working towards fulfilling the same vision?"

Shaun, the IT director, who had been very quiet up until this point, stood up, picked up the whiteboard marker and drew a whole set of arrows in a triangle formulation pointing up.

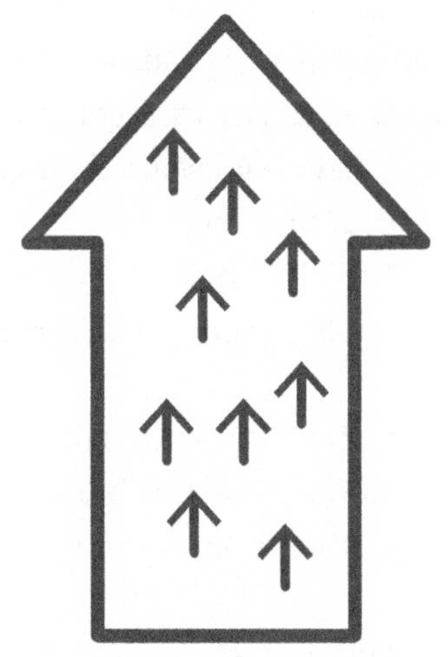

Everyone took a deep breath.

"We all need to work together, think together, and lead together," said John.

But there was a problem. The vision existed, but it was only in John's head. It had not been defined or expressed, let alone integrated into the **culture** and **brand assets**.

The values existed, but they meant nothing to the people or staff in the real world. They were just posters on the wall they walked past on the way to the humdrum of their old **status quo** world of business as usual. The BIG goals were there, but the only people who knew about them were the executive **team**, and they only spoke about them when it was time for their quarterly offsite meeting. The standards of how to conduct yourself existed, buried away in process manuals that no one read or referred to. Hardly a reference point to live your life by.

If this company wanted to grow and scale without sacrificing **results**, they needed to make these things real and known, and we had work to do.

JOHN'S NEW NORMAL

A few months later, things had changed. The **north star** was here, loud and proud. The vision, mission, and values of the company were known by all. Every meeting at every level of the company began by referring to the **north star**. You could walk up to any member of staff and ask them what it meant, and they could share their interpretation of what it meant to work at the company.

They had built the foundation of a strong **culture**. Each decision was guided by three questions:

1. Does it move us towards our vision?
2. Does it match our values?
3. Does it meet our standards?

There was a buzz about the place, and people felt certain of what it meant to work there. Staff felt safe in the direction they were going and empowered to make the choices knowing how to guide their thinking in the right way. Their **north star** had set the direction for the work that needed to be done.

The **events** of **team** ethos, **games**, and the selection and development of **players** that would follow aligned to this guiding set of clear direction and principles set out in their **north star**. They had a sense of safety in the decisions they made because they were empowered by **leadership** to create the **new normal**.

WHAT YOU'LL LEARN AND DO IN THIS INSTALLATION

In this instalment of **north star**, we will get to work creating an **asset** that defines our vision, mission, values, BIG goals, standards, and principles of our company. We will use this **north star** to guide the creation of all our **assets** and to direct the hearts and minds of the **players** in our company towards our **new normal**.

MOVING IN THE SAME DIRECTION

> *"If you could get all the people in an organization rowing in the same direction, you could dominate any industry, in any market, against any competition, at any time."*
>
> —*Patrick Lencioni*[45]

45 Patrick Lencioni, *The Five Dysfunctions of a* **Team**: *A Leadership Fable* (San Francisco: Jossey-Bass, 2002).

The idea of getting people to move towards the **north star** is powerful and so often overlooked or underplayed. In fact, if everybody could develop the thinking required to be able to move in the same direction, imagine how much time and energy we would save. Imagine how much conflict we could avoid and imagine how productive and profitable our companies would be.

The **TLC** provides the system to move in this direction and expand and grow as we go through the journey together.

When creating our **north star**, we create a direction for every department, **team**, and person within our company to calibrate their own **TLC. North star** inspires the hearts of your people to look towards a better, more compelling future. It excites and directs the minds of your people to think in a way that contributes to the BIG goals of the company.

If we don't have a clear **north star** communicated throughout our company, people will be stuck in the day-to-day activities. They won't see beyond the task they are doing, and their thinking will be limited to the problems immediately in front of them. Their engagement and motivation will be lacking. Without an aligned **team** ethos, it is likely they will only be turning up for their job and not with a shared mission and worthy cause bigger than themselves.

To create a unified and whole **culture** with everyone facing the same direction, we need to define what the vision, mission, values, and BIG goals of that compelling future look like and share the bigger picture, so they might be able to find the best way to contribute and be a part of the emerging **culture** and **brand.**

North star is a reference point we can build on through our **events** and our **asset** creation. It helps our **players** decide within the system what to do next and how to effectively think and grow together. It does not tell us exactly how to get to the vision. Rather, it enables them to align their own thinking and internal **TLC** to the bigger direction of where the **culture** and **brand** are moving.

By providing this direction from the top level of **leadership**, we're then able to calibrate, arrange, and become very organized in our **leadership** and management of the organization without suffocating their creativity or micromanaging every step of the way.

THE NORTH STAR COMPONENTS

North star is made up of the following components to guide and direct movement of the **TLC**. I will give you the brief definitions of these, and then we will dive deeper into how to create them in the following pages.

CORE VALUES

Statements that define who we are *now* as a whole and how we conduct ourselves (not who we would like to be in the future).

ASPIRATIONAL VALUES

Statements that define who we would like to become in the future as a **culture**.

MISSION

Why we exist as a company, what we stand and fight for, along with our worthy and just cause.

VISION

A picture of our desired future that gives clarity to where we are going as a company.

BIG GOALS

The biggest current objectives of our whole company.

STANDARDS (UNIVERSAL)

The simple and clear rules that apply to all of us, all the time, without exception.

PRINCIPLES

The guiding, good practice principles that define our collective identity and **culture**.

DEFINING CORE VALUES

A values system is a set of consistent statements used for the purpose of ethical and/or ideological integrity. **Players** have both a personal values system and a cultural values system. We can think of this in terms of their own **north star** and the company's **north star**. These values systems are considered to be externally consistent when they do not contradict each other, e.g., the **players'** values do not oppose the **north star** values.

> *"All the great things are simple, and many can be expressed in a single word: freedom, justice, honour, duty, mercy, hope."*
> —*Winston Churchill*

The **north star** can be simple. What is difficult and what requires effort and work are the conversations that follow the actual work of the **TLC**—the **events** and **rhythm**. The failure to have these conversations on a consistent basis until they become part of the company's **rhythm** and operation will be a failure to succeed.

Through inclusive **events** and **rhythm**, each values statement can be unpacked to find meaning for the individual **player** and the **team**. Thus, they can create their own **assets** and expressions of the core values, as well as belong, contribute, and identify with the **culture** so the company can grow and scale while remaining healthy.

GREAT THINKERS

The study of values is a field of philosophy called axiology. For the purposes of this book, we're going to look at the simplest way of defining core values that provide a useful **asset** for creating your **north star**.

> *"Greatness is not a function of circumstance. Greatness, in turns out, is largely a matter of conscious choice, and discipline."*
>
> —*Jim Collins*[46]

When Jim Collins examined the 10x companies (companies that had beat their industry index by ten times), he declared it is not the content of a company's values that correlate with

46 Jim Collins, *Good to Great: Why Some Companies Make The Leap...And Others Don't* (New York: HarperBusiness, 2001).

performance, but the strength of conviction with which it holds those values, whatever they might be. If Jim is right, the real work is in building the strength of values through **rhythm**, **events**, and **leadership** through **team** ethos, **games**, and **players**.

Your core values are who the company is, at its essence now. Not who we would like to be, not who we are some of the time; it's who we are consistently, now. These define what our behaviour reveals as the most important virtues. To us as a group, this is best defined not by what we say, but by what we say and do.

In defining core values, there is a series of **events** that needs to take place to create the **asset** of **north star**. We go further into how to run **events** and create **assets** in a later installation. For now, the most important thing is to give people—your **players** and your customers—a say and to involve them in the creation of this **north star asset**. This is a great opportunity to get a better understanding of the **status quo** and also to facilitate engagement and enrolment on the transformation journey.

If you already have a **north star** and it's working, great! Use or improve what you already have. If you don't, or it's not well-defined and embraced, let's get to work building or rebuilding it together.

There are three approaches that are useful here. I'll outline them first and then go into further detail.

1. Inclusive **events** and workshops that create value **assets**.
2. Surveying the company's people to gather data on what your people value.

3. Interviews with the company's people to document their stories and the narrative they have about the company.

1. EVENTS

If you are a very small company with a dozen or so staff, it's much easier. You can do this in an **event** where you bring people together, facilitate discussions, write all of the key words up on a board, and identify the themes and patterns to settle on the **asset**. Together, through the skills of a facilitator, you will decide collectively on four or five core values that really define you as a company.

With larger businesses and organisations of twelve to one hundred, to two hundred, or even five thousand people, it becomes a little more complex, but through **events** and surveys, we can make this easier. By holding simple workshop **events** in groups at all levels of the company, we offer the **players** the opportunity to have a hand in creating this **asset**, and we increase engagement from the very beginning.

I encourage you to record this and document it as you go because it is likely you will see very similar patterns across all of the groups. This information holds great value in forming your transformation strategy and for studying the **events** and **assets** installation in this book.[47]

2. SURVEYS

Another way to approach this is to send out value assessments, engagement surveys, and behavioural questionnaires

---

47 You can also go to the **event** installation for further guidance on this.

to obtain your **players'** insights. There are quite a few useful tools available. The selection of a specific tool to use will depend on your context. For a recommendation of what will suit you best, you can email me: *benny@bigchange.group*. Add Values Tools in the subject line.

You can also look into the following assessment tools on the market:

- ValueMatch
- Barrett Values Centre
- OCAI (Organisational Cultural Assessment Inventory)

We use the tools, collect the data, and then involve as many people as possible in the discovery of what the current values are. A great example is Toyota doing their **culture** jam, where they had tens of thousands of employees contributing to this conversation. They used algorithms to find the patterns in the words that came up to distil the core values based on the responses of their hive mind. This is powerful stuff in constructing a **north star**.

3. INTERVIEWS

I believe the most accurate method for finding your **north star** is the process of interviewing your people. If you can, set the right tone and intention for these conversations. The easiest way of doing this is by asking the following three questions and documenting their answers.

Here are the questions and prompts:

- Tell your story of working at this company.
- What do you think the company values most?
- Who do you think we are as a company?

Once we've collected this information, we've involved people in the process, and we've started to drive engagement and inclusion in the process of creating these core values. Then it is up to the **leadership team** to look at this information and the patterns. They must make the decision and define what the core values will be. For more specific instruction on how to formalise the creation of the values **asset**, read the installation **asset** chapter.

This will be signed off as a one-page from the **leadership team** in an **event**, and it will become an **asset** of the **culture**. This will provide the beginning framework for the **north star**.

EXAMPLES OF FUNCTIONAL VALUES SYSTEMS

ADIDAS

- **Performance**: Sport is the foundation for all we do and executional excellence is a core value of our group.
- **Passion**: Passion is at the heart of our company. We are continuously moving forward, innovating, and improving.
- **Integrity**: We are honest, open, ethical, and fair. People trust us to adhere to our word.
- **Diversity**: We know it takes people with different ideas, strengths, interests, and cultural backgrounds to make our company succeed. We encourage healthy debate and differences of opinion.

IKEA

- Humbleness and willpower.
- Leadership by example.
- Daring to be different.
- Togetherness and enthusiasm.
- Cost-consciousness.
- Constant desire for renewal.
- Accept and delegate responsibility.

VIRGIN AIRLINES

- We think customer.
- We lead the way.
- We do the right thing.
- We are determined to deliver.
- Together we make the difference.

STATING ASPIRATIONAL VALUES

Aspirational values are statements that point towards who we would like to be, who we aspire to be, and who we are not yet but could be with the right focus and direction. Useful questions to assess this are: What are we missing as a value? What is something that we really need to value in order to create the **new normal** we all desire?

As you develop a clear picture of the vision, the mission, the core values, and the BIG goals, this will provide some good indication of what needs to change in the **culture**, what needs to become the **new normal**, and what the aspirational value(s) need to be. The gap will become obvious as you move through this process.

REFLECTION POINTS

Grab your journal, consider your company core values and ask the following questions of your **leadership team**:

- Are our values a reflection of how our **players** truly see themselves in the **culture**?
- Is this how our customers see us?
- Is this what our customers also value?
- Is this how the market sees us when we work?
- Are we living this already, consistently?
- Are they memorable, clear, known, and regularly discussed by all?

Get your journal and calendar and plan the **events** to create the **north star asset** of core values.

The **events**, surveys, and interviews you run in this process will help inform the other elements of **north star** and will tell you a lot about the **status quo**. For further guidance on creating this **asset**, refer to the **events** and **assets** installations in this book.

Once we have set core values, let's begin to run the discussion of who we would like to be in our **new normal**. This is where we begin defining our aspirational values. While core values reflect who we are, aspirational values are statements of who we want to become.

Beware of the temptation to put forward a long list of aspirational values, the things we would like to become. Trust me, one or two aspirational values generally create more focus for change than a long list of wannabe statements. Consider one or two aspirational values that we will actively talk about in our **rhythm**, we will build into our **games** and conversations with our **players**, and that will help us to shift our behaviour.

You may even consider running a series of **events** around aspirational values where you can get **players** to discuss and decide on this **asset** of **north star**. The obvious benefit is that involvement will increase engagement. The less obvious benefit is that it will have a greater value as an **asset** of your **culture**.

An example of an aspirational value I encounter often is *collaboration*. Do you find your company **status quo** is always driving outcomes through individual effort? Would you identify the need to communicate and contribute across departments and areas as a gap? Then consider setting collaboration as an aspirational value—one you do not yet possess as a **culture** but are working towards developing.

Here are some of the most frequent aspirational values my clients desire:

1. Accountability
2. Ownership
3. Service
4. Continuous improvement
5. Open communication

In setting this aspirational value, we are setting the **north star** for how to align to **games**, how to improve those **games**, how to lead the discussion of **team** ethos in the **rhythm** at all areas of the business, and how to move us towards our **new normal.** Once we decide on and define the aspirational values (go for one or two), it will become part of how you run your **events** and how we coach in **rhythm.**

CREATE THE VISION

> *"A shared vision is not an idea...it is, rather, a force in people's hearts...at its simplest level, a shared vision is the answer to the question, 'What do we want to create?'"*
>
> —*Peter M. Senge*[48]

Your aim in creating the vision **asset** is to set a blaze of fire in the hearts of your people. Not an actual fire, but an emotional one. The kind that "brings thinking to a boiling point."[49] It is to give them something bigger than themselves to strive towards, so they may lose themselves in the pursuit of excellence by stating where we are going and what the **new normal** is and even giving them a glimpse into what the compelling future looks like. This gives people the opportunity to move towards the vision together with bravery and courage in their hearts.

Coming from a solid base of understanding through inquiry, **events**, and listening to your people, you will now have a set of core values the **leadership team** decided upon.

---

48 Peter M. Senge, *The Fifth Discipline: The Art and Practice of the Learning Organization* (New York: Doubleday/Currency, 2006).

49 Chip Heath and Dan Heath, *Made to Stick: Why Some Ideas Survive and Others Die* (New York: Random House, 2007.)

It is up to the leader to be able to articulate the vision for the company, the vision for where we are going, and to define this in a statement that frames the top of the **north star**.

The understanding of where we are and where we want to expand to provides a useful base to articulate where we are heading.

Great vision statements include where we are going, and what success looks like. It's a foundational **asset** that sets the sights of the company focused and in the same direction. They paint a picture of a better tomorrow that includes the staff, customers, and society. Vision statements exist to inspire possibility in thinking.

Here are some examples of short vision statements:

- Disney: To make people happy
- Oxfam: A world without poverty
- Microsoft: Empower every person and every organization on the planet to achieve more
- Nike: To bring inspiration and innovation to every athlete in the world
- Nike in the '60s: Crush Adidas
- Honda in the '70s: We will destroy Yamaha
- Ford: People working together as a lean, global enterprise to make people's lives better through automotive and mobility **leadership**
- Kraft Heinz: To be the best food company, growing a better world.

Here is an example of a longer vision statement:

THE COCA-COLA COMPANY

> *"Our vision is to craft the* **brands** *and choice of drinks that people love, to refresh them in body and spirit. And done in ways that create a more sustainable business and better shared future that makes a difference in people's lives, communities and our planet."*

When we create a vision **asset**, we are really talking about the idea of the company's promised land: where the **leadership** is taking people, where we ultimately want to go, and what the future will look like because our company exists.

When we define this, bring language to this, and we make this known, we begin to transform the language and the behaviour of our organization. It will serve you well to construct a concise and powerful statement, a promise of a better future, a promise that if we do this work, if we go above and beyond, this is what it'll look like, and this is how the future will be better. After all, to lead is to take us somewhere we've never been before.

To create the vision **asset**, the leader has to spend time in reflection on the core values, spend time analysing **results**, and plan the strategic direction of the company while being thorough in asking questions and consulting with the clients and customers of the business about the contribution the company makes and the potential to expand the **TLC**.

Once the leader has prepared a draft of this or captured this idea, it is to be shared with the **leadership team** for some robust conversation.

This is an **event** to facilitate an open and safe conversation that leads to the output of the best vision **asset** you can create right now. This will be reset over time, as the company goes through the continuous cycle of learning and development. How often you reset and redefine this very much depends on the company, but a good place to start is a three-year vision.

CRAFTING THE MISSION—OUR WORTHY CAUSE

> *"Life is a mission, not a career. A career is a profession, a mission is a cause. A career asks, what's in it for me? A mission asks, how can I make a difference?"*
>
> —*Sean Covey*[50]

Your mission statement is *why* you exist, what you stand for and fight for.

In crafting your mission statement, you will inevitably come to something that speaks of a worthy cause that your **brand** expresses and your **players** can identify with. It aligns with their own personal mission. It should be short and sharp, but people should immediately realize that this is a common cause of everybody within this **culture** and environment. If the vision statement is a reference of where we are going, the mission statement gives an overarching direction of how we're all going to get there together. It's a broad statement that describes what we must do in our hearts continuously to reach the vision. It's the mission we're all on together, what

50 Stephen R. Covey, *The 7 Habits of Highly Effective People* (New York: Simon & Schuster, 2020).

REFLECTION POINTS

Here is a list of useful questions to get your juices flowing. Take your journal and work through this.

Imagine you travel three years into the future in a time machine:

- What do you see?
- What do you hear?
- What are clients saying about your **brand**?
- How would you describe your **culture**?
- What does the market say about your **brand**?
- What sales, operations, and innovation **games** are we playing and winning?
- How is the company running day-to-day in its **rhythm**?
- What do the company's **results** tell us?
- What **games** are we winning in the market?
- What are our **players** all about—their attitudes, their words, their relationships?

Reflect and document this in your **leadership** journal, and then take this thinking and distil it into memorable language that everyone can commit to head and heart.

we stand for and fight for, and our worthy cause.

Like the vision, it needs to be inclusive. It needs to be something people can identify with and understand. It needs to be defined clearly and expressed through the company **events** and the **rhythm**.

Here are some examples of mission statements as worthy causes:

- Uber: We ignite opportunity by setting the world in motion.
- Kickstarter: To help bring creative projects to life.
- Tesla: To accelerate the world's transition to sustainable energy.
- Google: To organize the world's information and make it universally accessible and useful.

Create this **asset** when you are ready and refer to the **assets** installation in this book for more guidance.

BIG GOALS

Now the next point for **north star**.

We have a guiding and well-thought-out set of core values, our vision of what our compelling future looks like, our mission, what we stand for, and how we get the vision together in line with our values.

We also need to set some concrete **north star** goals. FranklinCovey calls them WIGs: wildly important goals. We call them BIG goals: BIG important goals. Whatever you want to call them, one thing is worth considering: less is more.

Studies from FranklinCovey have shown that companies with fewer BIG goals and fewer large objectives tend to perform better over time.[51]

BIG goals point towards the vision and quantify the focused aspects of it. By focusing our **north star** around the two or three biggest goals of the whole company, we are well-positioned to establish our **north star.** Then we can begin to align our organisation towards this point. When we have BIG goals in place that are known by all, it allows us to align our **games** toward a shared outcome.

The obvious BIG goal for any growing business is a profit number. The problem with having a BIG goal around profit is it doesn't necessarily inspire or speak to the **players** that make up the **games** within the **TLC.** Consider creating your BIG goals around performance and profit and then consider how to articulate this in terms of purpose.

For example, if we know that we need to make fifty million in revenue, don't set the goal to make fifty million in revenue. Set the goal to serve X many customers with Y amount of value (which will equal fifty million in revenue). This achieves the same **results**; however, the language aligns and balances the **north star** because it matches our values, mission, and vision, and it's defined in a way our **players** are more likely to relate to and embrace.

In the effective setting of BIG goals, we can create a BIG **game** where every single department, **team**, and individual **player** can find their own contribution through their own

51 Chris McChesney, Sean Covey, and Jim Huling, *The 4 Disciplines of Execution* (New York: Free Press, 2012).

REFLECTION POINTS

Here are some useful questions to consider when creating your BIG goal **asset** of your **north star**. Grab your journal.

- Do the BIG goals align with our mission?
- Can we get every person in the business to contribute to a **game** that helps these BIG goals happen?
- Can we measure our progress toward the BIG goal?
- Does the BIG goal move us towards our vision?
- Is it a reflection of our core values, and is it aspirational?
- Are we happy to share this with everyone in the business?

Once the BIG goals are set, the work begins in aligning everybody towards their games to point towards the BIG goals (more on this in the games installation). Remember, every game in the business exists to contribute towards the BIG goals. That's every Goal, Activity, Measurement, Expectation, and Support system.

The BIG goal of **north star** informs the thinking of everyone in the company to what the greatest priorities are.

games. Quite simply, the goals of every **game** align to the BIG goal of **north star.**

COMPANY-WIDE STANDARDS

The next part of creating a **north star asset** is to set the company-wide standards.

With a solid base of our core values—a vision of where we're going, our mission of how we get there, our aspirations of who we need to become to get there, and our BIG goals in place—we are well on our way towards our vision and the creation of the **new normal.**

The next step we need to take care of is the company-wide standards. Company-wide standards are defined as:

1. Nonnegotiable
2. Applicable to everyone all the time
3. Clear and obvious

By creating a small list of very clear standards, we are now setting the basic and clear rules that govern the **TLC** of the company. Later, there may be standards that apply to each **team** in each department in each group that are more specific and more relevant to their **team** ethos and the expectations in the **games.** At the level of **north star**, however, company-wide standards are the nonnegotiables that everybody needs to live by in order to be part of your organization.

REFLECTION POINTS

Here are a few considerations in setting your company-wide standards. Reflect on these and make notes in your journal.

- Standards should be clear-cut when possible. The best standards are set when it is obvious and clear whether someone is on-standard or off-standard.
- Your **culture** will be shaped over time by the lowest and highest standards you are willing to tolerate.
- The standards are truly set by what happens when they are broken.
- The standards become the **new normal** when somebody does something that does not adhere to the standards, and the **players** respond with a correction.
- It is more effective to have fewer standards that everyone knows by heart and can identify and share than a long list that does not get brought to life.

Consider this: the standard of standards is affected when any one of these standards slips away. The whole system tends to weaken and shrink. When you set a standard and let it slip, the entire meaning of standards in your **culture** slips. This causes your **TLC** to shrink and the system to move off-direction towards the **north star**. Remember, this is very different than creating a policies and procedures manual that nobody reads. This is about creating the ground rules that apply to everybody in the company. Done well, this specific set of rules exists within the core and aspirational values that promote direction towards the vision. It is one of the best things to get right in creating your **north star asset**.

Your company-wide standards can be as simple as a communications standard around response time. For example, McKinsey & Company, the most profitable consulting firm in the known universe, has a company-wide standard that every email from someone from the alumni gets a response within twenty-four hours, even if that response is simply, "I'll have to get back to you in a week." The point is that the standard around communication applies to every partner, every principal, every graduate, everyone. They all live by this rule.

Here are some more examples of company-wide **north star** standards:

- Show up on time for meetings or send an apology in advance.
- Follow through on every commitment you make.
- Reply to emails within twenty-four hours.
- Never lie to our customers.

- If you see something unsafe, report it immediately.
- Connect with one person from the company you have not met yet each week.

You get the picture. These universal standards are the more specific rules that support your values system. They set the broad set of expectations for our **culture**.

Ideally, we create this in a series of **events** that involves people in the process, gathers their input, and co-creates this **asset** for them, so they can have a sense of ownership over the expectations. Your **north star** aligns the **TLC** through these very simple and obvious but unquestionable standards of behaviour.

Again, try to make this as simple and clear as possible because we are going to express this through your business, and clarity creates focus, and focus time consistency equals change.

YOUR COMMUNICATIONS PLAN

When your **north star asset** is ready—you've run the **events**, you've had conversations, you've created a very solid, clear direction for the whole company—then we need to make it known, understood, and practiced by all. To do this, you take it to the **rhythm** and make it part of the conversation. We'll go deeper on how to do this in the **rhythm** installation.

If the **asset** of **north star** is not communicated consistently in the **rhythm** for every department, **team**, and **player** in the business, including visually, orally, and through the actions of the **leadership team**, the **asset** of **north star** will be devalued. In turn, the **TLC** will shrink, and **VUCA** will prevail.

So how do we communicate **north star** through the business? We can begin by making it visual and everywhere, as in posters, cards, videos, etc. Pretty much everything you can think of to keep this front of mind for people. Look at the **assets** section of this book and get creative.

As we bring the north star into the conversation of the **rhythm** on a consistent basis, these **assets** serve as a reference point of what we focus on and how we align on decisions and actions. If you've done your **events** well, people will feel involved in the process and will experience a sense of identity and ownership of the **assets**. This is a good thing because we are now going to use the **north star** to guide every **event** that produces every **asset** that follows for **brand**, **team**, **games**, and **players**.

Display your **north star** everywhere! Online, offline, verbally, visually. You shouldn't be able to walk into a room without seeing it. Include it in every correspondence at some level. It should be expressed clearly and articulately throughout the whole business, building it into the language of your **culture**. It should be visible to everybody in the company. Over time, as those **assets** become part of the conversation, they can then be expressed as an authentic **brand**.

Over time, as the **new normal** is established and everybody in the business understands **north star** through the **rhythm** of communication and understands how to talk about it and work towards it, it can then be expressed to the market in terms of "this is who we are" as an identity.

The **asset** of **north star** is an **asset** of higher purpose. When everybody understands, it becomes an artefact of who we are at our core identity. It becomes the most valuable **asset** in the business. The **asset** of **north star** exists to inspire. It exists to influence. And it exists to shape the thinking of every department, **team**, and person in your business towards the greater goal and greater purpose. You are creating a future state people can think through and move towards.

In this instalment, we learned how to go about creating our **north star asset.**

We have our vision, mission, values, BIG goals, standards, and principles that will serve as the guiding light in creating our **assets** for our **players, teams, games,** and **results.**

We can now begin bringing this to life by working through each of the elements of our **TLC** and running **events** that create the **assets** that we will use in our **rhythm** to create our **new normal** and direct our company towards our compelling future.

As we move into the next part of this book, we're going to start aligning the **TLC** to every dynamic element of your company. But first, let's get some **change agents** to help us lead the charge.

INSTALLATION 5

CHANGE AGENTS

JOHN'S OLD-WORLD STATUS QUO

"This all seems like a lot of work," said John. "Yes, I get that we need to be active and involved to make this transformation happen, but I'm only one guy, and we have thousands of staff. It's a huge thing to take on."

John pulled out his list again. "Developing leaders? How do we go about doing this? I need people who really get this stuff to help lead it and help bring the changes to life."

John was spot-on.

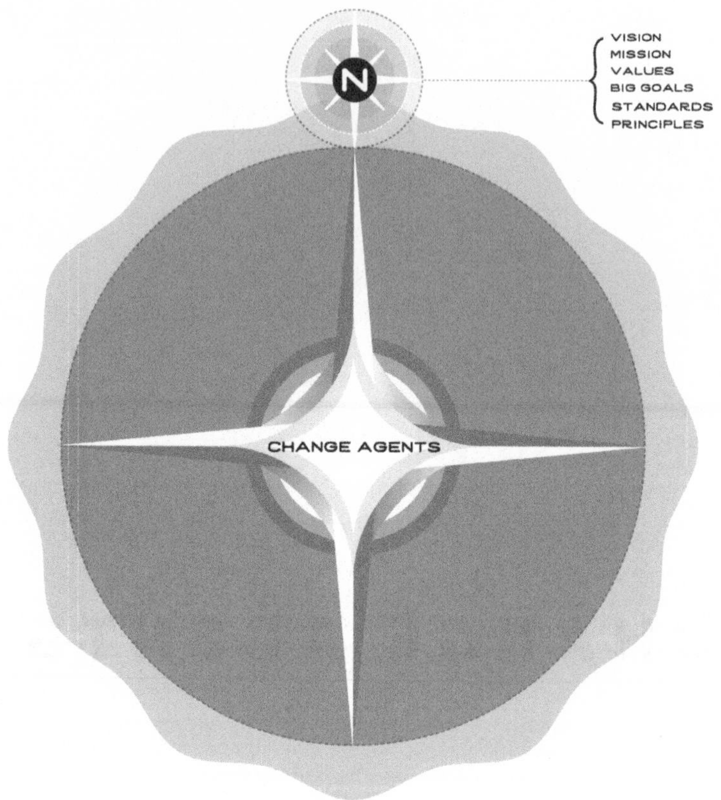

We needed to develop a group of people capable of leading these changes and helping to build the **new normal**, so we set about selecting and developing the **change agents** at John's company.

JOHN'S NEW NORMAL

John's **change agents** had been assembled across every function of the business. They did not come exclusively from levels of management with authority. They were selected based on their personality, their natural flair for inspiring people, and their potential to be future leaders in the business. They came from the front-of-house, the shop floor, and cleaners. They came from offices and factories, from all levels of the business, and they represented every area in the company.

These **change agents** were the ones best suited to go out and have the conversations in the daily **rhythm** to challenge people's thinking, to encourage the conversations that mattered to take place, and to share the stories that brought the **culture** to life. They would discuss what was going well in the **culture**, and what needed their careful thought and attention. They ran this group like a **team** of **teams**, obsessed with making the company a better place to work and moving the **culture** towards the **north star**.

It was exciting to see people at all levels sharing their insights, not by management, position, or authority, but through a genuine desire to improve the **culture**. Through our sessions, we shared the **TLC**, models, and language of **leadership** that helped these people develop to lead from the front—to inspire, influence, and impact those around them.

They set out to go to every meeting, to plaster the walls with the **team** ethos of the company, to make it their own personal mission to find the areas that weren't part of the **culture**, and to help them improve. This was truly an empowered **team** of **leaders**. They became the **change agents** that led and improved the **culture** and helped lead the transformation to the **new normal**.

WHAT YOU WILL LEARN AND DO IN THIS INSTALLATION

In this instalment, we get to work in putting together our group of **change agents**. We'll look at the dangers of change and develop our understanding of good practice through the best models of change management. We'll also create our **change agents** charter **asset** and use this to amplify our impact through hands-on **leadership** development as we transform our company and build the **new normal.**

To transform the world around you is no easy feat.

Leaders have two fundamental challenges to meet:

1. Making things better than they are now.
2. Developing other people to help make things better than they are now.

Simple, wouldn't you agree?

The practice of change management has moved from the domain of the consultant hired when we launch a new IT system to a central skillset of **leadership** and management. It may even be said that these days, all management is change management.

The responsibility to create and respond to change is the most important mission of the leader. As the great Seth Godin put it:

> *"Your art is the act of taking personal responsibility, challenging the* **status quo**, *and changing people."*[52]

---

52 Visit the Mighty Seth Godin here: https://seths.blog/.

This change can come from necessity or possibility. Some companies and leaders change because they have to. The world around them shifts, and a new technology or crisis emerges. They need to make changes to survive. Some companies and leaders change because they see the possibility of constant improvement, of always finding a better way to do things, to learn and strive for growth through embracing the fact that the only thing that does not change is that the world will change.

The beautiful irony here is that the leaders and companies who get good at changing out of possibility are ready and able to change fast and effectively when they have to change out of necessity. Some call this "change readiness," and I think Jack Welch said it best when he advised us to "change before you have to."[53]

As you look at the **TLC**, notice the ripples from the ocean of **VUCA** coming inwards towards the centre. Waves that rock the **status quo** and shake up the way we have always done things forces us to adapt or die. They demand we face the changes of the world or fall away and lose relevance. The waves crash on our **brand**, and the external forces flood through our **culture** and into our **results**, **teams**, and **players**. Action must be taken to create a **new normal** fast and restore balance to the **TLC** in the most effective and least damaging way possible.

When crises become the first order of the day, our **north star** can be whacked out of orbit as we face a market takeover, a new and threatening technology, or a global pandemic.

---

53 Jack Welch, *Jack: Straight from the Gut* (New York: Warner Business Books, 2003).

The **TLC leader** is all about constant transformation and change. It is change because you want to improve and grow infinitely.

The ripples come out from the centre.

Transformational leaders are constantly working with their **teams**, **players**, and **games** to improve the **results**, shape the **culture**, and shift from the **status quo** to a **new normal**. They are constantly running **events** of change and innovation. Their **rhythm** is one of infinite improvement and growth, and their actions and innovations ripple out from the centre and create waves in **VUCA**. They reshape the world through changing from the inside out. When a tidal wave of change crashes in from the **VUCA** world outside their **TLC**, they are ready; their **players**, **teams**, **games**, and **culture** are strong, agile, and even "antifragile" as they become skilled and experienced in dealing with the change. They can roll with it and weather the storm while their complacent competitors capsize in **VUCA** and wash up on the shores of bankruptcy and irrelevance.

THE DANGERS OF CHANGE

It is important that **leaders** have a handle on good practice when it comes to making effective change happen. Far too often, I find **leaders** in all sorts of difficulty for two main reasons:

1. They don't take into consideration how each element of the **TLC** affects every other element when they make decisions.
2. They don't take the right steps to involve the people in the change process and end up with resistance

and engagement issues that damage the **culture**, the perception of **leadership**, and ultimately, the **brand** and long-term **results** of the company.

To help us become great at change, let's have a very brief look at the evolution of change management theory. From there, we will equip you with the latest thinking and get ready to shape your company's **TLC**. As we move through this history of thought, I will share the most valuable parts of each theory or way of seeing things, and I'll explain how this works in terms of **TLC** thinking.

A VERY BRIEF HISTORY OF CHANGE MANAGEMENT

As you read through this, note your observations and ideas in your journal.

Pioneering psychologist Kurt Lewin gave us his Three-Step Change Theory.[54]

It basically worked like this: *unfreeze* the **status quo** by increasing discomfort and shaking up the existing "mindset" and bypass defence mechanisms. Then make *change* by adopting the new ideas, communicating and training people, *refreeze*, and lock in to make the permanent the **new normal**. Simple, huh? No, there is a bit more to this.

Elisabeth Kübler-Ross gave us a model of change that recognised that the human side of change correlated strongly

54 Kurt Lewin, "Frontiers in Group Dynamics," *Human Relations* 1, no. 1 (June 1947): 5–41, https://doi.org/10.1177/001872674700100103.

with the emotion of grief, and it mapped morale and competence over time with the stages of:[55]

1. Shock
2. Denial
3. Frustration
4. Depression
5. Experimentation
6. Decision
7. Integration

It is of great importance to be aware that emotions around change often follow the emotional journey of grief, particularly when the change is out of necessity and is a requirement to continue amidst **VUCA**. The practice here is to be aware of the emotions people are experiencing when faced with change. This requires the emotional intelligence or EQ we looked at in the **leadership** installation. Of course, further training in EQ is beneficial and recommended.[56]

As change-thinking evolved, Everett Rogers classed **players** into groups based on how they responded to change:[57]

- **Early Adopters**: those who jump into change fast
- **Early Majority**: those who join the early adopters

---

55 Elisabeth Kübler-Ross, *On Death and Dying: What the Dying Have to Teach Doctors, Nurses, Clergy & Their Own Families* (New York: Macmillan Publishing, 1970).

56 Look at Daniel Goleman's work and training on offer.

57 Everett Rogers, *Diffusion of Innovations*, 5th ed (New York: Free Press, 2003).

- **Late Majority**: those who join because it's becoming the **new normal**
- **Laggards**: those who fight to keep the **status quo**

Finally, we were getting into an integration of the models of the past and were moving towards an integrated approach.

The great Virginia Satir added the dip in performance over time as the "Virginia Satir Change Model."[58]

1. **Status quo** and new element coming in
2. Resistance
3. Chaos and a drop of performance as the new change comes in
4. Integration—rise in performance as the new change stabilizes
5. New **status quo** (**new normal**)

What we learn from this research is there is a dip in performance that often comes when change is introduced. As we go through the process of integrating and creating the **new normal**, we work through the dip. With longer-term initiatives, you should plan for and expect a temporary drop in performance at times. In some **results** areas, as you work through the changes in your **status quo**, set your expectations and strategy accordingly.

In the 2000s, Linda Ackerman wrote *Beyond Change Management* and shared that top leaders had recognised that

58 Virginia Satir, *Satir Step By Step: A Guide to Creating Change in Families* (Palo Alto, CA: Science and Behavior Books, Inc., 1984).

many of their top-down changes failed, and the trend was moving towards creating a role for a change leader to take responsibility for the human side of change.

The evidence was in. Change works best with a top-down and bottom-up approach involving and consulting your people on the journey of transformation. There are a few golden principles to consider brought to you by change expert, John Kotter.

Kotter boiled it down to eight steps:[59]

1. Create urgency
2. Form a powerful coalition
3. Create a vision for change
4. Communicate the vision
5. Empower action
6. Create quick wins
7. Build on the change
8. Make it stick

Kotter went on to provide academic research on what my colleagues and I had been practising for years. In his book, *Accelerate*, Kotter proposes something called a dual operating system.[60] He discovered this by studying the practices of the most effective **change agents** in the field.

A dual operating system is made up of two groups:

---

59 John P. Kotter, *Leading Change* (Brighton, MA: Harvard Business Review Press, 2012).

60 John P. Kotter, *Accelerate: Building Strategic Agility for a Fast Moving World* (Brighton, MA: Harvard Business Review Press, 2014).

1. A traditional management hierarchy responsible for the goals of the business.
2. A networked group for all levels of areas in the company that is responsible for delivering the change.

You have the best of both worlds as these groups work together to navigate the change from the **status quo** to the **new normal.**

We call this networked group your **change agents.**

Your **change agent's** group can consist of people who lead by title, so it will include your executive **team** and your management **team.** It can also include your **change agents team.**

To identify who should be on the **change agents team,** you can look for the following behavioural qualities:

1. They speak the language of the **TLC** quite easily, and it comes naturally to them.
2. They may not necessarily have positions of authority in the business, but people listen to them.
3. They show potential for future **leadership** positions.
4. They are natural facilitators.

You will find that they may develop as leaders through the **TLC** process and can help carry this work through the whole company.

Journal it, chose them, and let's start the journey. We bring these people together in a room for **events** to create the **assets** and to set out the scope of work required to make this change of who we are, to move us towards **north star,** and to help do the work in the installations that follow.

Before we get to that, let's create a charter for this group, an **asset** that we can use to align these fine **players** to our **north star**.

CREATING THE CHANGE AGENTS CHARTER ASSET

The charter **asset** exists to charter the course of change for the company.

This document will be an **asset** to show the objectives, the **events**, and the standards of your **change agents** to be able to go forth and lead this initiative. We go through this process in more depth in the **events** and **assets** installations. For now, grab your journal and think this through.

EXERCISES AND APPLICATIONS

EXERCISE: CREATING THE CHANGE AGENTS CHARTER

Get your **change agents** together by scheduling a workshop event.

You will need two or three hours, a whiteboard, a good facilitator, some butcher paper, and most likely coffee.

FIRST: TELL THEM THE *PURPOSE* OF THIS SESSION

The purpose of this session is for us to define and document one single page that explains what we are doing as **change agents**. This will be our **change agent's asset**.

SECOND: SET *STANDARDS* FOR THE ROOM AND THE DAY'S EVENT

Let them know you want them to set the standards for how we spend the next few hours together and ask them what the standards for this **event** should be.

I have done hundreds of these and the standards that always come up are:

- Everyone contributes
- Do not talk over each other
- Speak now or forever hold your peace
- We agree to do what we commit to do in this room

Keep the session purpose and standards on the board and point back to them whenever you get off track in the session.

THIRD: INTRODUCE THE CONCEPT OF THE *ONE*-PAGE CHARTER

Clearly define that this one page will serve as the main document for the **change agents**.

- They must understand that this is, in fact, their first **asset**.

FOURTH: WRITE THE **CHANGE AGENT** CHARTER AT THE TOP OF THE PAGE/BOARD/SCREEN

Take your marker or digital platform and write this as your headline.

FIFTH: SET A TIMEFRAME: THREE MONTHS/ SIX MONTHS/TWELVE MONTHS

Keep in mind that you will reset this charter at the end of this timeframe, and you will do it again in a future **event**. You will also be likely to get better and better at this over time.

Document the next **event** *RESET date in your calendar.*

SIXTH: WRITE *PURPOSE* AT THE TOP OF THE PAGE

The Questions:

- Why are we doing this?
- What is the purpose of running these sessions?

- Are we moving towards our **north star**?
- What are we going to change next?

A good facilitator here will dig. They will make sure everyone in the room speaks and refers back to the standards. They will help the room articulate a very refined and distilled purpose for doing this work.

Write the purpose on the board.

SEVENTH: WRITE *OBJECTIVES* AT THE TOP OF THE BOARD

Include what you have decided from your **status quo** thinking as the most important next change. At the same time, be open to the ideas that the group brings forward in this session.

The Questions:

- What will change as a **result** of this group?
- What will be different?
- What are the top three BIG changes that we need to make in your area of the company?

Place these on Post-it notes or butchers paper all around the room for reference in the event.

Keep this to the PROGRAM objectives, not the company objectives. The company objectives will be set later in **north star**.

EIGHTH: WRITE *MEASURES* AT THE TOP OF THE BOARD

The Questions:

- How will we know this change has occurred? Refer to objectives.

- How will we monitor the progress?
- Make sure each objective has the one (max two) clear measure of progress for each.

NINTH: WRITE *AREAS* (OR CATEGORIES) AT THE TOP OF THE BOARD

The Questions:

- What major areas will we address?
- List them by department or function related to the objectives.

TENTH: WRITE *THEMES* NEXT TO EACH AREA (USE THE PROVIDED TEMPLATE)

The Questions:

- In one sentence, what is the biggest *theme* change for each area of the company?
- Limit this to *one* per area and make sure this aligns to the purpose.

ELEVENTH: THE SIGNING CEREMONY

Leave space at the bottom and invite everyone in the room to come up and sign this one-page document.

We now have a clear and agreed **change agents** charter defining exactly *why* we are doing this, what we will change, how we will work together to make it happen, and how it aligns to our **north star**.

You now need to print this and put it up at the following **events**:

- Whenever this group meets (this should be a regular and consistent **event**)

- Whenever you are introducing the transformation program to other groups
- Whenever there is distraction or lack of focus

Remember, this is an ongoing process of change and improvement. Put the RESET date in your diary and schedule the **event** ahead of time with *all* involved. Get ready to build the company **culture** in line with the changes you have imagined and dreamed of.

In this installation of **change agents**, we selected our group of **change agents** from all areas and levels of our company. We have developed an understanding of how to go about the process of change based on the best models and practices available.

We created the charter that defines the **change agents'** group and began the work of developing our transformational leaders through the **TLC** process. Now you have a group of **change agents** and a chartered course for development. Let's go deep into the element of **culture** to understand the BIG picture of the **TLC** system.

INSTALLATION 6

CULTURE

JOHN'S OLD-WORLD STATUS QUO

"I'm just trying to do my bloody job. There were a few 'incidents' and complaints from staff again this week. This is not unusual for us," John's HR director said. He looked tense as we sat in his office.

"That's just the stuff we know about. Most of the time, I feel that people don't speak up. It's like they just assume there is nothing that can be done to change things. No one calls out bad behaviour. Hell, we don't even recognise what good behaviour looks like a lot of the time. It's like everyone is out

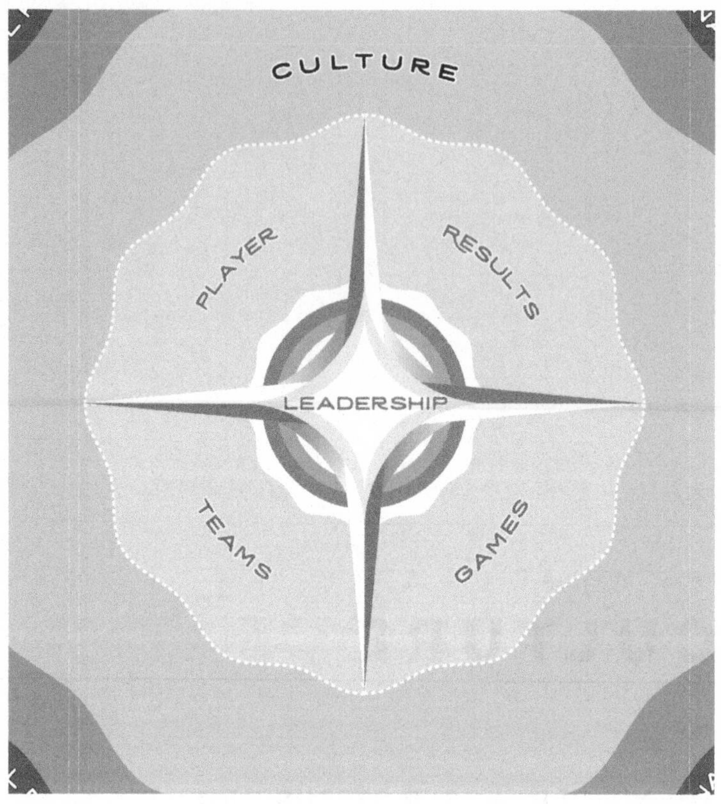

for themselves. People don't trust each other. It sometimes seems like our world is very selfish."

People were doing their best to fly under the radar, and when things went wrong or times got tough, everyone blamed everyone else. Every issue was met with a "Wasn't me." Posters on the wall about trust and **team**work had become the butt of sarcastic jokes, and it seemed there was a grave assumption that **leadership** would do what **leadership** does and there was not a damn thing the workers could do about it. If you were to ask them candidly, which I did, the people would tell you that they were just there for a paycheck and then they'd go home with no greater cause and nothing to be truly proud of. Another day and another dollar. Stay safe. Survive.

Maybe if you kissed enough ass, you would be promoted, or maybe if you played the right political cards, you could get ahead. The ones who did get ahead would carry on the cycle of defensive, scared, protective talk and behaviour. They knew that all their symptoms of lower productivity, nasty customer service complaints, poor or average performance, high absenteeism, and even higher turnover came from this nebulous and strange term called **culture**.

The word *culture* had become popular in business books, but until now, it had been seen as fluffy feel-good stuff, something that could be fixed by having more barbecues and benefits, more systems and software, more ropes courses and trust falls, maybe another off-the-shelf **leadership** development workshop.

John was not having it. He had woken up and realised that if he really wanted to make a difference and leave a lasting legacy here, he had to, as he said, "get our **culture** right." John had decided to make the ultimate shift. He wanted to intentionally move away from the **culture** that just happened as an afterthought and move toward the work of creating a **culture** on purpose. He would put the **culture**, the leading and shaping of the hearts and minds of his people first. So, of course, we set to work in creating the **new normal** and the new world.

JOHN'S NEW NORMAL

Twelve months later, the air felt different. You could hear people speaking in empowered tones and sharing new stories. In the beginning, they wondered when **leadership** would get tired of these new **events** and this new meeting and speaking **rhythm**. But it didn't go back to the old ways. They stuck at it, and this became the **new normal**. People were given the permission and empowerment to move towards the **north star**. They were given the **events** and encouragement to make their company a community they all had a hand in shaping. There was a huge sense of pride. You could hear it when they spoke about where they worked. When something was out of whack, they called it out, loudly, and without blame or shame. They learned this through **TLC leadership**.

In the old world, when something was off, everyone looked the other way and waited for management to deal with it. In the new world, the **culture** managed itself. It was empowered and engaged by the system of the **TLC**. The people felt a new sense of trust in **leadership** and had found the courage and empowerment necessary to make a difference and the **rhythm** of getting a bit better every day. Sure, it was hard work, but man was it worth it.

Performance and profits skyrocketed, and it was abundantly clear that each member of the company shared and celebrated a strong sense of purpose and pride. The new world was a **culture** built carefully, intentionally, and for a much bigger purpose than the agendas of a few individuals. This was a truly great place to work, where you could, with the right effort and attitude, have a magnificent career and a deeply fulfilling life.

So how did they do it? With a bit of the **TLC**, of course.

WHAT YOU WILL LEARN AND DO IN THIS INSTALLATION

In this installation, we deepen our understanding of **culture** and what it means to change **culture**. We will draw on a wealth of knowledge on the topic of organisational **culture** and emerge with insights on how to shape the **culture** of our company using the **TLC** system.

By reading, reflecting, and taking notes in our **status quo** journal, we will form a map of what our **culture** is and how we will go about shaping it.

THE BIG PICTURE

When we step outside the daily whirlwind of responsibilities and take stock of what is really going on in our company, we can develop a view of what we call **culture**. The BIG picture challenge in transforming a company is that of changing **culture**, and this is probably why so few **leaders** take up this challenge.

It seems that so many CEOs play musical chairs. Driven by quarter-to-quarter thinking, they jump into the seat, the next role at the next company, make some large, hard, and fast changes to strategy and budgets, and move on to the next assignment. Very few **leaders** dare to tackle the larger challenge at hand—changing the **culture**.

Changing the **culture** means changing the deep assumptions, the taken-for-granted norms and collective mindset of the company. In **TLC** terms, this is creating the **new normal.** In large companies, this presents a complex challenge with serious work required to change and rewire the organisation's mindset and operating system. Yes, the **TLC** provides a way to do this. In small and growing businesses, there exists a wonderful opportunity and also a terrible risk. The opportunity is to get the foundation right from the early stages. The risk is to put this off and have to deal with the complexity of **culture** change later down the track.

As our world becomes more **VUCA**, the thinking of **leaders** is changing with these times. In the past, **culture** change work was seen as a nice to have luxury for companies with a dedicated training and development budget that was okay to spend, provided that it did not get in the way of the immediate **results** and short-term strategy.

In the words of the great philosopher, James P. Carse, celebrated by Simon Sinek:

> ***Culture** is an infinite **game**.*[61]

It's deep and true. You cannot win **culture**, although, in understanding and improving **culture**, everything is won. **Culture** is a living system, a never-ending challenge to shape and improve. The invitation here for the **leader** is to understand how **culture** is everything and how everything affects

---

61 James P. Carse, *Finite and Infinite Games: A Vision of Life as Play and Possibility* (New York: Free Press, 1986).

culture. By understanding this and applying the thinking of the **TLC** to your **culture** and to your **leadership** practices, you will make better decisions, and you'll ultimately transform your company.

CULTURE MATTERS

This is a hot topic right now. What was once seen as a domain of HR and an afterthought to strategy and planning is now being recognised as a major responsibility of leaders. Bubbling under the surface for years as an ambiguous term used by organisational development consultants, **culture** is fast becoming a mainstream topic of strategy in boardrooms and executive meetings. It may soon become a requirement of accounting and reporting.

So, where's the data? What are the facts and stats that inform the thinking that **culture** has an effect on our **results**? According to research from Human Synergistics across four industry sectors, here are just some of the statistics indicating how having a strong **culture** tends to affect our **results**.[62]

When looking at companies across the following sectors, companies that have a strong **culture** (a **culture** where people can demonstrate an understanding of what their **culture** is and clearly articulate their **north star**), tend to outperform the average **results** of companies that have a weak **culture** (a **culture** that cannot be clearly understood and articulated by their people). Here are a few examples:

---

62 Strong Culture: People clearly can understand and articulate the culture. Weak Culture: People have difficulty defining and explaining.

- Transportation: 30 percent increase in profits
- Water Utility: 4x increase in shareholder returns
- FMCG: 5x increase in shareholder return over five years
- Healthcare: 500 percent increase in profits over one year.

At best, company **culture** can positively influence how well a company performs and how effective it is, how productive employees are, their sense of morale, and how well we can attract and retain talented **players**. For example, one study found that companies with a healthy, well-functioning **culture** had a 682 percent average increase in sales and a 901 percent stock increase, compared to the 166 percent sales increase and 74 percent stock increase for their counterparts with more neutral or less healthy **cultures**.[63] For an organization to reach its **north star**, company **culture** must be given attention. In that sense, it should be a primary focus of all managers, and managers at all levels should be invested in the **culture** of an organization, which has the power to establish behavioural norms.[64]

On the other hand, failure to change a company's **culture** doomed the other kinds of organisational changes.

> *This dependence of organisational improvement on* ***culture*** *change is due to the fact that when the values, orientations, definition, and goals stay constant, even when procedures*

63 D.D. Warrick, "What Leaders Need to Know about Organizational Culture," *Business Horizons* 60, no. 3 (May 2017): 395–404, https://doi.org/10.1016/j.bushor.2017.01.011.

64 Gholam Ali Ahmady, Aghdas Nikooravesh, and Maryam Mehrpour, "Effect of Organizational Culture on Knowledge Management Based on Denison Model," *Procedia—Social and Behavioral Sciences* 230 (September 2016): 387–95.

> *and strategies are altered—organisations quickly return to the* ***status quo***.[65]

So, we know that as **leaders**, we need to challenge the **status quo**, to shape the **new normal**, and shift the norms of what our people take for granted. In order to do this, let's take a look into the theories of organisational **culture** so we can emerge with some fresh thinking and a plan of what to do next. Buckle up and grab your journal.

A BRIEF HISTORY OF ORGANISATIONAL CULTURE THINKING

The first mention of organisational **culture** was made by Dr. Elliott Jaques in his book *The Changing* ***Culture*** *of a Factory*. In this early work, Jaques studied a publicly-held British factory to document findings of the social life and community and the behaviours of the groups within this company. Jaques noticed that "the **culture** of the factory is the customary and traditional way of thinking and doing things, which is shared to a greater or lesser degree by all of its members and which new members must learn and at least partially accept in order to be of service to the firm."[66]

For sixty years or so, Jaques developed his concept of the "Requisite Organisation" where he outlined a list of primary

---

65 Caldwell, 1994; CSC Index, 1994; Gross, Pascall, and Athos, 1993; Kotter and Heskett, 1992.

66 Elliott Jaques, *The Changing Culture of a Factory* (London: Tavistock Publications Limited, 1951).

company values or entitlements that tended to gain organisational commitment and formed part of the credo. This inspired the **TLC system.**[67]

Here are the values:

- Fair and just treatment for everyone
- **Leadership** interaction for all, including shared context, personal appraisals, feedback, recognition, and coaching
- Clear articulation of accountability and authority
- Articulation of long-term vision
- Opportunity for everyone to participate in policy development
- Work for everyone at a consistent level of their potential capabilities, values and interests
- Opportunity for everyone to progress as their potential capabilities mature within the opportunities available

Jaques developed requisite organisations much further into a triple bottom line management methodology; social, financial, and environmental, and developed a system of the managerial accountability hierarchy. More on this in the **results** installation.

The thinking developed from there. The 1980s saw corporate **culture** becoming an area of interest for business theorists, sociologists, and learned managers, and the

67 Elliott Jaques, *Requisite Organization: A Total System For Effective Managerial Organization And Managerial Leadership for the 21st Century*, Rev. 2nd ed. (New York: Routledge, 2016).

organisational communication perspective emerged to define **culture** in three different ways:

- Traditionalism: objective things; stories, rituals, symbols
- Interpretivism: a network of shared meanings
- Critical interpretivism: a network of shared meanings as well as the power struggles created by a similar, yet competing network of meanings.[68]

In 1982, Deal and Kennedy famously and clearly stated that **culture** is "the way things get done around here." Deal and Kennedy took a very '80s no-jargon approach to types and measured them by the way **players** get rewards and the risks they are prepared to take.

- Work Hard, Play Hard **culture**
- Tough Guy, Macho **culture**
- Process **culture**
- Bet Your Company **culture**[69]

This is a very self-explanatory and simple view of types of **culture**, useful in the sense that we can immediately understand and recognise these types. But of course, it is a very limited view of what **culture** actually is and the complexity of thinking required to change it.

---

68 Daniel P. Modaff, Sue A. DeWine, and Jennifer A. Butler, *Organizational Communication: Foundations, Challenges, and Misunderstandings*, 3rd ed. (Boston: Pearson Education, 2011).

69 Terrence E. Deal and Allan A. Kennedy, *Corporate Cultures: The Rites and Rituals of Corporate Life* (Boston: Addison-Wesley, 1982).

Linda Smircich gave us a tonne of great work around **leadership**, **culture**, gender, and the dynamics of these elements. Linda was highly critical of all theories that tried to pigeonhole and categorise **culture**. She preferred to use the powerful metaphor of a plant's roots as the **culture** that shapes everything on the surface.[70]

Then in the '90s, Daniel Denison describes Org **culture** in four general dimensions. *I have included the* ***TLC*** *terms with these to show you where they fit into the development of transformational* ***leadership*** *capability. This will help you deepen your understanding of the* ***TLC*** *and your ability to teach it to your* ***players***. The four dimensions are as follows:

- Mission; strategic direction and intent, goals, vision (**north star**/goals/**games**)
- Adaptability; creating change, customer focus, and org learning (**events/assets/rhythm**)
- Involvement; empowerment and individual development (**player/games**)
- Consistency; core values, agreement, coordination and integration (**team/rhythm**)

Denison described **culture** as externally or internally focused and as flexible or stable. This is a model often used to diagnose cultural problems in companies to this day.[71]

70 Linda Smircich, "Concepts of Culture and Organizational Analysis," *The Anthropology of Organisations*, 255–74, Routledge, 2017, https://doi.org/10.4324/9781315241371-20.

71 Daniel R. Denison, *Corporate Culture and Organizational Effectiveness* (Ann Arbor, MI: Denison Consulting, 1997).

In **TLC** terms:

- Externally Focused: **brand**
- Internally Focused: **culture**
- Flexible: **events** and **rhythm** that changes the **status quo**
- Stable: **new normal** or existing **status quo**

From there, Edgar Schein, Deal, and Kennedy noticed that companies have different sub**culture**s and these sub**culture**s are more often than not linked to different **teams** of management and are either co-existing or in conflict. (A hero and a legend, Edgar Schein is a former MIT professor and pioneer in the field of organisational culture development. He is one of the few truly respected experts in the area of organisational culture change.)

Kim Cameron and Robert Quinn conducted extensive research on organisational success and effectiveness and created something called the competing values framework and the OCAI instrument that notes four types of **culture** and their polarities of internal/external focus and flexibility/stability.

1. **Clan Culture**: Internal flexible—leaders are like heads of family
2. **Adhocracy**: External flexible—leaders stimulate innovation
3. **Market Culture**: External stable—leaders promote competition and act like hard drivers.
4. **Hierarchy Culture**: Internal stable—leaders act like formal coordinators.

To this date, the OCAI is the most widely used cultural assessment tool.[72]

Edgar Schein brought us breakthrough thinking and research. He declared **culture** as the most difficult part of a company to change, and he took the standpoint of the outside observer to describe **culture** with three basic concepts:

1. **Artefacts:** The things you can see, furnishings, visible rewards
2. **Espoused Values:** The values, beliefs, philosophies, and justifications that are not directly observable but can be uncovered by questioning and investigating through a process of surveying and interviewing **players**—*see* ***north star*** *installation.*
3. **Basic Underlying assumptions**: The foundations of a **culture** that are so widely shared that people are unaware of them. These deep beliefs are taken so much for granted and are the perceptions, thoughts, and feelings that are the ultimate source of the reason behind people's actions.

In short, basic underlying assumptions and the collective internal **status quo** is at the heart of **culture.**

Flamholtz and Randle saw **culture** as a "corporate personality" and the values, belief, and norms that influence the behaviour of the **players** and the **teams** in a company. Through this thinking, it can be quite helpful to think of

72 Kim S. Cameron and Robert E. Quinn, *Diagnosing and Changing Organizational Culture* (San Francisco, CA: Jossey Bass Inc., 1999).

culture as the collective mindset and **brand** as the attitudes and behaviours, the internal collective, and the external collective. They also defined strong and weak **cultures** in a very clear manner that we referenced earlier in this chapter.

- **Strong Culture:** People clearly can understand and articulate the **culture.**
- **Weak Culture:** People have difficulty defining and explaining the **culture.**

So, you see, if your people can't describe your **culture** well, we have work to do.

Flamholtz and Randle also identified a model of company **culture** components that drive financial **results** and shows us the five biggest areas of impact:

1. Treatment of customers
2. Treatment of people
3. Performance standards and accountability
4. Innovation and change
5. Process orientation

Flamholtz did us proud when he showed empirically that **culture** is not just an **asset** in the economic sense but also an **asset** in the conventional accounting sense.[73]

---

73 Eric G. Flamholtz and Yvonne Randle, *Corporate Culture: The Ultimate Strategic Asset* (Stanford, CA: Stanford Business Books, 2011).

DEFINING CULTURE

In order to change anything, we must first understand it, so let's get clear.

The definition of company **culture** is quite a matter of contention. In fact, I have found over 180 definitions while researching this book. All these definitions fall into two categories:

- Sociological: organisations *have* **cultures**
- Anthropological: organisations *are* **cultures**

Here is one golden definition for your consideration:

> *The shared beliefs, norms and expectations that govern the way people approach their work and interact with each other.*
>
> —*Robert A. Cooke, PhD*[74]

And my favourite definition:

> *"The accumulated learning of the group that is a pattern or system of beliefs, values, and behavioural norms that come to be taken for granted as basic assumptions and eventually drop out of awareness."*
>
> —*Edgar Schein, PhD*[75]

Let's look a bit deeper at Schein's three levels to get an

74 Robert A. Cooke PhD, Professor Emeritus University of Illinois at Chicago.
75 Edgar Schein PhD, Professor Emeritus MIT Sloan School of Management.

understanding of what is going on here, so we can start creating our **new normal**.

Artefacts are visible organisational structures and processes. These are easy to see but hard to decipher or figure out what they actually mean in your **culture**.

Espoused values are strategies, goals, and philosophies that make up the justifications for our actions in the **culture**.

REFLECTION POINTS

When looking at your underlying assumptions, a useful guiding question is: *What do we take for granted?*

"**Culture** is the deeper level of basic assumptions and beliefs that are shared by members of an organisation that operate subconsciously and define in a basic 'taken for granted' fashion an organisation's view of itself and its environment."

To change the **culture** is to create the **new normal**—the next set of taken-for-granted assumptions, the new why, and the way we do things around here. The magic of the **TLC** comes to life by defining, designing, and aligning these elements on purpose through **events**, creating **assets** that bolster this, and sustaining the change through a consistent and disciplined **rhythm**.

Through **leadership** of the **TLC**, we are able to shift these basic assumptions and over time, reshape your **culture**.

Underlying assumptions are the subconscious, taken-for-granted beliefs, habits of perception, thoughts, and feelings.

This deeper level is the ultimate source of values and action. It is the BIG circle in the **TLC.** This is what we use the **TLC** process to shift to ultimately change the **culture** by using ALL the dynamic elements to create the **new normal.**

KNOWING THE DIFFERENCE BETWEEN CLIMATE AND CULTURE

It is important for us to understand the difference between **Culture** and Climate.

Culture implies stability and consistency over time, shared meaning, repeating patterns, reoccurring dynamics, and all aspects of life within the **TLC**. The **new normal** becomes our stable **culture.**

> *Climate is "the meanings people attach to the interrelated bundles of experiences they have at work."*
>
> *—Benjamin Schneider, PhD, Professor Emeritus, University of Maryland*[76]

> *It can also be defined as "people's perceptions and attitudes about the organisation—whether it is a good or bad place to work, friendly or unfriendly, hard-working or easy-going and so forth."*
>
> *—Wendell French, PhD, Professor, University of Washington*[77]

---

76 Benjamin Schneider, PhD, Professor Emeritus University of Maryland.
77 Wendell French, PhD, Professor, University of Washington.

Edgar Schein uses the metaphor of an iceberg to explain how **culture** sits beneath the surface of climate. Climate sits at the top as visible artefacts, feelings, engagement, structures, and systems. It is seen as easy to recognise, easy to change, and as a predictor of short-term performance. Deeper under the surface, we find **culture** as the **status quo** basic assumptions. These assumptions are the norms and basic expectations, characterised as harder to see, harder to change, and a much more powerful predictor of performance over the long-term. Again, it is through ongoing **events** backed by disciplined and consistent **rhythm** and a lot of shared growth and collaboration that we create the **new normal.**

CULTURE AS A LIVING SYSTEM

I find it most useful to plan for **culture** using the elements and dynamics of the **TLC** and to think of your company **culture** as a living system, like an ecosystem or a garden. When anything in the system changes, everything within the system changes. You can think of your **culture** in terms of a carefully curated environment, the outer circle of the **TLC**.

HOW DO WE MEASURE CULTURE?

Measuring **culture** is a matter of contention, and there is a vast range of tools out there to be able to take a baseline measurement, map potential change opportunities, and track the progress. This can be complicated territory. Here is a list of a few tools that you can research and consider:

- OCAI—Organisational **Culture** Assessment Inventory
- **Culture** Amp
- ValueMatch
- Barrett Values Centre
- Interviews and narrative process
- Engagement surveys

Choosing an effective way of measuring **culture** is something you can reach out to me to help you with. Simply email me: *benny@bigchange.group* with the subject: Measuring Culture.

My **team** and I will be happy to learn about your journey and assist you with this choice.

BUILDING YOUR NEW NORMAL

> *You never change things by fighting the existing reality. To change something, build a new model that makes the existing model obsolete.*
>
> *—Richard Buckminster Fuller*

When we talk in terms of transformational change, it is a bit like riding a wild elephant. Sure, you can lean and steer, but at the end of the day, the elephant is going to go where the elephant wants to go.

You can't affect transformational change overnight by ordering the company to change its **culture**. You can, however, through careful examination of what we have already, influence the direction of people's thinking and decision-making processes.

REFLECTION POINTS

When we can begin the journey of making changes, we need to keep in mind how these changes fit into the bigger picture by asking the simple question: "Is this creating the **culture** that we want?"

By thinking of **culture** as a living, learning system, constantly evolving and adapting within your environment, we start to step out of the whirlwind of day-to-day doing and step into the shoes of the true transformational **leader**, the creator, the constant gardener.

Frederic Laloux noted in his popular book *Reinventing Organisations*, "Living systems have an innate capacity to change."[78]

When we create an organization as a living, breathing system that has the structure required to grow organically, this innate capacity to change is built into the organization as an organism.

By using the **TLC**, we are able to build and bake change within the operating system of the organization, allowing us to deal with a complex and uncertain future by having the right operating system in place.

---

78 Frederic Laloux, *Reinventing Organizations: A Guide to Creating Organizations Inspired by the Next Stage of Human Consciousness* (Brussels: Nelson Parker, 2014).

> *Company* **cultures** *are like country* **cultures.** *Never try to change one. Try, instead, to work with what you've got.*
>
> *—Peter Drucker*[79]

Understanding your **culture** is the first step in the process of being able to shape it. Remember, you can't change **culture** directly. You need to influence it through the **TLC**, through the **team** ethos, through the **games** and **players**. The **TLC**, when applied, can help you consciously shape the **culture** and create the **new normal.**

79 Peter Drucker, *The Essential Drucker: In One Volume the Best of Sixty Years of Peter Drucker's Essential Writings on Management* (New York:HarperCollins, 2001).

REFLECTION POINTS

It may be useful for you at this point to start thinking of **culture** through the following elements:

- The mindset of the individual, the **players**
- The sub**culture**s and ethos of the **teams**

The set of assumptions held by a group of people will determine the behaviour of that group over time. When we assess values and we assess our **culture**, essentially what we're doing is mapping the mindset of our company. Your task as a transformational leader is to alter the mindset of the company and, of course, this is not a small task. You only need to think of what is required for an individual to make a shift to their **new normal** in their own behaviour and habits to recognise the magnitude of shifting the collective **new normal**.

The way to alter the mindset of the company is to lift the awareness of the individuals through communication of the **TLC** and the prioritisation of the **north star**. The individual **player** perceives the world through a series of filters, through their own belief system, assumptions, and predeterminations about the world. The company perceives the world through a broader set of filters, a wider net.

It's hard to measure and document. However, working to do this will certainly increase your effectiveness as a transformational leader. The best way to get a gauge on this is to look at the language of your **culture**, the words we use, the stories we tell, and the truths we share when we feel safe to do so. All **cultures** have their own language, be it the **culture** of a nation, the words, the slang, and the language that the nation speaks, or a sub**culture** of genre of music. Those who control language and shape language control **culture**. Words create worlds.

The magic term "abracadabra" loosely translates to, "as I speak, I create." It is interesting to observe that the language and chosen words of a transformational **leader** consciously reflect the environment they are creating within their company. Your task here is to create the language required to shape the **culture** that will best serve the people and the customers. With the **TLC** system, we do this through running **events**, creating **assets**, and embedding **rhythm**.

In this installation, we have learned how our deep, taken-for-granted assumptions are the essence of who we are as a company. We also have an understanding of what can be done to measure **culture** and how to begin to use this data to inform our progress and strategy.

In the next installation, we'll go deep on **brand** and how our **culture** affects and is affected by our authentic **brand**.

INSTALLATION 7

BRAND

JOHN'S OLD-WORLD STATUS QUO

"It's a lie," John's brave customer service representative said as she pointed to the sign saying, "We always put our customers first."

"We don't. We put our targets first, then ourselves, and then we bullshit to get around the promises we make. It's a front, and no one really believes it. We don't have a real mission. We are just here to get by, and no one feels proud to work here."

Brave and candid feedback like this is hard and valuable, and yes, there was work to do.

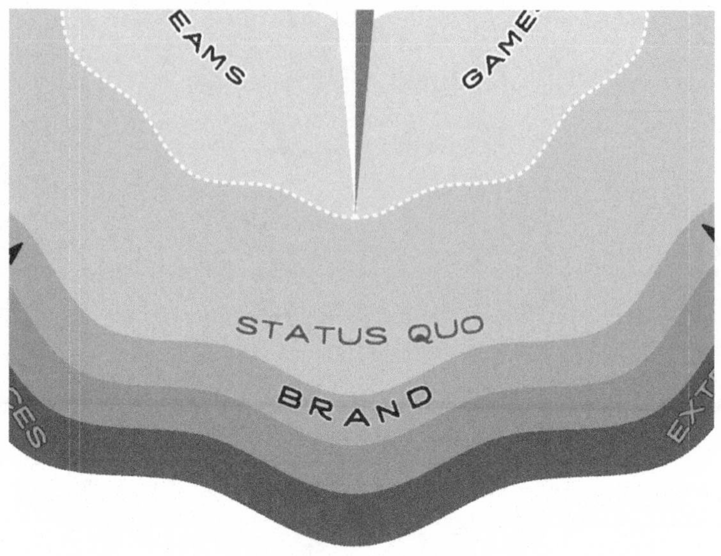

JOHN'S NEW NORMAL

Twelve months later, John's authentic **brand** matched the company's emerging **culture**.

The inner world and workings of the business were expressed honestly out to the BIG wide world, and people could feel authenticity. They bought in and voted with their wallets. They joined the club and became part of the wider **culture**.

The doors were open, and the people did not hide what it was like to work at the company. Rather, they celebrated it. The market fell deeply in love with the unique realness and honesty of this company, and their new **culture** became the most powerful **brand asset** for attracting new customers.

WHAT YOU'LL LEARN AND DO IN THIS INSTALLATION

In this installation, we define what an authentic **brand** means and how to create it for your company. We will go through the evolution of **brand** thinking and arrive in a world where the most powerful **brands** are open expressions of a company's **culture**. We will explore the values of your market and create a market **player** avatar to help us understand how to be more valuable to the world around us. Finally, we will create a plan to bring your **brand** to the language of your people and expand your **TLC** to grow your presence and market share.

THE GREAT THINKERS

Let's begin by turning to some great thinkers to define **brand**.

> *"A* ***brand*** *is the set of expectations, memories, stories and relationships that, taken together, account for a consumer's decision to choose one product or service over another."*
>
> *—Seth Godin*[80]

Pretty great, Seth. Thanks, man. Here is another one:

> *"Mass advertising can help build* ***brands****, but authenticity is what makes them last. If people believe they share values with a company, they will stay loyal to the* ***brand****."*
>
> *—Howard Schultz, Starbucks*

80 "define: Brand," *Seth's Blog*, December 13, 2009, https://seths.blog/.

And finally, one more from some guy named Jeff Bezos who claims to be from the Amazon:

> *"**Brand** is what people say about you when you are not in the room."*
>
> *—Jeff Bezos, Amazon*

If you are following closely, you will be able to see how every element of the **TLC** has a part to play in making great **brands** work. To deepen our understanding and inspire our thinking, let's look at how **brand** has evolved over time.

THE EVOLUTION OF BRAND THINKING

Ancient seals were used as **brands** to differentiate the quality of products in Mesopotamia. Eggheads continue to argue about whether these "seals" were the first **brands** or not, and whether it matters. It doesn't.[81]

By 2700 BCE, Egyptians were thought to **brand** livestock in order to identify one person's cattle from another. Seared into the skin with a blistering hot iron allowed them to claim ownership in the **event** of a dispute. How do we know this? Paintings told us so.[82]

Over time, buyers started to recognise that the **brand** on the cattle not only told them who owned the beast, but it also was a

---

81 Zohrab. S. Demirdjian, "The Rise and Fall of Marketing in Mesopotamia: A Conundrum in the Cradle of Civilization," *The Future of Marketing's Past* 12 (May 1, 2005).

82 Harold Wheeler, *The Miracle Of Man: A Survey of Humanity's Upward March through the Ages* (London: Odhams Press, 1946), 84.

good indicator of the quality of the stock, because certain farmers had the ability to produce higher quality animals. Through their **brand**, they earned and shared their reputation and status. Once this was known to be effective, the practice of **brand** spread into all types of farming and into pottery and ceramics.

The year 1300 marked the earliest known use of "Makers Marks" found in India, and the oldest example of this is a **brand** of herbal paste health product called Chyawanprash made by a Rishi (wise Yoga dude). This product is still available to this day, though I doubt his family is still collecting royalties.[83]

White Rabbit sewing needles from China's Song Dynasty of 960 CE shows the first examples of a sophisticated **brand** including posters printed on copper, a tag line, a trademark, and even a target market of women as homemakers[84] and around 490 BCE in Ancient Greece, there was a vase made and later dug up that was inscribed with the words "Sophilos painted me."

Third-century Gaulish pots have been found bearing the names of well-known potters and their places of production. Around the first century, there is evidence of English potters using stamps to leave their makers mark.[85] The year 35 CE saw

---

83 Saif Ullah Khan and Owais Mufti, "The Hot History & Cold Future of Brands," *Journal of Managerial Sciences*. 1, no. 1(1) (January 2007): 75–87, https://www.researchgate.net/publication/235937759.

84 Stefania Borghini (Ed.), Mary Ann McGrath (Ed.), and Cornelia C. Otnes, *European Advances In Consumer Research* (Duluth, MN: Association for Consumer Research, 2008), 221, http://www.worldcat.org/title/european-advances-in-consumer-research-vol-8/oclc/441485226.

85 Karl Moore and Susan Reid, "The Birth of Brand: 4000 Years of Branding," *Business History* 50, no. 4 (June 19, 2008): 419–32, https://doi.org/10.1080/00076790802106299.

Romans marking up ceramics, shipping containers, oil lamps, and apparently, even some bread makers were getting in on the action.

A guy named Umbricius Scaurus **brand**ed his fish sauce, which was a BIG hit across the Mediterranean, and then all sorts of products began coming with their **brand**s as we saw jewellery, wine, and other lovely things imprinted with the names of their producers.[86]

Then the Romans, who were very into hierarchy and rank at the time, developed a system and language of symbolism as the guilds of merchants stepped up production and makers marks started to go beyond the insignia and started to make use of this symbolism to begin creating logos.

By 1266 in England, if you were going to sell bread, you were required to have a hallmark, and these stamps of authority of value were applied by silversmiths as a certification and regulation of purity and value.[87]

In 1777, Bass and Company, a British brewery was founded and had started marking their barrels with a Red Triangle with Bass written on it. By 1876, this became the first registered trademark issued by the British government. You can still drink a nice glass of their "World's Finest Pale Ale" to this very day.[88] The *Guinness Book of World Records* ecognizes Tate and Lyle and their golden syrup as the oldest unchanged

86 Robert I. Curtis, "A Personalized Floor Mosaic from Pompeii," *American Journal of Archaeology* 88, no. 4 (October 1984): 557, https://doi.org/10.2307/504744.

87 Tony Martino, *Trademark Dilution* (Oxford: Oxford University Press, 1996), 21.

88 "Intellectual Property Office," British Government, accessed October 21, 2020, http://Ipo.gov.uk.

branding, which has been around since 1885, although some say Twinning's Tea has done this since 1787.[89]

As the Industrial revolution rolled on in and factories started to come up with ways to compete with the artisan local products and producers, this is where it gets really interesting. They started to realise that when they personalised their **brand** to the buyer they wanted, their products outsold their competitors. In the 1880s, **brands** started to pop up that had personal traits of fun, sexiness, youthfulness, status, and significance.

The product was now linked to the personality of the buyer, and things would never be quite the same. People started buying the **brand** instead of the product and going with the **brand** that spoke to them instead of just asking their local retailer for a recommendation.

Quaker Oats, Coca-Cola, and Campbell's soup all started to personify their **brand** using images of mascots and people tied to the **brand's** identity, a personification of the link between the company and the consumer.[90]

The 1900s brought us trade press publications, and the first advertising agencies were spawned to life. Companies started to bypass retailers and advertise directly to consumers. A dude named James Walter Thompson started publishing his

---

89 Colette Hibbert, "Golden Celebration for 'Oldest Brand'," *BBC News*, last modified January 10, 2008, http://news.bbc.co.uk/2/hi/uk_news/england/london/7180268.stm.

90 Ross D. Petty, "A History of Brand Identity Protection and Brand Marketing," *The Routledge Companion to Marketing History*, 97–114, Routledge, 2016, https://doi.org/10.4324/9781315882857-6; Tony Martino, *Trademark Dilution* (Oxford: Oxford University Press, 1996), 21.

ideas of trademark advertising, which shared some of the earliest thinking behind modern **brand** management.[91]

The 1920s brought us radio and television, and mass media was not far off. Mass media was awash with jingles, slogans, and sponsors from soap makers for soap operas (bet you didn't know that).[92]

By the time we got into the 1940s, the psychologists and anthropologists got into the mix and worked with advertising agencies to study buyer motivations. These supercharged campaigns and endowed products with **brand** personalities matched products with the buyers. What does your couch say about you as a person?

As we rocked into the heady and material eighties, quantified concepts of **brand** value and **brand** equity came into play. Now **brand** was a serious consideration of the company's value. Phillip Morris bought Kraft for six times more than what the company was worth by its financials because of goodwill and the **brand** name.[93]

By now, **brand** management had become a science with high stakes and a great BIG premium price tag.

Brand management concepts came to light. For example:

- **Brand** Names
- **Brand** Trademarks
- **Brand** Personality

---

91 Ross D. Petty, "A History of Brand Identity Protection and Brand Marketing," *The Routledge Companion to Marketing History*, 97–114, Routledge, 2016, https://doi.org/10.4324/9781315882857-6.

92 Mary Ann Copeland, *Soap Opera History* (Chicago: Mallard Press, 1991).

93 Naomi Klein, *No Logo®* (New York: Picador, 2000).

- **Brand** Awareness
- **Brand** Recognition
- **Brand** Recall

They worked through the elements of:

- Name
- Logo
- Taglines
- Shapes
- Graphics
- Colours
- Sounds
- Scents
- Tastes[94]

These were all purposefully engineered to be as attractive as possible and expressed through as many communication touchpoint channels as possible. They had figured out all the touchpoints, or so it seems.

Kapferer in 2007 noted six facets of a **brand's** identity:

1. **Physique**—iconography and physical characteristics
2. **Culture**—the principles and values on which a **brand** bases its behaviour.

---

94 Lisa Merriam, "Beyond Name and Logo: Other Elements of Your Brand," Business 2 Community, September 8, 2011, https://www.business2community.com/branding/beyond-name-and-logo-other-elements-of-your-brand-055547.

3. **Personality**—expressed through its communications, tone of voice, collateral, and **assets.**
4. **Reflection**—the avatar (a term coined later) profile of the generic stereotype of a customer from which the message is crafted and delivered.
5. **Relationship**—the relationship between the **brand** and the customer.
6. **Self-Image**—the **brand**'s portrayal of its ideal self, the aspirations, and what the company wants to achieve and how this messaging matches the buyer.[95]

At this point, the idea of **brand** management was in full force. Not surprisingly, you need to manage all of this work.

A bunch of categories came through under the heading of **brand** management, and it's useful to be aware of these:

- **Brand Equity** is the **result** of doing all the things below:[96]
- **Brand Preference** is the customer's preference for certain **brands.** What is the understanding of how they think about the choice of this and what stimuli can influence this?
- **Brand Image** is the image that the **brand** wants the world to see, who the **brand** says it is, and the meaning the **brand** conveys.[97]

95 Jean-Noël Kapferer, *Strategic Brand Management: Creating and Sustaining Brand Equity Long Term*, 4th ed. (PublisherLondon, Kogan Page, 2008).

96 Jean-Noël Kapferer, *Strategic Brand Management: New Approaches to Creating and Evaluating Brand Equity* (Sydney: The Free Press, 1994).

97 Dawn Dobni and George M. Zinkhan, "In Search of Brand Image:...

- **Brand Personality** is the human trait represented in the **brand** and hopefully reflected in the personality of the buyer.[98]
- **Brand Attitude** is the buyer's collective assessment of whether the **brand** meets their buying motivations.[99]
- **Brand Associations** means getting into the realm of systems thinking. It's all of the things above that come together to influence the next term, Self-**Brand** Congruity.[100]
- **Self-Brand Congruity** is the notion that people prefer **brands** that match their own personality and image.[101]

So, where are we now?

As the age of the internet reshaped the world, there was a growing post-modern scepticism[102] of **brands** and marketing in general. The conversation was no longer one way, because as social media, review sites, and all the world's information

...A Foundation Analysis," *Advances in Consumer Research* 17, no. 1 (January 1990): 110.

98 Audrey Azoulay and Jean-Noël Kapferer, Do Brand Personality Scales Really Measure Brand Personality?" *Journal of Brand Management* 11, no. 2 (November 2003): 143–55, https://doi.org/10.1057/palgrave.bm.2540162.

99 Larry Percy, and John R. Rossiter, "A Model of Brand Awareness and Brand Attitude Advertising Strategies," *Psychology and Marketing* 9, no. 4 (July 1992): 263–74, https://doi.org/10.1002/mar.4220090402.

100 Zamri Ahmad, and Rahmat Hashim, "Customer's Brand Equity and Customer Loyalty: A Study on Hotel's Conference Market," *World Applied Sciences Journal* 10, Special Issue of Tourism & Hospitality (2010): pp 115–20, http://citeseerx.ist.psu.edu/viewdoc/download?doi=10.1.1.390.6420&rep=rep1&type=pdf.

101 Jennifer Lynn Aaker, "Dimensions of Brand Personality," *SSRN Electronic Journal* (1997), https://doi.org/10.2139/ssrn.945432.

102 Ibid.

became accessible from a smartphone, **brand** was no longer a declaration and an announcement. It was an interaction, an ongoing dialogue among your customers, their experience, and the internal working of your **brand** and how the world experiences it.

As the internet enabled the market to communicate faster and to a larger and more targeted audience, customers became king. The **brand** was no longer a choice informed by the limits of shared information. Now we go online and find the truth we choose for ourselves. Our customers get more information and begin to demand even more information about the companies they buy from by assessing if the promise matches the reality.

In order to fulfil a **brand's** promise and to be authentic and real so the world does not either call bullshit or say nothing at all, we need to make as many of our internal people **brand** ambassadors as possible. Our behaviours must match our promises, and our core values and identity must match our image in order to be authentic in the **VUCA** world.

CROWDSOURCING TRUST

The collective of existing and potential customers is our market. It is obvious but often forgotten they are the ones who keep the lights on, help the company grow, and pay the salaries. The age we're living in is the age of information. In this age, the customer is the king of the internet, and word of mouth now has the world's biggest soapbox and megaphone.

Think about it: if you were a time traveller, the strangest thing you could tell somebody from the past would be that

REFLECTION POINTS

Imagine if your company **culture** was made entirely of **players** who were evangelists and promoters of your **brand**.

Imagine letting the world into the internal workings of your company, taking them into the lives of your people, and connecting your authentic message to a movement of the market.

What would this look like? Sound like? How would it feel?

As we move further and faster into the future, one thing has become very clear: **brand** is an inside job. The moment our customers experience our **culture** not reflecting and matching our **brand**, we risk losing them, unless we crowdsource the currency of trust.

you have a device in your pocket that's capable of accessing almost all of the information in the known world. What does this mean for our customers and our clients?

It means they have more power than ever over their choice and their influence over the value of your **brand**. It means they're constantly dancing on the edge of being loyal and staying with your company and exploring other cheaper, better options. They have the power to inform the market the moment they interact with your **culture** and have a valuable or terrible experience. It means that they have the power to celebrate your **brand** or damage it based on how your **culture** treats them.

We must provide a way of expressing who the company is as a whole and how it is different in the market, because these days, we crowdsource trust. We live in social communities on the internet where we're able to ask those we trust and whose opinions we value about the products and services we buy and the companies we engage with. Gone are the days when a company could make a promise to the market and not fulfil that promise.

The reviews, the forums, and the comment section will reveal the amount of market trust in that **brand**. The advantage of this is companies who back their **brand** and make promises with a **culture** that supports, understands, and nurtures their loyal customers and attract them in a cult-like following. The best PR and marketing these days is through your existing customers. When they proudly declare, "I trust this **brand**," they are sharing that they belong to your company. They believe you are doing the right thing by them and are aligned with what they value, how they see the world, and how they want it to be.

No ad campaign, slogan, or radio jingle could ever compete with the power of the consumer and the client recommending you to their nearest and dearest in a circle these days to build trust. **Brand** loyalty is now in the realm of community and **culture** development.

JOIN THE CLUB

People are looking for something beyond a product or service. They are looking for an aligned identity, and the best **brands** project a values system the customers align and belong to. In this, they move beyond the realm of logos into belonging to the membership of a club.

Mercedes Benz is a club.

Jeffery West shoes is a club.

Apple is a club.

Harley Davidson is a club with many clubs within it.

These clubs reflect a **culture** with a particular values system that resonates and with the internal **TLC** of the customer. People look for products and services that define themselves as an expression of who they are and how they want the world to see them as a person.

What does this mean for us? It means that there is an opportunity to connect with the market through our **culture**. If the **culture** is well-defined in who it is and what it values, and the people within the company understand this, then they will constantly attract the right type of customers who see value in what the company values.

The idea of your cultural values being an internal system is very limited.

The market will never care about your core values unless they match with their own values.

Keep this in mind as we get to work in defining your **north star**.

When we curate and create alignment here, we move from being a product or a service to a community the customer belongs to. This is key. When there is alignment, **brands** grow and the **TLC** expands. We earn the right to serve more of the market. When there is misalignment in the **brand's** promise and the experience does not match the behaviour of your **culture**, the **TLC** will shrink as we lose business.

BRAND AND CULTURE

The Purpose of **brand** is to bring people into your company, customers, and **team. Brand** brings the right hearts and minds into the **TLC** to help them stay there—loyal, growing, and thriving.

To expand the **TLC** and have more influence over the **VUCA** world, we express our **culture** through the **assets** and messages of our **brand.** By understanding an authentic **brand,** we are able to shape our **culture** to become that which attracts more customers towards your movement. This **culture,** informed by who we are in relation to the larger market **culture,** then feeds back and expands our **culture.** When done with consideration and the right **events** bolstered by a steady **rhythm,** then we are able to constantly develop and improve our authentic **brand.**

Culture and **brand** are constantly evolving and influencing each other. In considering this, we can conduct a deeper inquiry into the hearts and minds of our customer and develop a greater understanding of their values and needs as we shape our **culture** to serve those needs. In this process, we learn to align our **cultures, north star,** vision, mission, values and BIG goals to that of the greater **culture** of the market.

Authentic **brand** is the outward expression of your **culture** and **culture** is the inward development of **brand.**

The feedback cycle of **brand** and authentic marketing goes like this:

- The company makes a promise to the market expressed through a **brand asset.**

- The market then experiences that promise through the service and the products created by those within the company's **culture**.

REFLECTION POINTS

- How do we create attractive, reasonable, and realistic promises to the market that our **culture** can fulfil and overdeliver on?
- How do we take that even further and improve and expand over time?
- How do we take the promise from a small promise to a slightly larger promise?
- How do we continue this cycle of authentic feedback?
- How do we do it in such a way that we're constantly dancing with an ever-changing market, and our people can believe in and deliver on the promises we make to the world?

I'm sure you agree, we must choose our **brand** promises very carefully and give our **culture** the best possible chance of fulfilling this. We do this by running the **TLC** as ongoing, continuously improving, and learning **events** of **brand**, celebrations, and calibrations of our cultural message that become a larger movement in the world around us.

The **culture** then receives feedback from the market, based on its loyalty and an inquiry into their experience to see whether or not this promise was delivered.

Culture shapes and develops its own beliefs based on the feedback of how the market perceives it. Over time and **rhythm**, this creates the **new normal**, for better or worse.

MESSAGE TO MOVEMENT

Great movements deliver a simple message that wins the hearts and minds of followers. That message is carried on like a meme within the greater market **culture**. To lead a movement of any magnitude, we need to consider the strength of the message delivered and how we are going to encourage your people to share this message in as many ways as possible.

Great messages become the catch cries of the market. They become memes. They become something that you couldn't forget if you tried. There is a combination between the power of the message and critical mass—the initial communication.

Within **brand**, I encourage you to decide on a powerful message that reflects your **north star** through the buyer's needs. Your **north star** is the first point of alignment towards **brand** integrity. The **TLC** allows you to develop a plan to socialize this message throughout the business, teach people this language, empower them with the right words, and be able to influence everybody they come into contact with inside your company.

INDUSTRY AFFINITY

Another great opportunity within **brand** is industry affinity.

There have been many clients I've worked with who have operated in an industry that has traditionally low trust in the market. Recruitment firms, lawyers, and salespeople typically have a low-trust reputation as a profession. This can be a difficult obstacle to overcome, or this can be one of the greatest opportunities and challenges in **brand**.

If the vision for a company is to be the most trusted, then every action must align to this through the **TLC**. If you find yourself in a low-trust industry, perhaps your **culture** could be pointed towards the **north star** of being the most trusted or earning the most trust in the market. Everything we do is to develop more and more trust by showing how you do ordinary things extraordinarily well.

The value of your **brand** grows through the feedback of the market and the alignment of your internal **culture** to your market's values. While we are here, let's explore that thinking.

EXPLORING MARKET VALUES

Management guru Peter Drucker once said the purpose of all business is "to add value to the customer." Simple, right?

MARKET PLAYER AVATAR

Demographic profiling is only a very small and limited part of the picture of your customer. Their age, socioeconomic status, location, etc., all play a part. The study of psychographics

REFLECTION POINTS

The first question here is: what does the customer and ultimately, the market truly value?

The second is: how do we get clear on the external value of what we are creating, and develop a strong understanding of how we serve the market in order to shape our **culture** to deliver this?

These questions can be answered by asking the right questions to the market and by diving deeper into the psychology of who our customers are and what they value at the deepest level. In the **VUCA** world of constant change, this is not a single inquiry. This is an ongoing process of learning, development, and evolution through **events**.

By creating **events** of understanding our customer, we are diving in and looking at these needs and values from every angle possible. We are able to create **assets** that inform our **team** ethos, shape our beliefs, construct our **games**, and develop our **players** toward a **rhythm** of service. Then we can focus on what we all need to do to allow our **brand** to expand.

We all have a self-concept of who we'd like to think we are. When the language of our **culture** and **brand** align to the market, we go beyond the transactional purchase and into the realm of transformational **brands**. Through study and inquiry, we can develop the language that resonates with our audience and our buyers. Beyond this, we teach that language to every person in the business. That action thereby influences the way we speak to each other and turns this into our own taxonomy and our own value that we put on certain words. This is what creates **brand** movements and transformational **brands**.

Being able to define what certain words mean to us with clarity and conviction is very close to arming your people with the tools they need to be able to go out there and win a greater market share. In order to craft and communicate this language, we need to get very clear about who it is we are talking to in the BIG wide world.

is the study of activities, interests, opinions, attitudes, values, and behaviours of people that you can serve. When given an option, people will tend to do business with companies they can relate to. When we say we like something, quite often we mean that we *are* like something, someone, some group, or **brand**. We buy things for a number of reasons. One of the most powerful motivators is to change the way the world sees us and to change the way we see ourselves. **Brands** impress labels upon us. These are often self-imposed and tell the world we are a certain type of person. To understand an authentic **brand**, we must consider the status and the signal that comes along with choosing to do business with your company.

EXERCISES AND APPLICATIONS

EXERCISE: BRAND AVATAR ASSET

The exercise of **asset** here is to create and continually develop an avatar.

Write the answers to the following questions in your **status quo** journal or grab a template from our website at *www.bigchangeagency.com/brandavatar*.

The avatar is a character that is a representation of your ideal customer.

Their own personal **TLC** matches the **north star** of your company.

To further understand your customers, it is useful to assess the following **TLC** questions. You can do this by guessing, but it is much more effective to conduct the research and ask them through interviews. Most people do not know their own answers, and it can take an interview exploration to uncover the gold here.

Take these questions and get to work defining your market **player** avatar.

- What is their **north star**? Their highest purpose and values?
- What is their **team**'s ethos? Sets of beliefs that they hold and share with their closest ones?
- What are their **games**? **G**oals, **a**ctivities, **m**easures, **e**xamples, **s**upport?

- What **results** do they want in all areas of their lives?
- What are they trying to achieve through your **brand**?
- Who are their **players**? Their relationships with the people in their world?
- What **culture** and sub**culture** do they identify with and belong to?
- What are their **rhythms** and patterns of communication and behaviour?

As we answer these questions, we begin to paint a picture of the greater alignment, and we can expand the **TLC** further into the market. Start asking your customers deep and curious questions.

Find out where the value is for them, and you will then be able to be well-placed to start defining and refining your **north star** in no uncertain terms.

In this installation, we have built an authentic **brand** into our **TLC** capability, and we understand how our **culture** is shaped by our **brand** in the world around us. We have a better understanding of our market **player** avatar and their values, and we can begin to run our **events** to create the **assets** of change to transform our company and create our **new normal**. In the next installation, we will learn how to get set up to facilitate our **events**.

INSTALLATION 8

EVENTS

JOHN'S OLD-WORLD STATUS QUO

Another workshop session. "F*ck, I have to take time out of my day to attend some bullshit talkfest. I have targets to hit, meetings, and real stuff to do!" said John's burley sales manager. "I am not happy to be here."

This time HR had managed to scrape together a budget for a training session for goal setting and frontline **leadership**. The facilitator was pretty good by all accounts. The group was engaged, the commitments had been set, and people felt pretty energised by the experience. Twelve months have

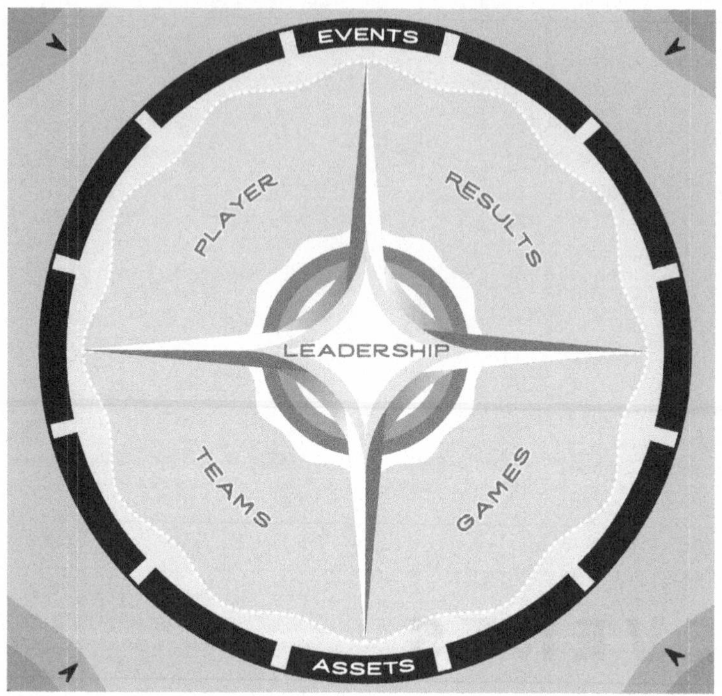

passed since the last **event** of this type, and the issues flowed from the mouths of all participants.

The Flipchart outputs were papered on the walls of the **event** space like a confession log of 1,000 problems and difficulties. It felt like a great, long overdue purge of the year's sins and transgressions. To the credit of the facilitator, the people were open, sharing, happy to vent, and put forward their best ideas to make things better.

Everyone leaned in and played "full-out" as the facilitator suggested.

John was impressed by the level of "radical candour," and in some moments of lucidity, he even caught a glimpse of a **culture** that was not afraid to speak up and tackle tough issues together.

There was, however, a problem, and it was certainly not a small one.

After the group had aired their dirty laundry, made their suggestions, committed to 1,000 changes, and faced their problems, they left the room feeling lighter, better, and truer to who they really wanted to be as a company. But three weeks later, nothing had changed.

The warm, fuzzy, safe space of the **events** room had faded, the excitement of the conversation had subsided, the people had returned to their **status quo** modus operandi, and went back to the daily grind. Nothing stuck.

"Why do we do this?" asked John.

"It's like everyone has the best intentions and says the right things, but nothing seems to really stick. We just return to the same old way of doing things, the infamous **status quo**. We go back to what is easy and what will create the least amount of noise and inconvenience until next year when we do another **event** and list all the same issues we identified the year before. It's like having the same New Year's resolutions every year and just changing out the date at the top of the list.

I get that these are important. It's great to get these groups together and hear their input, to vent, to build the **team**, but I need something that has impact. There has to be a better way, a way to make this really affect lasting change."

He was right; there *was* a much better way. However, it's going to take a lot more than a once-a-year **event** to shift the **status quo** and create the **new normal**.

JOHN'S NEW NORMAL

Three months into the transformation program, the world had changed.

Events were now a monthly cycle for all **teams**. Not just **teams** of departments, but cross-functional groups, project **teams**, and mastermind groups were all committed to improving the business step-by-step, month by month, and day by day. Gone were the days of a yearly dump of concerns and ideas that never became a reality. Now we moved fast, agile, and committed to action.

Groups would create **assets** together:

- **Assets** of **team** ethos that brought the company's **culture** to life
- **Assets** of **games** that constantly improved their performance, scoreboards, and measures of success

Employees co-designed **games** that people helped create and in which they found meaning and focus in their development. The **new normal** was about constantly stepping out of the business-as-usual whirlwind and fast-paced, get it done blizzard of tasks and to-dos.

Employees began to work together improving and innovating their company. The groups tackled this one month at a time. They worked ON the company to improve their strategy when they went back to work IN the company. They put their heads together, found answers, made commitments, and most importantly, they made it the **new normal** through their communication and action in the daily **rhythm**.

Month by month, they experienced progress and failure. Failure, mind you, was now celebrated as learning and growth, and the whole company began to evolve. These regular **events** were forums where people could set change in place and be empowered to bring the changes to life through their **rhythm.** Bit by bit, with the help of steady and committed **leadership,** we created the **new normal.**

Their success in transformation was not due to a single **event.** It was a committed and patient series of **events,** backed by a solid **rhythm** of communication and action. It helped them transform the purpose, performance, and profits of the company and ultimately their **culture** and **new normal.**

Good change had become the **new normal.** The calendar of **events** was in place, and everyone knew how they could be part of this.

WHAT YOU'LL LEARN AND DO IN THIS INSTALLATION

In this installation, we learn the basics of running our own **events** to bring our people together and work on improving our company. We use the best of organisational development thinking to create forums where we can build our collective intelligence and make the changes we need to make to keep going and growing. By working through a consistent calendar of **events,** we make constant improvement a part of who we are, and we build our capability of responding to external **events** that require us to change the way we work as a company.

THE EVOLUTION OF ORGANISATIONAL DEVELOPMENT THEORY

Before we go charging in to run **events**, let's have a look at the thinking behind this.

Org Development (OD) emerged as the study of human relations as psychologists woke up to the idea that the structures and processes of an organisation have an effect on workers' motivations and behaviour.

OD is the continuous and systematic process of implementing effective change. It is a field of applied science and ongoing interdisciplinary study that includes thinking from psychology, sociology, personality, motivation, and learning.

Kurt Lewin is widely considered to be the founding father of organisational development, although his ideas did not come to prominence until the mid-fifties.[103] Lewin gave us the ideas of group dynamics and action research, which formed the basis for the organisational development process as he founded the research centre for group dynamics at MIT where he created a learning method called T-Groups or Training Groups.

In the 1950s, Douglas and Richard Beckhard were consulting together at General Mills and coined the term OD (organisational development) to describe an innovative bottom-up change approach that was vastly different from other consulting methodologies at the time.[104] They found that offsite,

---

103 John Child, *Organization: Contemporary Principles and Practice* (New York: Wiley, 2005), 292.

104 Marvin R. Weisbord, *Productive Workplace: Organizing and Managing for Dignity, Meaning, and Community* (New York: Wiley, 1991).

lab, and classroom training was not doing a lot for developing leaders in terms of their effectiveness in changing structures, communication, and behaviour. They found that by placing people in groups with no fixed agenda, their ability to learn these critical skills increased.

Herbert A. Shepard conducted large-scale experiments on this in the late fifties, and along with Robert Blake, they brought the study and practice of org development and behaviour to become a recognised field of research in psychology.[105] They used these Training Groups, usually from different companies and backgrounds and called these "stranger groups." But after a while, they found that the knowledge and experience in these groups didn't really translate into **results** when they went back to their respective workplaces. So, they tried something different. They ran the group as what they call "Family Groups." These were groups from within the same organisation, and they recognised that this made the learning far more applicable and tended to improve **results** within the company.

Margulies and Raia (1972) stated the objectives of OD were as follows:[106]

1. Increase levels of interpersonal trust
2. Increase levels of satisfaction and commitment
3. Confront problems instead of neglecting them
4. Effectively manage conflict

---

105 Herb Shepard, *Essence of a Proactive Life: 2 Practical Essays on Life & Career Planning* (Irvine, CA: Professional Development Institute, 1994).

106 Newton Margulies, *Organizational Development: Values, Process, and Technology* (New York: McGraw-Hill, 1971), 3.

5. Increase cooperation and collaboration among employees
6. Increase organisational problem-solving
7. Put processes in place that continually improve the operations

Pretty much all OD programmes set out to achieve the following (I've added **TLC** language here to highlight where we do this in the **TLC** system.):

1. Make everyone aware of the vision (**north star**)
2. Encourage people to solve problems instead of avoiding them (**events/rhythm**)
3. Strengthen interpersonal trust (**teams**)
4. Encourage people to be part of the planning (**events**)
5. Create a **culture** where people are encouraged (**culture**)
6. Put knowledge and skill over formal authority (**player**)
7. Prepare people to align to changes (**status quo**)
8. Create a **culture** that is trusting and accepting of change (everywhere)

The basis for OD was rooted in behavioural science. Now the emerging trends are around systems thinking, organisational learning, decision-making and coaching. As the **TLC** shows us, OD must deal with the company as a whole and all of the subsystems within it. These elements cannot exist in isolation, as everything affects everything else.

It requires a holistic view from **leadership** of the whole company. Fortunately, this is what the **TLC** system is designed to create.

WHY EVENTS?

When we gather people together, we are well-placed to create the emotional states that enable changes to happen. When we bring people together and facilitate a conversation around how to make things better, we involve people in the process, and we invite people to become part of this change. We challenge peoples' existing thinking as we bring them together and discuss and unearth their insights. We can harness the wisdom of the people in our company to better understand and commit to the changes they're going to make.

Events done well change the emotional state of the participants, and they become aware of the possibilities to do things differently. By running **events** in a structured way, we are able to continuously improve the **assets** we create and constantly improve the **TLC**. It is the invitation for you in this installation to consider a schedule of **events** that you're running at all levels of the business.

EVENTS CREATE TRADITION

Culture norms are formed on tradition, as we consistently repeat them time after time. **Events** are about creating a tradition where people return to and grow from, by giving them structure around the **events** that will take place. Over time, we can build a framework for tradition. Through this practice, they will know what **event** is coming up and what the demands and expectations are of them to be able to contribute towards that **event**. The **assets** that come from the **events** and the outputs will get stronger and better every time.

REFLECTION POINTS

What kind of **events** do you run? What kind of **events** do you need to run?

- **Events** with the **leadership team**.
- **Events** with your management **team** and supervisors.
- **Events** for the people closest to the frontline, doing the tasks, involving them, and bringing them together to find better ways.

When we create **events** that move people, that encourage them to speak up and be heard, that involve them in the process, we're well on our way to creating an environment and a **culture** that rewards and celebrates improvement.

> *Very great change starts from very small conversations, held among people who care.*
>
> *—Margaret J. Wheatley*[107]

When bringing these **events** together, we are creating the conversations that allow change to happen. We can reset the **rhythm** and shape and influence

107 Margaret J. Wheatley, *Leadership and the New Science: Discovering Order in a Chaotic World*, 2nd ed. (San Francisco: Berrett-Koehler Publishers, 1999).

the **new normal**. Yes, this requires time, energy, and effort to be able to let these conversations take place, but even the very act of arranging these **events** shows that you care and can boost engagement. That's just the tip of the iceberg.

> *I think a major act of* **leadership** *right now, call it a radical act, is to create the places and processes so people can actually learn together, using our experiences.*
>
> *—Margaret J. Wheatley*

When we create **events** for people to learn from each other in a forum setting, we're creating the structure around people being able to come together, share ideas, and produce **assets** of value to the company. By doing this regularly in a disciplined way, we are actually improving the power of our company through our people. You can claim to know things about the **culture** of the company, but unless people can engage in conversation, and unless people can express how they feel, this will be a very limited set of perspectives.

By providing the right forum and asking the right questions, we can use these forums to work through issues, shift our deeply held collective assumptions, and create new traditions in our **culture**.

When we do this in a consistent and disciplined way, we can create movement towards improvement. We create a tradition of **events** that people value the more you involve them. By involving them, you give them the certainty that this will be an ongoing process. You create engagement by letting them know that their thoughts, their opinions, and their knowledge, and wisdom matters and helps shape the company you are creating. Practice **events** over time, and you will create tradition.

THE PROBLEM WITH EVENTS

We can create amazing **events.**

We can lift the energy of the group.

We can inspire new conversations and new ideas.

We can encourage our groups to share their insights and their wishes.

This, however, is not enough to make transformation work.

Have you ever attended an **event** that was high energy and you felt something was different afterwards? You felt a lift, you felt compelled to take action, but then found yourself back in the day-to-day whirlwind of the business, and nothing changes. Yes, indeed, we need to have an occurrence, a gathering, or a conversation that lifts our thinking and lifts our emotional state to want to take action. But the problem lies in execution. The question is, how do we take an **event** and turn that into the daily behaviours of what we do to make good change happen?

REFLECTION POINTS

How do we create that follow-through after we run an **event**?

How do we take the amazing things that happen in **events** that we create and turn that into our daily behaviour?

When we create an **event**, we must involve everybody in the conversation and facilitate consensus that's committed and clear. Then we document the output and create an **asset**. Through **assets**, we can guide our daily **rhythm** and bring focus and change into the conversation in our company and ultimately transform our **culture**.

One of the core concepts of this book is that great **events** can help us create **assets**. Strong, owned **assets** your people have been involved in creating can then be a part of that daily conversation. This requires discipline, but the things we talk about become the things we do. The things we do become our habits, and as we are aware, our habits become the character, identity, destiny, and legacy of ourselves and our company.

In the chapter that follows this one, we will go deeper still into using design thinking to create your **assets**. For now, let's get into practicing our facilitation skillset.

THE ART OF FACILITATION

There are many definitions of facilitation. In **TLC** terms, we define it as:

> *A collaborative, creative, consensus-based decision-making process used to run an effective meeting or* **event**.

This definition is closely related to ideas of experiential and active learning and has been covered with in-depth research from John Heron at the University of Surrey and the International Centre for Cooperative Inquiry.[108]

Now, let's take this a bit further, and I'll share some key ideas for how I bring this to life.

To facilitate a great **event**, a few things need to occur. First of all, we recommend that you get somebody who is good or even masterful in the art of facilitation. If you don't have somebody available, we can recommend somebody. Email me: *benny@bigchange.group* with the subject line: **TLC** Facilitators.

The transformational leader must work to facilitate these **events** as part of the skillset.

The following framework will show you how to set the facilitation frame for the **event**.

This can be applied to every installation in this book to run your **events** of **teams**, **games**, **player**, **north star**, and **change agent** charter.

---

108 John Heron, *Co-operative Inquiry: Research into the Human Condition* (London: Sage Publications, 1996).

EXERCISES AND APPLICATIONS

CREATING EVENTS

STEP ONE: SET THE PURPOSE OF THE EVENT

The first thing a facilitator needs to do is work with the room to clearly define the purpose of the session. Yes, they know they are there to create an **asset** of **teams**, **games**, **players**, **results** or, once you are up and flying, all of the above.

We need to further define what outcome is. This is important to get right.

You must do this in the session with the **players** present, even if you have defined it in the calendar invitation or the email inviting the participants to the **event**. This may sound obvious. Maybe it is to you, but it will not be obvious, clear, or aligned to the **players** at the **event**. You must do this so everyone in the room can start to be pointed in the same direction and begin to focus on the same outcome.

Here are some examples of the purpose of **events** for each of the areas of **team** ethos, **games**, and **players**.

- The purpose of this **event** is to define the ethos for our sales **team**.
- The purpose of this **event** might be to design a **game**, so we can track our progress in an engaging, visual way.

Ask them, "Do you know why we're here today?" Then, to encourage a deeper conversation into why this **event** matters, this open discussion creates the collective commitment to the **event**.

As we shepherd them along this journey, the core skill of a facilitator is to bring insight from the people. The facilitator's goal is to have the people think and express why they think it's important. When we get the conversation started about the clear reason why we are doing this, we set the frame for the room to engage in a valuable discussion.

Ask, "Why is this important?"

Ask, "What will this give us?"

Ask, "How do you think we should do this?"

Ask, "What will make this session a great use of everyone's time?"

Stoke the fire of this conversation with clarifying questions. Dig, explore, encourage, and reward participation with thanks and praise. The deeper you go into discussing the purpose of this, the more transformative the **event** will be.

Don't settle for everyone immediately agreeing with each other. Gently ask each person to share why they think it's important.

As the insights and contributions are shared, write them on the board or the butchers paper. Document the thinking, display it, and let them know that their perspective and voice matters. They will reward you with engagement and, quite often, golden insights.

Once you have invested the time and energy in gathering these insights, work to distil the frame into a clear consensus of the **event's** purpose.

Ask the group, "Is this it?"

"Is this what we are here for today?"

"Are we committed to this session and its value?"

Write it clearly at the top of the board.

The purpose of this **event** is to ________________, so we can ________________.

Through this process, we develop buy-in, and we teach the room that it's okay to speak up, that this environment we are creating within the **event** room is one of sharing and participation.

STEP TWO: GET CLEAR ON THE OUTPUTS

Once you have defined the purpose of the **event** with the group, you need to clearly outline the outputs and **assets** of the session.

In the **TLC**, the outputs of **events** are called **assets**. Let participants know we will be creating an **asset** together, and this will be a clear, concise document of what we create together.

Include everyone, encourage everyone, and ask the following questions:

"How will we know we've been successful in this **event's** purpose?"

"What are the objectives?"

"What are the outputs you want to see?"

"What are our specific goals for this session?"

They might say, "We have a clear one-page plan **asset**."

"We have all agreed on a strategy for the next month."

"We have chosen the right words for our **team** ethos, and we've decided that is how we're going to define ourselves."

"We have set our **g**oals, **a**ctivities, **m**easures, and **e**xpectations for the quarter."

It's important to note here that you do not need 100 percent agreement on every item. What you want is to find common ground for the majority and a safe environment to challenge the **status quo**.

Write two or three clear goals for the session on the board under the Purpose column.

STEP THREE: CREATE THE STANDARDS FOR THE EVENT

The next step the facilitator needs to take is setting the standards for the room.

The standards for the room are how we're going to behave and work together in the **event** to be able to create the **asset**. These are different from your **north star** standards in that they set the ground rules and boundaries for the specific **event**. You can customise these in collaboration with the room based on the requirements of the purpose, goals, and **assets** you are working to create.

Invite the room to come up with the standards.

Do this by asking the room the following questions:

"What nonnegotiable standards do we need to work by in this **event** to fulfil its purpose and create our **asset?"**

"What should we expect from each other in this **event**?"

"What are the ground rules for this **event** session?"

Make sure that while I'm doing this that every single standard that goes on the whiteboard is something that everybody in the room commits to and agrees to. You need a full consensus on this to set the group up for success.

Standards that often come out of this process are:

- Everyone contributes
- There are no bad ideas
- Don't talk over each other
- Speak up and speak now
- Whatever we agree to in this room we carry out into the workplace

Another standard I like to set in every session is that the facilitator has the right, the privilege, and the honour to facilitate, to bring the conversation back on track, and to keep people pointed towards the purpose of the session so we can achieve the objectives together.

Once you set the standards with the room, write these on the board underneath the goals and **assets**.

We refer to these throughout the session, especially if you feel like the group is getting off-track or not moving towards the purpose and goals.

Once you've set the standards in place, you're ready to go. You're ready to bring the discussion to the group. In the next installation of **assets**, we go through the process of how to design the **assets** in each event once you have set the facilitation frame using the method above. But first, let's set aside some time for the **events** we need to run.

EXERCISES AND APPLICATIONS

THE CALENDAR OF EVENTS

This is where you take action.

This part of the installation is about mapping out what **events** need to take place over a twelve-month period. You do not need to be specific. In fact, it is best not to, because you will be much better placed to decide on the details closer to the date and to base this on what your company needs at the time. You do, however, need to allocate the resources of time, energy, and money and commit to a series of regular **events** that align your organization and create the **culture** and **brand** that you've envisioned in your **north star**.

It is a requirement for the right people to attend and contribute to each of these **events** in order to create effective **assets** of change.

When crafting your calendar of **events**, consider the following.

- Have we allowed enough time?
- Are we involving everybody?
- Is it regular and consistent?

Remember, the key here is engagement through involvement. Benjamin Franklin famously said, "Tell me and I forget, teach me and I may remember, involve me and I learn."

We no longer live in a time where we are hiring labour hands in most businesses. The robots are taking that over. So, what business are we dealing with now? We're dealing with the business of thinking.

If we want to shape people's thinking to harness and point in the same direction, we need to host **events** that involve people who have clear outcomes toward the **assets** and the tangibles and the outputs they're creating. The **events** you will schedule must enable the creation and ownership of valuable **assets** for every **team** and **player**.

The **assets** detailed in the following installations will be **assets** of **team**, **game**, **results**, and **players** that all point towards **north star**.

CREATING ASSETS THROUGH EVENTS

As I've referred to in every point in this installation, the purpose of an **event** is to create a transformative environment that **results** in engagement and a clear definition and understanding of what we're going to do. **Assets** are the clear, agreed-upon commitments to outputs of the **events**. It's what we agree to do after the **event** when we step into the **rhythm**. When we create **assets** through engagement and facilitation, and we align this toward **north star**, we create a map for people for the next distance that they need to travel, so they can be aligned and agree that this is what we're doing. We run continual **events** for the simple reason that today, we are the dumbest we will ever be and the smartest we have ever been. We are always learning, improving, and growing.

In this installation of **events**, we learned how to set the facilitation frame, create a calendar, and bring people together to work *on* the company. We improve our **teams**, **players**, **games**, and **results** as we move towards our **new normal**. The next installation is going to be a deeper dive into the **assets** that are created at these **events**. I'm going to unpack each of the areas and share with you what the defined **assets** can look like, what they should be, and what they need to include. In the next installation, we will dive a bit deeper into the practice of creating your **assets** through **events**.

INSTALLATION 9

ASSETS

JOHN'S OLD-WORLD STATUS QUO

We are standing over the boardroom table looking at a BIG pile of values posters, management reports, operations manuals, an org chart, and a stack of marketing material that make promises of a better world. There were keyrings with taglines on them and coffee cups with "people first" stickers with the company logo tattered about the place.

"What does this stuff mean to you?" I asked John.

John looked impatient this morning and replied, "What's the problem, Benny?"

"John, does anyone know these values?"

"Not really. I mean, if you asked someone out in the office or the warehouse what they were, I reckon you would be stuck for answers."

"What about the management reports?" I asked. "Do people read them?"

"Well, I do, and I think some of the **leadership team**, maybe half, reads them through."

"Interesting. You send them around to everyone, though?"

"Yes," he said.

"Do you want them to read them?"

"Yes, I wish they would care enough to pay attention. We need people to understand this stuff for our **culture** and **leadership** development."

"How about the org chart? How do people use this?"

"Well, it's something people use to plan their next career move or to figure out where they need to go to get something approved. All companies need an org chart, right?"

"Okay. How about the manuals?" There were so many manuals and operating procedures. "How do we go with them? Do people use them?"

"Not really," John said, sounding defeated. "They were part of our ISO process. We needed to document all of this stuff in order to get accredited."

"Okay. What about how people actually work? Do they follow these procedures? Do they know them?"

John sat back and thought. "Well, I think they know enough to keep their jobs," John chuckled nervously.

"What are we noticing here? What's missing?" I asked.

"Well, when you put it like that, a lot. These documents don't really mean much to our people. We only refer to these when there is a BIG problem or a crisis. When that happens, no one really cares about them, though. They don't think about them on a daily basis. They don't work this way.

I want to create real **assets** in the company. **Assets** people value and refer to constantly. Cultural capital. Can we do this?"

"John, I thought you would never ask," I said. "Let me help you use your **events** to create **assets** and make them habits by bringing them into the **rhythm**."

JOHN'S NEW NORMAL

Six months later, the world had changed.

Through a series of highly engaging **events**, the staff had co-created the company manifesto, a solid statement of what mattered to them. They had live charts tracking their own progress they helped put together. Everyone set and knew the standards of what was required to make their **culture** work. Management was visual, engaging, clear, and unquestioned.

Every conversation seemed to reference the vision, mission, values, standards, **team** ethos, **games**, and the **assets** that represent them. The daily **rhythms'** agenda constantly referred to the **assets** the staff had input in creating. They appreciated in value every day because they were used to driving and leading the conversation back to what matters most. The language of the **culture** was changing. Over time, people were changing their assumptions about what it meant to work at John's company.

Through the **events**, we created powerful **assets** of **team** ethos, **games**, and **players**. We created a manifesto, a living org chart, a **culture** deck that was used to start every meeting in the company's **rhythm**, **game** plans, scoreboards, and **player** profile cards. All **assets** of the company's **culture**.

Through the **rhythm**, we embedded these **assets** in the daily thinking, words, and habits of the people. The value of these **assets** appreciated because we gave the people the forum and space to appreciate them. Through the consistent and patient process of this, the **culture** and the assumptions of the people moved, day by day, inch by inch, toward the **new normal**—towards the **north star**.

WHAT YOU'LL LEARN AND DO IN THIS INSTALLATION

In this instalment of **assets**, we will learn how to build powerful, one-page plans and reference points for our transformation. We will draw on the basics of design thinking to create these **assets** with our **players** through our **events** and take this to our **rhythm** so we can increase the value of these **assets**, create our **new normal**, and transform our company.

THE POWER OF THE ONE-PAGE ASSET

There is great power in concise, clear, synthesised thinking.

By limiting the amount of space we have to capture the output of our **event**, we harness the power of succinct thinking. The method we use for this is a one-page asset. Why one page? Simple, one page is memorable and clear. One page makes us think in concise, precise, no-nonsense terms. The limited real estate helps create clarity and simplicity, and this makes it easier to communicate clearly in a noisy, distraction-filled, time-poor world.

The output of each **event** is to create a one-page document. Your **assets** can be shorter than one page but no more than one page each. These documents frame what we will do next. They define what we will agree upon and act upon.

Toyota runs its entire operation through visual one-page plans. The reason for this is that we do not waste words, we do the work to be as clear as possible, and we use the fewest words possible to explain the clearest concept possible. At the end of an **event** when everybody has discussed, argued, considered, and been challenged by the facilitator, the output and **asset** is summarised in the clearest way possible in one page.

Let the group co-create this, frame it, and capture it as a one-page **asset**. From there, this **asset** can be signed by people. It can be published, and then it can be communicated through your daily **rhythms** and through your channels of communication. It will serve as the reference point to where we are going. Done well, the one-page **asset** provides the focus we need to achieve our goals and the communication required to get there.

Follow the facilitation notes in the **events** installation to set up the facilitation frame for the **event** and then use the framework to create your **assets** using the following basic principles of human-centric design thinking.

ASSETS APPRECIATE OR DEPRECIATE IN VALUE

When we think of **assets**, we are describing something that has ongoing value. **TLC assets** created in a company lose value for two reasons:

1. The **asset** is not very good and needs to be redesigned either through an event or by the leader.
2. The asset is not referred to and not talked about in the **rhythm**.

A classic example of this is walking into an organization that has a poster in the lobby, or a plaque in the hall, or a small piece of paper in the CEO's office that states the vision, the mission, the values, **assets** of **north star**. However, when you ask people, "What does this mean? What are the values? What are the BIG goals of the company?" they can't provide an answer or an insight, or reflect into their own day-to-day workings. In such instances, the **asset** has no value. The **asset** only existed as an **event**. It was captured, but it wasn't talked about.

The biggest problem with creating **assets** in workshop **events** is bringing them to life. How do we bring them to life? **Assets** must be brought to life by talking about them and bringing them into the language of the business. The daily conversations must refer to the **assets**, so the compass points towards **north star**. If we're not discussing it, it was just an **event** that came and passed. Maybe it felt good, but without creating the clear **asset**, it's not likely to change anything.

As we define these **assets**, you will learn to bring this back and bake it into the **rhythm** of your daily operations. **Assets** come to life when they become part of the **rhythm** of our communication. When we appreciate them through discussion, they appreciate in value.

If you create an **asset** but do not refer to it, value it, or spend time and energy on it, it not only loses value but the entire value of creating **assets** diminishes. If the momentum subsides, people start to say, "Here we go again! Another workshop that won't change anything!" This is one of the most destructive things in transforming a **culture**.

We need to have **events** that create **assets**, that then get baked into the **rhythm**. If the old cycle continues, all you're doing is putting words on a page that won't change diddly-squat! **Events** can be transformational emotionally, but they require a solid output to be felt, to be referred to, and be accountable for.

Well-defined **assets** create a reference point, but this reference point alone is not enough. Behaviours and habits only change when they become consistent, when they become part of our daily conversation. Remember, our thinking eventually becomes our destiny. This adage applies to the individual, to the **team**, and to the entire company.

To bring an **asset** to life and increase its value, we need to bring it into a **rhythm** of communication and regularly reset and improve it through **events**. We need to bring it into the daily conversation to reinforce it until it becomes our language. Once everybody is sharing the same thinking, we experience a shift. We experience a change in the **status quo** because we are talking in a focused way about what matters most.

How do we make this communication constant? How do we make it what we come back to each day to guide our thinking, shape our actions, and develop habits that create the character, identity, and destiny of our **teams** and our company? We take it to the **rhythm**.

In this instalment, we learned how to create our **assets** using design thinking. We brought everyone together and worked on improving the company. Now we are able to create the plans and reference points to practice in our **rhythm**.

In the next installations, you can create your **assets** through **events**, **teams**, **games**, **players**, and **results**, and we will share examples of each.

EXERCISES AND APPLICATIONS

EXERCISE: CREATING AN ASSET USING DESIGN THINKING

Getting ready—Get plenty of Post-it notes, a whiteboard, markers, blank paper, and coffee and follow the **events** facilitation process in the **events** installation to set the frame for the room.

If you are running this online, you can use Zoom, Google Meet or your choice of video conferencing software and some virtual whiteboarding tools such as Stormboards or MURAL.

Make sure everyone understands what the **TLC** asset is. Educate them on what a **game** is, teach them about **team** ethos, and show them the elements of the **north star**. You should know this well by now.

Once you have set the purpose and the standards for the event and everyone knows the **asset** we need to create, then follow this basic formula of design thinking. Do not worry about getting it perfect. Just work through the steps and develop your facilitator and coordinator skillset as you go. You will apply this thinking to running an event and creating an asset for every instalment in this book. The next instalments contain further examples and more guidance in doing this. For now, get familiar with the basic design-thinking process.

STEP ONE: EMPATHIZE

Ask open-ended questions about the asset you are trying to create with your **players**. Let everyone write down their responses on Post-it notes or alternatively have someone write down all of the group's ideas.

- What is most important to us in creating this asset?
- What are your ideas on how we can create this?
- What do we need to consider in creating this?
- How do we want it to serve us, our **team**, our company, our **north star**?

Put these ideas on the board where the group can see them and use them to think about the next step.

STEP TWO: DEFINE

Ask everyone to discuss and look for the themes. What are the main problems and best ideas that come from the discussion? Clarify the answers and write the outcome down.

STEP THREE: IDEATE

Come up with a range of ideas on how to create this, taking input from everyone in the room. Write them up, have some healthy tension within the room standards, work the issues, and encourage new thinking and ideas.

STEP FOUR: PROTOTYPE

Build the draft one-page asset. Get everyone's input but lead the process through your understanding of the **TLC**. You will have a great understanding of many of the **assets** you can create through reading and considering the examples throughout this book. Put a start and end date on the page and get everyone to sign it as a commitment to testing the **asset**. Close the session, thank everyone, give high fives all around, and let them know we will be bringing this **asset** into our daily **rhythm**.

STEP FIVE: TEST

Take the one-pager and practice using it in the daily **rhythm**. If it's a **team** ethos statement or an **asset** of **north star**, discuss it in the daily **rhythm**. If it's a **game** plan, discuss it and mark up your scoreboards in the daily **rhythm**. Through this process, we test the **assets**, find ways to make them better, and we can get started to make it part of our **new normal**.

STEP SIX: IMPLEMENT OR REPEAT

Here we either love the asset, and it works perfectly to create our **results**, or we run the next **event** to repeat the process and improve it. In **culture**s of continuous improvement, the **assets** are constantly improved and updated. This cycle continues in the calendar event getting more and more effective every time and producing better and better quality **assets** each time.

These steps are the broad formulae for creating **assets**. All installations in this book contain more specific instructions and guidance for the types of **assets** to create in the transformation process.

Use the guidance and examples in each installation but also get creative. What **assets** can you create? Think of each element of the **TLC** and come up with a few ideas of the **assets** you want to develop with your people.

INSTALLATION 10

TEAMS

JOHN'S OLD-WORLD STATUS QUO

"They just don't get it!" said John, brow furrowed, clearly frustrated.

I know.

"We went through this **north star** stuff, we asked them, we ran the surveys and **events**. We really tried. The **teams** still don't get it."

Interesting.

"The posters are up, but people don't seem to be able to see my vision like I do. I see them parrot the values, and I worry

they are just paying lip service to what we want to hear. I wish we could do better. I wish they could really understand that we are doing something great here, and they can be part of it. We have over 1,000 staff, and this is not an easy thing to achieve.

"How do we get them all in? How do we help them find purpose in what they are doing?" John asked.

"John, do you think anyone has a clear sense of purpose here?" I asked.

"Some of them. There are patches of it. I see it in some **teams**, in some people, but it's still like a surface veneer, like they don't really get it. Our engagement scores have gone up, but there is so much more needed to make this transformation work. What can we do?"

"Well, John, I'm glad you asked."

JOHN'S NEW NORMAL

A few months later, the world had changed.

Everyone had been involved in the creation of the **team** ethos **assets. Events** challenged peoples' thinking, coached their frontline **leadership**, and invited them to contribute to creating meaning together. Everyone knew the **north star** by heart and understood what it meant to them.

Each department had set a clear purpose statement supporting this and clear standards for what it meant to be in the **team** and be a part of the company's **culture**. They all had a hand and a voice in creating their Yearly **Culture** Deck and almost everyone in the business felt proud of these **assets**.

People would constantly refer to the **team** ethos and **north star** in conversations. It was a bit spooky in the beginning. This was not like anything they had ever experienced in any workplace.

Because we involved as many people as possible in the process of creating the **assets** of **team** ethos, they bought into it. It was their decision and commitment, and together they knew where they stood and how to act. The **assets** of **team** ethos were built through facilitated **events**, bolstered, and made habits through the **rhythm**, and over time, totally shifted the *basic* assumptions of the **culture**. They created the **new normal** with pride and involvement, because their fearless leader, John, had decided to empower them to do this.

WHAT YOU'LL LEARN AND DO IN THIS INSTALLATION

In this instalment, we will learn how to develop highly functional **teams** by understanding our organisational structure and building shared **team** ethos **assets** for every group in our business to align with our **north star**.

Before we jump into building our **teams**, let's zoom out and consider the organisational structure and the best thinking behind this.

A BRIEF HISTORY OF ORGANIZATIONAL STRUCTURES

Organizational structures can be created and developed in many ways depending on the requirements of the company's **north star**. One thing is for sure; they need to allow allocation of responsibilities while being flexible and efficient enough to deal with **VUCA**.

Here are the main organizational structures and a quick history on this.

Weber, in 1948, identified the major org structures as follows:[109]

PRE-BUREAUCRATIC STRUCTURES

These were companies with no standard tasks, totally centralised, all key decisions made by one hopefully strategic leader.

109 Max Weber, *Economy and Society: An Outline of Interpretive Sociology*, trans. Guenther Roth and Claus Wittich (London: University of California Press, 1978).

- High control, low scalability.
- Can be dominating or charismatic **leadership** styles going on here.

BUREAUCRATIC STRUCTURES

Like a machine, the machine tries to go for speed, precision, and optimisation, a certain amount of standardisation, tall structures, mechanistic and not organic, hierarchy, clearly defined roles, respect for merit.[110]

Levels upon levels of management decision-making passes through layers and takes time, depending on how functional the "machine" is and tight restraints and policies, reluctant to change and adapt, authority at the top, close supervision, tremendous command and control, but not so good for creativity and innovation, and as such, quite vulnerable to **VUCA**.

POST-BUREAUCRATIC STRUCTURES

Here the company practices **culture** management, quality management, and matrix management, but adheres to the core tenants of bureaucracy.[111]

Hierarchy of authority still there, however as Gideon Kunda wrote in his classic studies of **culture** management, "the formalisation, codification, and enforcement of rules and regulations does not change in principle. It shifts focus from org structure to company **culture**.

---

110 Max Weber, *From Max Weber: Essays in Sociology*, trans. H. H. Gerth and C. Wright Mills (London: Routledge, 1991).

111 Chris Grey and Christina Garsten, "Trust, Control and Post-Bureaucracy," *Organization Studies* 22, no. 2 (March 2001): 229–50, https://doi.org/10.1177/0170840601222003.

Charles Heckscher went on to develop an "ideal type" of a post-bureaucratic structure where he stated that decisions are based on dialogue and consensus instead of the old school of authority and command. It's kind of like involving your people in **events.**[112]

This is a shift from a hierarchy style org to a networked style that exists within a set of rules, and it empowers people to make rules within the rules. Think of it like this: the **north star** sets the rules, the **games** align to the goals and standards, the **player** and **team** align to the values and principles.

Now, let's consider functional, divisional, matrix, flat structures, and the merits and limitations of each to help us get a handle on what will best serve your company and its **north star**.

FUNCTIONAL STRUCTURES

This structure organises people based on their realms of expertise. This can be great for efficiency in each department, though it brings problems when cross-functions are not established when different departments fail to communicate, and when silos can be problematic if we try to foster collaboration across the company. It's a bit like trying to juggle when the left hand won't talk to the right hand.

DIVISIONAL STRUCTURES

Self-contained businesses within the company that operate as separate profit centres are one of the most common business

112 *The Post-Bureaucratic Organization: New Perspectives on Organizational Change*, eds. Charles Heckscher and Anne Donnellon (Thousand Oaks, CA: SAGE Publications, 1994).

structures we see today. On the bright side, it can increase flexibility and speed up decision-making and allow for innovation, it delegates authority, and performance can be measured in a focused way with each group. While many have evidence showing that this does promote better morale and higher engagement due to smaller groups that allow for more meaningful relationships, there can be an unhealthy competition going on. It can increase costs as more qualified leaders and managers are needed for each division. Furthermore, there tends to be an emphasis and focus on divisional goals rather than company goals, so this must be considered when planning for in relation to your **north star** and divisional **teams** and **games**.

MATRIX STRUCTURES

Matrix structures can be best described as cross-functional **teams** that are assigned based on the function and the product or output that the company offers. Project managers recruit **teams** from different departments and areas to produce something together. The difficulties of this include power struggles and uncertainty in the authority of **leadership**, and it can be difficult for people to identify and understand who is in charge.[113] The bright side is that it busts down silos and gets the functions of the business talking to each other, which helps information spread and leads to better decision-making for the org as a whole. It also can be useful in utilising talent across a range of different project applications.

113 Stanley M. Davis and Paul R. Lawrence, "Problems of Matrix Organizations," *Harvard Business Review* 56, no. 3 (May 1978), https://hbr.org/1978/05/problems-of-matrix-organizations.

THE FLAT STRUCTURE—ORGANISATIONAL CIRCLES

The flat or horizontal structure consists of very few zero levels of middle management among executive **leadership** and the staff or **players**. The benefits of this are well-documented in increasing **player** engagement through autonomy and self-**leadership**.[114]

Flat structures are often utilised in small companies, though they are frequently abandoned for an authoritarian hierarchy, bureaucracy, or a matrix structure (like Starbucks, for example)[115] when they reach a certain size or have a requirement to urgently scale.

The downside of this is that companies often damage the **culture** that made them successful in the beginning in pursuit of growth and scale.

If only there were a system that allowed companies to effectively scale flat structures and maintain the cultural dynamics that made them special and successful in the first place.

Indeed, there are rapidly emerging structures and methods for developing this successfully.

One of these new structures is the Wirearchy, which enables the flow of power and decision-making to be based on information, trust, credibility, and **results**. This is made possible by the speed of communication technology.[116]

---

114 Edwin E. Ghiselli and Jacob P. Siegel, "Leadership and Managerial Success in Tall and Flat Organizational Structures," *Personnel Psychology* 25, no. 4 (December 1972): 617–24, https://doi.org/10.1111/j.1744-6570.1972.tb02304.x.

115 Starbucks Coffee Company, https://www.starbucks.com/.

116 Lynda Gratton, *The Democratic Enterprise: Liberating Your Business with...*

One of the benefits of the **TLC** system is that it enables the leader to bring together the relative merits of all of these structures through **north star** governance, collaborative **events, games** as systems of management accountability, and **results** as measures to trust and track progress.

We do this through the simple structure of **teams.**

TEAMS

Team is actually a relatively new structure in the twentieth century.

It is very simple and it goes like this: the org structure is the totality of horizontal (functional) and vertical (hierarchy) effectiveness. At the end of the day, a company is a BIG group of smaller groups of people coming together to create value for the world.[117]

I believe leaders always get the **teams** they deserve.

If we don't clearly articulate our **north star** and help people find their **team** ethos (their shared beliefs), they're not going to have a sense of meaning or a sense of purpose. If we don't give them **games** they can progress in, they're not going to find a sense of satisfaction, and they will be unproductive and inefficient. If we don't surround them with like-minded people and select the right **players**, their relationships will be full of conflicts, and the **team** will break down.

...*Freedom, Flexibility, and Commitment*(Upper Sadle River, J: Prentice Hall/ Financial Times, 2004), xii–xiv.

117 Priyavrat Thareja, "Each one is Capable (A Total Quality Organisation Thru' People)," *Foundry* 20, no. 4 (July/August 2008), https://www.researchgate.net/publication/228233868.

The **teams** that work well are usually the ones that understand the bigger picture and the part they have to play. They turn up because they want to be there because they believe in the **team's** ethos and the **north star**. They want to put in work for a company that shares their values and interests.

TYPES OF TEAMS

A **team** defined is simply this—a group of **players** working effectively together to achieve their goal. Academic research on **teams** has only really been around since the late twentieth century, and there is plenty of argument as to what **teams** are and if the concept even works.

There are two major categories of **Team** to look at:[118]

1. Independent **Teams**: Here, **games** are played individually, and the points are scored independently by individual **players**, e.g., track and field.
2. Interdependent **Teams:** Here, **games** are played together, and goals require the cooperation of every **player**, e.g., basketball.

From there, you can think of a whole range of types of **teams** and the types of **games** they play.

- Sales **Teams**
- Project **Teams**
- Service **Teams**

---

118 Marty Brounstein, "Differences between Work Groups and Teams," accessed October 22, 2020, http://www.dummies.com.

- **Support Teams**
- **IT Teams**
- **Maintenance Teams**
- **Leadership Teams** (a **team** of **teams**)
- Cross-Departmental **teams**
- **Change Agent Teams**

The power of effective and diverse collaboration is necessary for our battles against **VUCA**.

The better and faster we get at developing **teams** of all categories and types into **games** that produce effective **results**, the more success we will experience as we learn, adapt, and grow as a company. The invitation here is to build the practices and skillsets of effective **team** building.

In the **TLC** system, we work to build self-managing **teams** capable of sustaining their own growth and continuous improvement.

Wheelan teaches us the groups develop into **teams** in four stages,[119] and Tuckman's model tends to line up pretty well to this.[120]

1. Dependency and Inclusion—Forming Stage
2. Counter Dependency and Fighting—Storming Stage
3. Trust and Structure—Norming Stage
4. Work—Performing Stage

---

119 Susan Wheelan, *Creating Effective Teams: A Guide for Members and Leaders*, 5th ed. (London: SAGE Publications, 2014).

120 Bruce W. Tuckman, "Developmental Sequence in Small Groups," *Psychological Bulletin* 63, no. 6 (1965): 384–99, https://doi.org/10.1037/h0022100.

Now, let's look at accelerating this process by creating a shared **team** ethos within **teams** and across **teams.**

The **TLC** system is designed to establish self-managing **teams** through the practice of all of the elements that you are by now very familiar with.

Hackman, in 1976, showed the following behavioural characteristics applied to effective self-managing workgroups:[121]

- Personal responsibility
- Monitor own performance and seek feedback
- Manage own performance and take corrective action to improve their own and others' performance
- Seek guidance, assistance, and resources from the company in order to perform their job well
- Help other members of their **team** improve their performance and raise productivity for the whole company.
- All of this is made possible by getting your **team's** ethos right, getting the right **players** and the right **games** (more on this in the **games** installation).

THE LANGUAGE OF LEADERSHIP—CREATING TEAM ETHOS

To build and express your **culture** and **brand assets** by creating them with the people who live and breathe your **culture,**

121 J. Richard Hackman and Greg R. Oldham, "Motivation through the Design of Work: Test of a Theory," *Organizational Behavior and Human Performance* 16, no. 2 (August 1976): 250–79, https://doi.org/10.1016/0030-5073(76)90016-7.

we define, refine, create, and express valuable **assets** of each **team's** ethos.

Why do we need to create **assets** with every **team**? Why is that **north star** not enough? Well, it is great to express our **north star** and the direction of the company, to create a focal point for where we need to point our hearts and minds. But it's another thing entirely to have an **event** where people think together, communicate together, and create their own **asset** of **team** ethos, their own expression of language leading them to the BIG goals of the company.

This is as much about the process of creation as it is about the creation itself. You'll see as you go through this experience that not only will you have a clear map built with people about their **team** ethos and beliefs, but they will say, "We got there, we own that, and we're going to hold ourselves to it." Then, this **team** ethos can be brought into the daily **rhythm** of conversation. They identify who they are as a group and how they fit into the bigger picture.

By helping your people create their own **assets** of **team** ethos, we're helping them think in the way that helps us achieve our vision and our BIG goals for **north star**.

TLC leaders are able to articulate the **north star** of the company and also work with their **teams** and individual **players** to help them define and align their ethos. They're masters at facilitating alignment towards the **north star**. They're able to ask the right questions to draw out a group's deeper purpose and inclination.

This may seem basic, however, and it is always under-utilized and usually done quite poorly. A good practice here is not parroting off some sheet from management or poster in the hallway. It is the process of digging deep into the purpose and the story behind the purpose to discover a shared meaning. A shared meaning creates movement, stirs emotion, and brings inspiration to the world of work.

MAN'S SEARCH FOR MEANING (AT WORK)

> *The only happy people I know are the ones who are working well at something they consider important.*
>
> —*Abraham Maslow*[122]

People need encouragement to develop their own sense of courage. It is the responsibility and the task of the **TLC** leader to help people uncover the hidden meaning in their work by 1) helping them think of the value that they're creating, and 2) connecting with people's lives so they will improve through their work.

If you want to make your people happy, help them think about the value of the work they deliver and find ways to celebrate this as you go.

This is the art of facilitation of **team** ethos through **events**.

> *Large numbers of strangers can cooperate successfully by believing in common myths. Any large-scale human cooperation—whether a modern state, a medieval church, an ancient city or an archaic tribe—is rooted in common myths that exist only in people's collective imagination.*
>
> —*Yuval Noah Harari*[123]

---

122 Abraham H. Maslow, *Maslow on Management* (New York: Wiley & Sons, 1998).
123 Yuval Harari, *Sapiens: A Brief History of Humankind* (New York: Harper, 2014).

The invitation here is to help people build those myths together. Your **team's** ethos is the language of myth; it is what is seen to be true and held dear to your people. You can create this through having organized conversations, and you can sustain this by creating the **assets** and artefacts required to bring it to life over time until it becomes history.

Your company creates its own universal truths, and this is what becomes the **new normal. Team** ethos **assets** can become the defining vernacular of your **team**'s sub**culture**, shaped intentionally and aligned to your **north star**.

EVENTS OF TEAM ETHOS

Transformational **leadership** works to engage all the people in the organization to be able to understand the **north star** in a way that has meaning for each individual **team** and **player**. **North star** will show us the vision, mission, and values of the whole company. But until we have **events** where people are able to discuss, understand, and define their own set of beliefs (their own **team** ethos around that **north star**), they won't usually understand it.

An **event** of **team** ethos is an **event** that aligns each **team** and each individual towards the **north star**. It's a facilitated conversation where people develop the thinking required to create something of their own. An **event** of **team** ethos exists for the purpose of creating an **asset** that aligns to **north star**. An example of this might be that your **north star** is to become the most trusted number one widget manufacturer in America.

Now, you may run a **team** ethos **event** with the sales **team**. They may come up with a **team** ethos that is to sell in a clear, ethical, customer-centric way that never overpromises and always overdelivers on what they're selling, to work hard and drive towards this tirelessly to be able to fulfil the larger company's vision.

In doing this, we're shaping the thinking of people to be able to think towards the same purpose, towards the same ultimate goal. Remember, you can't just express **north star** through the business and expect everybody to be engaged with it, understand it, and hold it like their own. It does not work that way. The requirement to make this work is an **event** when people become emotionally involved, speak up, are challenged, and have to work to shape their thinking and come up with the answer themselves.

Within the **TLC** system, **events** of **team** ethos create **assets** that people own, feel responsibility and pride towards, that allow them to develop their beliefs in the direction of the **north star**.

An **event** of **team** ethos is all about aligning and engaging at every level, department, and with every **team** and every individual to create an **asset** that then can point us home towards **north star**. The **event** is there to create the initial energy. The **asset** then becomes what we refer to in our **rhythm**, what we come back to, what we lead our conversations with. In order to affect behavioural change, people need to consider their own beliefs.

We help them agree how they're going to show up together. They need to make this emotional shift between how they are normally and who they need to be to fulfil a larger vision.

This **event** is facilitated with every group in the business, and it becomes part of your **event** schedule. It's not set and forget. It becomes this act of coming together, discussing our identity, what we believe in, what it's about, and defining it as an **asset** that then becomes part of the daily conversation. **Assets** of **team** ethos can include manifestos, purpose statements, mottos, and creeds. **These events** and **assets** of **team** ethos create smaller belief structures that fit into our larger **culture** and point towards **north star**.

STORY TIME: THE FACTORY FLOOR MANIFESTO AND THE CEO'S DREAM

"You can't change the corporate values," I heard.

The corporate values were set from the parent company, the corporate office in Upstate New York, and here I am, standing in a training room in Australia, Dandenong, with a group of fifty factory floor workers.

The challenge that we face is that nobody in this room really understands the core values of the business. They know what they are. They see them on the poster in the lobby. They know the words, but the meaning doesn't ring true to them.

We began the process of discussing what matters most to them.

"We're going to create a manifesto," I said. "We're going to create an **asset** that shows and shares what you really believe and what you value. *We used the process from the* ***events*** *and* ***assets*** *installation.* You're going to use this to guide the conversations in your daily **rhythm**.

Immediately the group is taken aback. Nobody had ever asked them what they thought about this before.

We got to work and asked them:

- What do you believe in?
- What's most important?
- What do you value?

And we wrote all of the answers in a sea of text on the whiteboard.

After we had set the **event** frame, they felt safe enough to share dozens of desires, including:

- To get home safely
- To come up with ideas and to be heard
- To make better decisions
- To look after each other and champion our **results**.

Everybody had something to say, and every word got captured on the great BIG whiteboard on the wall. At the end of the session, when we looked through the themes and picked out the core messages, we put it all into one place.

After the session, we sent this off to some designers, and they came up with a poster with all different fonts and different lettering to really capture all the different beliefs and components of the factory floor manifesto. When it was done, we took the poster and showed it to the people in the marketing department.

They said, "This is ugly, this is off-**brand**, this doesn't follow our guidelines. You can have your poster, but please don't put the poster in the office. Please keep it out of the corporate room. Just keep it in the factory." This manifesto was for the frontline production workers. They'd made it, they owned it, and it was theirs. So, into the factory it went.

ONE CHOBANI MANIFESTO

WORK SMARTER

Be Safe

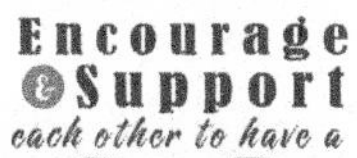

EVERYBODY NEEDS
TO CONTRIBUTE

Make
BOLD
INFORMED
DECISIONS

UNDERSTAND & UPHOLD
CHOBANI
standards

Take This
Opportunity
TO SHINE

RIDE THE BUMPY TRAIL
WE ARE ON A QUEST TOGETHER.

CHOBANI
DATE 29.03.2017
JOB SIZE 420mm(w) x 594mm(h)
JOB NO. REV. CLIENT. JOB NAME
042280/06_CHOB_One Chobani - Values Poster - A2

We put this poster up next to their **games** board where every day they would stand in **rhythm** and discuss the points of the manifesto, discuss what mattered to them. They'd discuss their **team** ethos. After they discussed their **team** ethos, they'd get into their **games**. They'd talk about their goals, activities, measures, and expectations, and get the support and coaching they needed to improve. They did this every day for a year, and day by day, their **results** got better and better.

A year later, the CEO and founder of Chobani yogurt visited the Australian site for the first time since it opened five years earlier. The CEO was the transformational entrepreneur, humanitarian philanthropist, and all-around great human being—Hamdi Ulukaya.

Hamdi walked into the building, went straight past the corporate office, and strolled straight out into the factory. He knew the workers on the frontline were the ones who made the magic happen. Once in the factory, Hamdi walked straight up to the manifesto poster, and said, "What's this?"

A young lady named Ruby said, "This is our manifesto. This is how we share our ethos, and this is what we talk about every single day as we start our **rhythm**."

Hamdi took a moment, stared at the poster, stared at the people, and shared that this is exactly how he wanted them to bring his vision to life.

You see, Hamdi had a vision for the whole company, but it needed to translate to the workers who were carrying out the work every single day. It needed to be theirs as well.

Hamdi asked for a copy of this poster for his office in Soho in Manhattan, and he hung it as a reminder that his dream had become the actions and the conversations every day of the people who run his business. So, it went. The poster was hung in the CEO's office, and the factory floor manifesto was an expression and an **asset** of the production **team** ethos and a realisation of the CEO's **north star** vision and values.

THE CULTURE BOOK

A famous example of an organization and company that puts **culture** first is the obvious example of Zappos. Tony Hsieh, the CEO of Zappos, believes that everything comes from **culture.**[124]

One of the ways Zappos bring their values to life is by collecting stories. Each year Zappos publishes what they call a **culture** book, a publication of their employees' stories and expressions of the values. It's their expressions of the values through the stories of their daily work. This is a great example of a cultural **team** ethos **asset**. They collect these stories; they put them together in a book, and they organize the book into categories of the value of **north star**.

This book then gets handed out to all staff, all new inductees. It's even available to the suppliers and fans of the company as well, on Amazon. The Zappos **culture** book is a beautiful example of how the stories we tell, how our ownership and expression of the values become an **asset** of **team** ethos.

We quite often work with clients to invite their people to collect stories that affirm the values.

We look for examples of the company living the values, capture these stories and statements, and put them in one

124 Tony Hsieh, *Delivering Happiness: A Path to Profits, Passion, and Purpose* (New York: Business Plus, 2010).

place. We put them into a book; put them into something that can express this and perpetuate good **culture**.

As such, we encourage you to start collecting stories that relate to your **team's** ethos and to your truth north. Then you will have all of these examples that can be used to teach people how to be successful in your company and how to move towards your **north star**.

STORY TIME: THE PURPOSE TREE

We once worked with an organization who had their **north star** firmly put in place. The vision, the mission, and core values were known to the entire company. Still, they had trouble communicating across **teams** and departments. They had siloed thinking that separated them from their aspirational value of collaboration. What they needed to do was create **assets** of **team** ethos for every department and **team** in the business.

So we ran **events** and facilitated with each **team** what the **team**'s ethos was, what the **team**'s purpose was, and what the **team**'s standards and goals were that contributed towards **north star**. We worked across the twelve departments that all had something to contribute for purpose and goals towards the bigger picture of **north star**.

Once we had collected all of these **assets** of **team** ethos, we thought to ourselves, "How can we display this in a way that people can understand this as a business? How can we turn this into an artefact? How can we turn this into something that will identify who we are and make it easy for people to navigate our company as we grow?"

What we came up with was a tree—a picture of the tree where the roots of the tree were the core values of the company. The whole tree was made of movable magnets that could be changed and modified, just like the company.

Each root showed a core value of belonging, gratitude, customer service, communication, and continuous improvement that formed the roots of the tree.

The trunk of the tree showed the goals for the company for that year what was core to the mission of what we were doing.

Each branch showed a department, and each branch had a purpose shown on the tree, clearly visualised that each department within this company had a purpose that was defined, clear, and understood.

We then put pictures of people on leaves for each department, and we used these pictures to move people into a department, so they had a visual representation of an orchard that came to life.

They took this even further and added emojis to show how each **team** was going and noted the progress towards their goals using pieces of fruit marked with their **team game** goals.

Across the sky within this picture, we put the vision of the company. The **north star** picture of where we were all going together and the mission formed the sky with all of the branches reaching up towards this.

What we created here is a full-purpose org chart.

Anyone can come into the business and stand in front of this artefact and gain a deep understanding of what the business is all about, what their **north star** is, but also the interdependent relationship among all of the departments and how they're all working, contributing, and communicating together to reach their vision in the sky.

The point is, when we take what's in people's hearts and minds and we synthesise it, we bring it together. We express it in a clear, visual, compelling way. People then stand around the tree and have conversations about how the departments are working together. The conversation becomes about how the whole organization benefits, not just one branch or one piece of fruit, but everyone can identify that they are part of a bigger mission and that they're moving towards a much bigger vision.

You can see a close-up of this asset at: *www.bigchangeagency.com/TLCresources.*

I'm sure you can think of many ways to express and share the unique ethos of every **team** in your company.

STORY TIME: FROM DATA ADMIN TO SAVING THE WORLD

The **team** was the data entry department of a background-checking company.

I asked them what they did, and they said, "We process background checks for people."

"Why?" I asked.

And they said, "So they can get jobs, and so the businesses know that there are no criminals in the organization."

It made me reflect upon an old Vietnamese proverb, which I shared with the group. The proverb goes, "When eating the fruit, think of the person who planted the tree."

This made them think again. They immediately started thinking a bit further.

"Why? What's the contribution that your work provides?"

They said, "Well, a safer workplace."

"Why?" I pressed.

"Because if we have the right people and the right systems in place, it makes us more secure, safe, and removes the risk from our day-to-day work life."

I started asking them more questions. "Well, why is that important? What are you really doing here? How are you contributing to the community, to the businesses, and to the world around you?"

After some careful thought and consideration, they realised that what they were doing was not simply background checks admin. Rather, they were making the world a safer place.

And they were doing it by helping businesses trust their people by being the guardians, the ones who would raise the red flag when there was a problem, when things required further investigation.

Everything they did was to increase trust in people. So trust in people became their **team's** ethos. They saw a world where the wrong people didn't end up in the wrong roles.

They saw a safer world, a more secure world, and most importantly, they saw how their daily actions and their work translated to creating a safer world. So instead of filling out their forms and merely going through the task in front of them, they thought of the consequences of their actions, and they could see their contribution to the world around them. They realised that through their work, through their diligence, they were creating trust in people, and they were creating a safer world around them.

That statement as an **asset** is now part of their daily **rhythm**.

Every conversation begins with the question, "How are we creating trust in people? How are we making the world a safer place?"

Every decision they make, every action they take comes back to their statement of truth.

The most important thing was that they owned it now. It was their statement and their contribution to the world. Through this, they developed a sense of pride and power in the **team's** ethos and the contribution that they made in working together.

POWERFUL GUIDING QUESTIONS

Gold Medal Olympian and motivational speaker, Ben Hunt-Davis, has a powerful question to ask. This Olympian was working with his rowing **team**, the Awesome Foursome to work towards winning gold at the Olympic **Games.** In order to do this, they decided that they would ask one guiding question that would guide all decisions made by all **team** members. The question was: "Will it make the boat go faster?"[125]

This one question allowed them to determine their behaviour and their actions for any decision that needed to be made.

Do you want to go to the pub? Will it make the boat go faster? No.

Shall we do hill sprints in the afternoon? Will it make the boat go faster? Stronger legs = faster boat. Yes.

There is an opportunity here to develop your own one guiding question as an **asset** of **team** ethos that aligns to your **north star** and helps you teach your business how to make the best decisions, and how to make the right decisions and guide them in this process.

TAKING IT TO THE RHYTHM

Through **events** we've worked with everybody in our business to create **assets** for each **team's** ethos. We've created **assets** that show the purpose, that define the standards, that express what matters, and we've visualised this by way of creating a poster, by way of a book, and by way of the **culture** tree.

This has been visualised.

---

125 Ben Hunt-Davis and Harriet Beveridge, *Will it Make the Boat Go Faster? Olympic-winning Strategies for Everyday Success*, 2nd ed. (UK: Troubador Publishing Ltd,2020).

The next, and critical, step is to take these **team** ethos into our daily **rhythm**.

Remember, the **assets** of **team** ethos are only as valuable as the value we put on them.

To be able to build the value of our **assets** of **team** ethos, we need to make this part of our daily conversation.

So now, in each daily stand-up, at each level of the business, we begin with a conversation around **team** ethos. We train people to run this conversation. They discuss what matters. They discuss their why. They discuss the bigger picture and how they're contributing to make the company and ultimately the world a better place. **Assets** of **team** ethos become part of the daily **rhythm**.

In this instalment, we learned how **teams** make up our organisational structure, and we developed an understanding of how to build different types of **teams** through the **assets** of language and **rhythm** of **team** ethos. With our shared beliefs in heart and mind, we can begin to build the systems of management, the **games** that allow us to perform at our best and achieve our BIG goals together. In the next installation, we get our **games** on.

INSTALLATION 11

GAMES

JOHN'S OLD-WORLD STATUS QUO

One hundred spreadsheets were open in tabs.

A nervous group of John's managers sat around the meeting table, the projector light as dim as the eyes of the tired managers as they prepared to talk of the myriad of KPIs and **results** of their various **teams**.

John sat there still, brow furrowed like he had a headache from the unrelenting noise and racket around him. He leaned over to me and said, "I'm over this shit." He let out a BIG sigh. The managers looked over what seemed to be a hundred goals

and a thousand KPIs noting a vague sense of progress over time and told stories to explain missing targets and unmet budgets.

I wondered how long this format had been going on, and for how many years they had done things like this. How could anyone find this useful?

Those dangerous words graced my ears once again, "This is the way we have always done things."

John looked at me as if to say, "Do something! What the hell am I paying you for?!"

I asked a few questions. "What behaviour are you trying to change in your people?"

"We just need them to perform better," was the answer.

"How do your people know they have had a great day?"

"They achieve a goal or complete a project that they set—those days are great."

"When do they get feedback?"

"We do our performance reviews and look at how they went for the year and what could improve."

"Are they focused on what matters most?"

"Well, they do tend to all have so much going on that they may not be as efficient as they could be," one manager conceded.

"Let me ask you one more question. Why are you having this meeting?

"To report our progress," said one.

"To improve our performance," said another.

"To plan for the future," added another.

"Is any of this working?" I asked.

"Not really," said the group. "What do we do?"

JOHN'S NEW NORMAL

A few months later, John's world had changed.

We had introduced the first round of **games** to every **team** in the business.

Games is an acronym that, in **TLC** language, stands for the following:

- Goals: set clearly with everyone and all aligned to the company's **north star**
- Action: leading activities made clear, efficient, focused, consistent

- Measurements: live, interactive scoreboards made progress visible and exciting
- Expectations: clear rules and benchmarked examples showed what success looks like; examples of success were constantly shared and celebrated.
- Support: coaching and support were readily available whenever required to help each **player** in the **rhythm**, not just from the **leader**. The whole **team** offered and received support.

The Kajillion performance indicators had been scrapped.

The eight goals per department had been reduced to two goals per month.

Every department, **team**, and individual had clear **games**, and every **game** made a clear contribution to achieving the BIG goals of the company's **north star**.

With this simple and clear system of management, you could see progress on the walls and on all the digital platforms. Every **team** and **player** had a **game** plan **asset**, and things were dealt with proactively with an attitude of trust, support, and growth. **Players** found themselves in states of FLOW where they were not only more productive and effective, they were happier. **Teams** worked together, and we began to see the early signs and signals of a coaching **culture** emerging as the **new normal**.

What's more, the management meeting had turned into something John actually looked forward to. No noise, no bullsh*t, just highly engaged and empowered people making progress together every day.

WHAT YOU'LL LEARN AND DO IN THIS INSTALLATION

In the **games** instalment, we will learn how to design and develop our systems of management using a simple yet powerful process. We will examine the evolution of management theory and emerge with a framework that allows us to improve our effectiveness, efficiency, and performance of our work. Through this process, we can help our **players** create their **game** plans as **assets** and reduce the need for management.

THE EVOLUTION OF MANAGEMENT THINKING

As always, let's look to the wisdom of the greats to help us get a deeper understanding of how this works. Yes, this historical account is flawed and incomplete. It is also brief and hopefully entertaining. Enjoy.

Around 4,000 BC, the Pyramids of Egypt were built through the construction of millions of blocks of stone by utilising and coordinating labour on a large scale.

By 800 BC, Rome was documenting how they organised the empire and army. These principles would later influence and shape western military corps and public administrations systems.

By 600 BC, Sun Tzu's *Art of War*,[126] arguably the first book on management, was all about utilising internal strength and exploiting external weakness. Chinese legalist philosopher Shen Buhai[127] showed us an early theory of managerial administration.

---

126 Sun Tzu, *The Art of War*, trans. Lionel Gales (Mineola, NY: Ixia Press, 2019).
127 Eirik Lang Harris, *The Shenzi Fragments: A Philosophical Analysis and*

In 300 BC, Chanakya's Arthashastra,[128] the treatise out of India deals with governance, **leadership**, policymaking and people management. It even covers how to create departments, job profiles, and selection criteria. This treatise influenced management in India for years, and the entire administration philosophy for the country. By 350 BC, Plato was describing job specialisation.[129]

Flash forward to 1776 and Adam Smith gave us an account of effective work through division of labour in *The Wealth of Nations*. He showed us how process changes could boost productivity in a pin factory going from 200–48,000 pins per day. Not bad gains, huh?[130]

As the Industrial Revolution came around, we needed more and more management.

Manufacturing of goods, large scale business, you know the story.

Business was getting more complicated and complex, and managers were required to look after tasks, resources, planning, and of course, people and labour. By the nineteenth century, the job and title of manager were widespread.

Eli Whitney, James Watt, and Matthew Boulton documented standardisation of work processes, work planning, and cost accounting quality control.

These early theories included:

Translation (New York: Columbia University Press, 2016).

128 Kautilya, *The Arthashastraa* (Australia: Penguin Classics, 2016).

129 Plato, *The Republic* (Australia: Penguin Classics, 2012).

130 Luis R. Gomez-Mejia, David B. Balkin, and Robert L. Candy, *Management: People, Performance, Change*, 3rd ed. (New York: McGraw-Hill Irwin, 2008).

- Scientific management
- Classical organisation theory
- Behavioural theory

Frederick W. Taylor published *Three Principles of Scientific Management* in 1911 and set out some founding principles:[131]

- Precise measurement of science to replace rule-of-thumb guesswork
- Obtaining harmony in group action
- Cooperation of human beings
- Working for maximum output

Henry Gantt worked with Taylor and introduced incentives to both workers and supervisors for tasks achieved and exceeded and made up charts to publicly acknowledge and rate performance, you know, Gantt Charts.

Frank and Lillian Gilbreth (1868–1972) were a husband and wife **team** that worked to add to scientific management and promote workers' welfare through fatigue and motion studies as they tried to find the most economical way to do each task to improve performance and reduce workers' complaints of fatigue.

Yoichi Ueno in 1912 took Taylor's ideas to Japan and the "Japanese Management style" came into development. His son, Ichiro, went on to pioneer Japanese quality assurance.

In 1921, Harvard offered the first MBA, and the first comprehensive theories began to appear.

131 Frederick Winslow Taylor, *The Principles of Scientific Management*. (New York: Cosimo Classics, 2010).

Max Weber (1864–1920) strictly defined hierarchy and bureaucratic management marked by strict regulation and clear lines of authority, technical competence, and performance based on the merits of the individual worker.

Mary Parker Follett (1868–1933) built on the classical framework and added the idea of human relationships and that people grew and developed through their relationships within the company.[132] Mary was a trailblazer in what would change management thinking over the next century.

The Behavioural School of Thought emerged in the 1930s largely because earlier theories were not seen to produce sufficient performance, and there were problems caused by disharmony in workplace relationships. Now that human relationship aspects of the company were part of the conversation, and the interest turned to how managers interact with their employees, it became clear that poor human relations lead to poor morale, which produces undesirable efficiency and **results.**

When Peter Drucker wrote *Concept of the Corporation* in 1946, it marked the release of the first book on applied management, and the 1940s brought in a tonne of management studies of applied mathematics and the birth of management science.[133]

We saw a bunch of developments summarised very, very briefly here:

---

132 Anne Smyth, David Legge, and Pauline Stanton, "Learning Management (and Managing Your Own Learning)," in *Managing Health Services: Concepts and Practice*, 2nd ed. (New South Wales: Mosby, 2006), 47–99.

133 Peter F. Drucker, *Concept of the Corporation*. (New York: Routledge, 2017).

- Theory of Constraints; Identifying the key blockers that stop us reaching our goals
- Management by Objectives: Setting objectives, involving people in goal setting, comparing performance with the standard.
- Business Process Reengineering: A full-scale restructure of workflows and process to improve performance and cut costs (1990).
- Six Sigma: A cult of tools and techniques for process improvements made in Motorola.
- Viable System Model: Systems organised to be autonomous and highly adaptable. Based on cybernetic theory, Stafford Beer.
- Agile Software Development: Build something fast and with fast customer feedback with self-organising and cross-functional **teams**.

With all of these tools and theories, you would think we'd have management down to an exact science and a fine art. Unfortunately, this is not the case.

In the recent book—*IT'S the manager* by Gallup, the largest survey of employee engagement ever conducted showed that 87 percent of staff are not engaged. This **results** in an enormous loss of productivity, and the number one reason they gave is—you guessed it—the manager.[134]

So, how do we develop highly engaged self-managing **teams**

---

134 Jim Clifton and Jim Harper, *It's the Manager: Gallup Finds the Quality of Managers and Team Leaders is the Single Biggest Factor in Your Organization's Long-Term Success* (Washington, DC: Gallup Press, 2019).

where coaching and constant progress becomes the **new normal**?

In the **TLC**, we do this by creating **games** as management systems. You can choose to use **GAMES** as your management system, or if you are already using OKRs, 4DX, agile scrum, or Hoshin Kanri, you can plug your system into the **games** window. Provided you balance the dynamics, it will work well.

GAMES: THE TLC SYSTEM OF MANAGEMENT

> *Everywhere I go, I see a lot of managers. I just don't see a lot of management.*
>
> *—My mate, John Bell (Ex-Toyota Chief Engineer)*

We tend to perform best when we see our progress. When we can get fast and useful feedback, we can use it to get better and better, faster and faster. By co-designing **games** with people, we create focus and communication, and we're able to continuously improve. Using a **games** management system will help your **players** know when they have had a great day, when they're doing well, and when to get help, coaching, and receive feedback. Plus, they can see their progress and improvement day-to-day.

By creating these **games**, we create not only performance, but engagement.

Motivation expert, Daniel Pink, speaks of something called R.O.W.E—the **Results** Only Work Environment. The idea of this is that as long as we track and trust the measures and **results** that matter most, everything else is superfluous to this. To be able to create an environment where the goals are so clear that people can have the freedom to get there in the way they see fit creates a highly engaging **culture** that tends to attract the kind of **players** we all want.

> *Control leads to compliance; autonomy leads to engagement.*
> —*Daniel H. Pink*[135]

Games bring together the best of these worlds by creating the right boundaries for people to play within and find their best performance without having to micromanage them. The better and clearer the **games**, the more creativity and performance can emerge through playing the **games**. We can see this when we look at **player** performance through the study of flow states.

THE FLOW STATE OF PERFORMANCE

Hero and breakthrough thinker, Mihaly Csikszentmihalyi, (Try saying his surname after a few glasses of wine) recognised and named a psychological state of being called Flow.[136] When we experience Flow, we feel engaged, alert, and alive. Flow exists on the edge between our level of skill and the level of challenge in a **game**.

Flow states have the following characteristics:

---

135 Daniel H. Pink, *Drive: The Surprising Truth About What Motivates Us* (UK: Cannongat books, 2018).

136 Mihaly Csikszentmihalyi, *Flow: Living At The Peak Of Your Abilities* (Wheeling, IL: Nightingale Contant, 1994), cassette tape.

- Complete concentration on the task
- Clarity of goals, reward in mind, and immediate feedback
- Transformation of time (speeding up/slowing down)
- The experience is intrinsically rewarding
- Effortlessness and ease
- There is a balance between challenge and skills
- Actions and awareness are merged, losing self-conscious rumination
- There is a feeling of control over the task

Games can help us engineer the conditions favourable to flow states where we're set up to find ourselves productive and lost in our work in a way that's meaningful to us.

To create a flow state, we need a few things.

- We need to be able to see our progress clearly and focus on it
- We also need to be able to receive feedback quickly, so we know how to improve
- We know how to get better through testing and failing quickly
- We need to find it meaningful and know it points towards a **team** ethos that allows us to contribute to something we believe in that's bigger than ourselves

Flow is being completely involved in an activity for its own sake. The ego falls away. Time flies. Every action, movement, and thought follows inevitably from the previous one, like playing jazz.

—Mihaly Csikszentmihalyi

EXERCISES AND APPLICATIONS

EXERCISE: CO-DESIGN GAMES

Here is how to create **games**—You can set each of these in an **event** and document it in an **asset**.

- Goals: Must be SMART and also on the edge of challenge and ability. (SMART: Specific, Measurable, Achievable, Relevant, Time-based)
- Actions: Must be focused and 80/20 effective. (Choosing the highest impact activities or the 20 percent of options likely to deliver 80 percent of the desired **result**.)
- Measures: Make progress as visible as possible. (Using scoreboards, physical whiteboards, or digital tables to track progress.)
- Expectations and Examples: Have clear rules and examples visualised and front of mind.
- Support: Coach in **rhythm** with a fast feedback loop to help improvement day by day.

This is the basic formula for setting out a simple **games** system of management. You can run this discussion in an event, and create your game plan and scoreboard based on these headings as an **asset**.

Not all **games** are simple, though. Let's look at the different types of systems to get a better understanding of the types of **games** we can design.

We can give purpose and direction to people even in the most mundane or complex work so they can be immersed in these **games** and perform better. Wouldn't you like that for your **players**?

CYNEFIN FRAMEWORK

We need to look at some different types of systems in order to understand how to create different **games** in your company. Here we will identify how simple, complicated, complex, or chaotic your challenges are and what type of **games** you need to create to manage this. We will do this by borrowing from another great thinker named Dave Snowden who created the Cynefin Framework.

The Cynefin (Kin-Eff-Enn) Framework will help us understand where you are at **status quo**, how to create the **new normal**, and what kind of **games** you will need to put in place.[137] Cynefin is a sense-making device, and by understanding this basic explanation, you will be able to make far better decisions as to how to set up your **TLC**. Here is what you need to know.

There are four different types of systems as stated by Snowden, and I have applied these systems to different types of **games**. *I hope Mr. Snowden won't mind.*

SIMPLE SYSTEMS

The relationship between cause and effect is obvious to everyone—we clearly know why things happen. In simple

137 Greg Brougham, *The Cynefin Mini-Book: An Introduction to Complexity and the Cynefin Framework* (New York: C4Media, 2015).

systems, we can put simple, best practice processes in place, like clear instructions of what to do next. We sense, categorise, and respond. Simple systems are tightly constrained, they have no degree of freedom, and you do things a certain way because this is the best, most efficient, and effective way to do them.

You can script what is going to happen next, and you don't need experts to solve problems. A simple system is one where all the problems have already been solved, and we know what to do next. Accordingly, we have documented it well, and we know the best practice to apply. Simple **games** are easy to create and relatively stable. Think of any well-documented process in your company, and you can create a simple **game** around it to engage your staff and improve your productivity and efficiency.

Think of anything in your company that you have down to a very tight process, and you can teach this to new people in a simple and easy manner.

SIMPLE GAMES

- **Goals:** clear SMART goals
- **Activities:** repeatable activities known to produce a desired **result**
- **Measures:** visual scoreboard for both **results** and activities
- **Expectations/Examples:** clear standards and best practice examples
- **Support:** coaching from **team** members with more experience and proven **results**

We can use simple **games** for any operation where you want to develop focus, better practice, and consistency.

Example: *Sales* Games

- **Goals:** $2 million in new sales this month
- **Activities:** making calls, writing proposals
- **Measures:** scoreboard and targets on how many calls to make and proposals to write
- **Expectations/Examples:** do your best to hit the activity scores, turn up on time, and share your learnings in the **rhythm**
- **Support:** Daily coaching with the sales coach in the **rhythm**

Simple **games** are great for focus and accountability and help to establish a coaching **culture** through daily **rhythm** and fast feedback. They don't need to be reset too often and can significantly improve productivity, engagement, and learning speed when done well.

Simple **games** are great for building habits and favourable behaviour, but not so great for more complicated roles. For this, we want to create **games** that allow for more flexibility and decision-making about what to do next. To create these **games**, we need to understand complicated systems.

COMPLICATED SYSTEMS

In complicated systems, the relationship between cause and effect requires analysis or investigation and/or the application of expert knowledge. In a complicated system, we have a general idea of what is going on, we know the questions we need to ask, but we need experts, people with knowledge, to solve the problems and meet the challenges on the road towards our goals. We can't put best practices in place because there are too many variables. We can, however, put good practices in place where we can sense, analyse, and respond to the requirements of the situation.

COMPLICATED GAMES

Complicated **games** require strong goals, expectations, and examples. The details of the activity, although complicated, can be discussed in the **rhythm** to help the **team** learn from each other and develop their expertise. Think of any process in your company that requires expert knowledge or experience, something that you need to know the right questions to ask in order to provide the right answers—perhaps your sales process.

- **Goals**: clear, SMART goals, usually with longer timelines
- **Activities:** key activities and behaviours without specific instruction
- **Measures**: scoreboards with **results**, key activities, and documented insights
- **Expectations/Examples**: clear rules and role model examples
- **Support**: ongoing mentoring by role models who have achieved **results** and align to your **north star**

In complicated **games**, we put fewer restraints on our **players** by having more general activities. We also add the component of documenting insights so we can build a knowledge base or Wiki that allows us to turn a complicated process into a distilled and teachable method. We may consider using a knowledge management system here to develop the learning **assets** through complicated game design. You can consider Litmos or Confluence as software for this.

Complicated **games** require strong ethos, good practice, and standards to allow for a multitude of variables and choices. They are great for building expertise in your company, but not so good for managing complex projects. For projects, let's look at more complex systems.

COMPLEX SYSTEMS

In complex systems, the relationship between cause and effect can only be seen in retrospect, when you look back at what is happening. Here we don't even know the right questions to ask. We don't know what we don't know, and we need to run experiments in order to find out what is going on. This is the realm of emergent practice: we probe, sense, and respond.

COMPLEX GAMES

In complex **games**, we are experimenting. This is where we use a scrum-board to constantly test and discuss our activities. This is where the world of Agile **games** come in to play (pardon the pun).

This book is certainly not a full training in Agile project management; however, here are some renowned thinkers to deepen your knowledge if required.[138] (See the footnotes.)

---

138 Stephen Denning, *The Age of Agile: How Smart Companies Are Transforming the Way Work Gets Done* (New York: Amacom, 2018).

Here is the basic framework for complex **game** design.

- **Goals**: a specific deliverable for the **team** in a short time frame.
- **Activities:** activities are set and reset in the **rhythm** and a backlog is created.
- **Measures:** a KANBAN board is used where cards or Post-it notes are moved from to-do, to doing, to done (see example).
- **Expectations/Examples**: the **team** sets clear expectations around the standards of the group and holds each **player** to these expectations.
- **Support:** in the daily **rhythm**, each **player** on the **team** declares three things:
    - Yesterday I did (moves card on scoreboard to done)
    - Today I will do (moves card on scoreboard to doing)
    - I need help with (asks the group for help to solve a problem required for the goal or deliverable to be met)

BACKLOG		TO DO	IN PROGRESS	TESTING	DONE
Feature 10 hrs HIGH	Bug Fix 2 hrs MEDIUM				
Update 4 hrs LOW	Research 3 hrs MEDIUM				
Content 2 hrs HIGH					

CHAOTIC SYSTEMS

Chaotic systems are just like they sound. There is no relationship between cause and effect at a systems level. It is the realm of novel practice: We act, sense, and respond. This is where shit gets crazy and off the rails, and the immediate priority is containment. We are just trying to correct the problem and contain the issue here.

CHAOTIC GAMES

In chaotic **games**, we are constantly acting, assessing the situation, and determining what to do next.

- **Goals:** what we need now to survive
- **Activities:** what we will do right now
- **Measures:** what worked and what did we learn in real-time?
- **Expectations/Examples:** what do we know from past experience and knowledge?
- **Support:** who do we need here fast?

We run this process in fast iterative loops to navigate our environment and manage the best we can. Over time, we move from chaotic to simple **games** by forming patterns of what works. This is the thinking of emergent strategy (more on this in the **results** installation).

There is also a fifth type of **game** that is not in the Cynefin Framework, something that James Carse, and later, Simon Sinek, call an Infinite **game**.

INFINITE AND FINITE GAMES

I'd like to introduce a simple, yet deep concept from an author named James P. Carse.

This concept is of infinite and finite **games**.[139]

Yes, I know the wonderful Simon Sinek wrote about The Infinite **Game**.[140] He got this from James P. Carse in his book, *Finite and infinite* ***Games***. Here is the gist.

Finite **games** are played for the purpose of winning the **game**. Infinite **games** are played for the purpose to continue playing the **game**. Business is an infinite **game**. Your golf swing is an infinite **game**. You continually get better at it, but there is no point where you've definitively finished or won. It goes on for as long as you stay in the **game**.

The ultimate infinite **game** is life. The central purpose of the infinite **game** of life is to keep living. Finite **games** are played for the purpose of winning and knowing that it will come to a definite end, which happens when someone has won or been declared a winner. Finite **games** are the **games** that we play with clear goals, clear rules, and a clear endpoint. We know the **game** is over when someone has been declared the winner. Finite **games** are the Saturday afternoon **game** of golf versus the infinite **game** of your golf swing. Think about it: you don't win your golf swing like you win a **game** of golf. You just keep getting better and playing for the experience of playing.

---

139 James P. Carse, *Finite and Infinite Games: A Vision of Life as Play and Possibility* (New York: Free Press, 1986).

140 Simon Sinek, *The Infinite Game* (New York: Portfolio, 2020).

Shall we go deeper? Infinite **players** play with boundaries. Finite **players** play within boundaries. This is an important distinction to make. When we use the **TLC**, we use the infinite **games** of **culture** and **brand** to expand the **TLC** into new territory, into **VUCA**. We push the boundaries and grow further, become better, and expand outwards.

When we create **games**, we are designing:

- Goals
- Activities
- Measures
- Expectations and Examples
- Support

These are the boundaries to keep us focused and moving. These are the finite **games** of management within the infinite **game** of **culture**, **brand**, and **leadership**.

Culture, Carse asserts, is an infinite **game**. **Culture** has no boundaries, and anyone can be a participant in a **culture** anywhere and at any time. **Culture** has no temporal limits, and to understand its past is not its destiny, but its history. A narrative begins to take place. **Culture**s are ongoing and not restricted by time or space. To the degree that the Renaissance was true **culture**, it has not ended. Anyone may enter into its mode of renewing vision. This does not mean that we repeat what was done. To enter a **culture** is not to do what the others do, but to do whatever one does with the others.

Carse uses the metaphor of a gardener in curating **culture**. All **culture** is like a form of gardening. He says, "The encouragement of spontaneity in others by way of one's own.

The respect for source and the refusal to convert source into resource. The garden is the metaphor for **culture**."

In creating finite **games**, we're able to measure progress. There is a definitive endpoint, and we know when to celebrate, get feedback, or learn. When we do this well, the finite **games** we design align with our **team** ethos and **players**, and they allow us to get into flow states and expand the **TLC** through the infinite **games** of **culture**, **brand**, business, and of course, life. By designing well-thought-out finite **games**, we not only manage and measure performance, we create a healthy tension and competitive environment where people can perform at their best because they know how to play the **games**.

If James Carse looked at the **TLC**, I like to think he'd say that what we are doing is "World Building." All finite **games** exist within a world, and that world is the infinite **game** of our **culture**.

EXERCISES AND APPLICATIONS

ALIGN THE GOALS AND CO-DESIGN THE GAME

The first thing we need to do in an **event** to co-design a **game** is to decide what our goals are.

How simple/complex your **game** is will determine how often you reset this process. Simple **games** can be set yearly or quarterly, complex **games** may require a monthly, weekly, or even daily reset. The goals of each **team** need to support the goals of the **north star** of the company, the BIG goals.

Each **team** is going to choose a maximum of **two goals** that they are going to focus on and best contribute towards achieving **north star** BIG goals. You can do more, but it won't work as well.

The next thing we're going to do is list the two activities most effective in getting us towards the goal based on the best thinking we have right now. By thinking this way and having to select only two reoccurring activities, we are forced to think effectively.

Now for the MEASURES. Remember, we want to make progress visible. Each person has two goals. Each **team** can also have two goals. All goals support the BIG goal of **north star**. For Measure, we want to create a scoreboard using a whiteboard, a spreadsheet, or some software like Trello, Asana, or Smartsheets.

Here is the basic layout:

- Month/Quarter/Year ____________________
- **north star**
- BIG Goal x 2
- **Team** Goals x 2
- Individual Goals x 2
- Daily **Result** Measure x 2
- Daily Action Measure x 2

FOR EXAMPLE

- **North star** BIG Goal: help 10,000 people with our product
- **Team** Goal: 1,000 new sign-ups

- Individual Goals: fifty new customers this month
- Daily **Result** Measurement: how many new customers today?
- Daily Action Measure: calls made, product demonstrations completed

We take all this, and we put it on to a scoreboard (something physical like a whiteboard if in person, or digital project management software as mentioned above if your **teams** are remote). Make the progress visible, and use this to drive behaviour or change, to focus us on what matters most, and to point us all towards **north star**. Most importantly, each day in our **rhythm**, we are going to have the conversations that matter to improve and grow bit by bit, day by day.

Check out *www.bigchange.group/Resources/TLC* for regularly updated examples and templates for creating your **games**.

A KAJILLION PERFORMANCE INDICATORS

The pitfalls of a kajillion performance indicators, and other mistakes.

I have noticed in my work that quite often managers think that KPIs stand for a kajillion performance indicators. People get lost in the complexity of lists and lists of things that need to be ticked off each day. There is no chance of flow without *focus*.

Games with a few clear goals are better than **games** with a thousand unclear goals. What we need to do is choose the things that require the most focus and communication, and then build our **games** around these things.

We employ the 80/20 principle. There is a BIG difference between efficacy and efficiency. Efficacy is effectiveness. It's doing the right things; it's choosing the right things to do. It's picking that 20 percent that gives us 80 percent of the **results** and focusing on that. For our **results**, we measure in **games** we need to have efficacy. Efficiency is about doing those things in the best possible way. Effectiveness or efficacy is doing the right things, and efficiency is doing those things the right way. If we have efficacy without efficiency, our **results** will suffer. On the other hand, if we have efficiency without efficacy, we're doing the wrong things in a way that creates a sense of busyness but is less likely to **result** in us achieving our goals or moving towards **north star**.

STORY TIME: 1,000 UNFINISHED PROJECTS

I'm standing with the continuous improvement manager of a large and growing business.

His head is in his hands, and he is grumbling about the thousands of unfinished initiatives that the business has with no completion. He said, "We only do the things that we have time to do, and we tend to do the wrong things at the wrong time." Here was a man at his wit's end.

I asked him, "For each of these projects, how do you know you've moved forward and made progress?"

He said that they're scattered among spreadsheets, various project management tools, and performed on an ad hoc basis. Basically, whenever someone has a bit of time, they go in and chip away. I could feel his frustration, and I could tell exactly why he felt like he was getting nowhere.

We needed to create a **game** to manage the projects where people could feel progress so they could maintain the momentum and the energy required to make it happen.

We looked at all of the initiatives going on in the business, and we chose the two that were the most important for the business to reach their BIG goals. We said it's only two, but it's a start.

Then we built a **game**. We took two **teams** of six people, and we used a Kanban board. The **game** was simple. Once a week, map out all of the tasks to achieve the goal for the week and write them on Post-it notes. The rules were simple: the Post-it note can't take more than fifteen minutes to do.

We will assemble each day for five minutes, choose one Post-it note and move it from to-do to doing and move one Post-it note from doing to done. We made agile scrum as simple as humanly possible.

Each week the **team** came together. They had their project's goal, and they formed a small group of inter-departmental individuals who would each choose one task for the day. We found that this profoundly simple **game** gave everybody the focus towards moving to completion. It allowed them to ask the right questions to learn and overcome the problems and challenges.

We realised we couldn't map out the whole project start to end, because we didn't know what the end was. What we did figure out was that by showing people they could move a little bit of paper across the board was enough for them to know that they were moving forward in ever so small steps. They realised that by moving these projects towards completion together as groups, they were able to achieve and maintain momentum. They were even able to have some fun while they were doing it, and they began closing out these projects one by one over a month by month **event**.

Soon, other people wanted to be involved in the **games** as well. Heck, it only took fifteen minutes a day to be involved in a project that would improve the business. By the end of the year, every single person in the company was involved in at least one improvement project.

We had these Kanban **game** boards all over the lunchroom. Every day, small groups would meet, discuss what they'd done, discuss what they were going to do, and discuss what they needed help with. It was so visual that anybody could walk in and see where the projects were, clearly, visually, and tangibly through these boards. This was the simplest version of agile scrum that was ever deployed in my knowledge. To this day, my client continues to run every improvement project in the business this way, because it's clear what's expected, and it's obvious when progress is made.

STORY TIME: LEARN TO MICROMANAGE YOURSELF

I once had a sales representative express to me that he thought creating simple **games** that measured progress and actions was micromanagement. After a lengthy discussion, we discovered his lack of **results** were mostly due to his lack of consistency around the actions he would take.

I said, "In order for you to remain in this role and to be successful here, you need to learn to micromanage yourself."

The idea of needing somebody to tell you what you need to do is limiting in the sense that autonomy can be taken away. The idea of a great **game** is to give somebody the framework where they can set their own score, rules, and parameters in which they might be successful. **Games** exist to be self-managing.

If we can empower people to manage themselves through these **games** and work with others to achieve them, there is no need for traditional management. People become accountable because they want to be autonomous and responsible.

STORY TIME: ZERO PERCENT MANAGEMENT

"I have a dream," the CEO said. "I have a dream where management is no longer needed."

I stopped to consider this proposition.

He continued, "Using **TLC**, if our **games** are tight, our **team** ethos is solid and true, and the right **players** are on board, why should we pay managers to look after this?"

I considered this line of thought.

He said, "My ultimate goal is to be able to run this business without having management costs because everybody knows why they're doing what they're doing, how to do it, and who to involve."

I fell in love with this idea. If we have clear **games**, with the right goals, activities, measures, and expectations that we all agree upon, why do we need managers to tell us how to play it?

I said to the CEO, "Perhaps we should rethink what management means within the world of **games**. Perhaps we should look at this in terms of coaching because it doesn't matter how clear your **game** is, we could all do with a little help in learning how to win it better, how to play better, and how to improve."

The CEO liked this idea, so we began our quest towards zero percent management with every conversation coming back to the **games** and **team** ethos, through the **rhythm**, and ending on a conversation of one thing we could do better.

In the beginning, it was the managers who ran this conversation, but over time, they found that by having clear measures, they were now able to focus their time on the **players**. The managers stayed in the business, but they got involved in the **games**. They had their own **game** plans. They were part of producing the **results**.

Through the **rhythm**, they became coaches who could show the way forward. They could stand in the bleachers and help their people play a better **game**. They were no longer an auxiliary function of command and control but rather captains of the **games**. They were now **players** providing support to the other **players**.

Not only did the management costs get replaced through the performance of the managers and their own performance, but now we had an increase in performance across all of the **teams** because every single **team** now had somebody on their side who knew exactly what to say so they could play a better **game**. All we had to do was make the goals and the rules very clear.

When the coaches became the ultimate champions of the **games**, the company achieved its quest for zero percent management.

EVENTS AND ASSETS OF THE GAME

The purpose of **events** of **games** is to align each **team** and co-design a **game** that points towards **north star**. An **event** of **games** is a discussion and collaboration to design and co-create the **asset**—the **game** plan.

We have set our **event** and created our **assets** of **team** ethos, and we have brought the hearts of people together. Now it's about getting our heads in the **games**. To run an **event** of **games**, we need to bring together a **team** working for the same objective. Within this **event** of **games**, the participants will talk about what they measure and the ultimate measures of success.

They discuss the 80/20 principle, where their **results** came from, and they'll ultimately land on a design for how to measure success in real-time (or as close to that as possible), and create a feedback loop with the **rhythm**. **Events** of **games** are about working with people who have knowledge in the business to design **games** where everybody can win and improve. They create the system for engagement. It is a bad idea to come up with the **games** without your people, and then insist that people play.

The purpose of the facilitated **games event** is to involve them in the conversation. It's for them to air their grievances and concerns. It's for them to experience the emotion and understand the why of creating **games** through a skilled facilitator. In a great **event** of **games**, people feel energised, excited, and their thinking is simplified in a way that gives them focus. Each **team** should go through this cycle monthly in the beginning.

A good facilitator can work with the room to create a **game** where there's clear progress measured visibly, as well as simple, clear rules and a good feedback loop that becomes part of the daily **rhythm** conversation. From there, the **event** of **games** reset occurs on a regular basis to improve the **games** until it becomes the **new normal.**

When we reset the **games** through an **event**, we update the **asset** and improve it each time by looking at what worked and what didn't. The entire point of this is to involve people in designing their own management system. Trust me; they will share valuable insights.

The **game assets** that are produced can become self-managing systems over time. These include the goals of the **team** aligned to the goals of **north star**. They include the simple, clear rules we will play by within this **game**.

An **asset** of **games** also includes the scoreboard and how we are going to measure and track progress. We create **assets** of **games** at regular intervals where we've reset the **games**. The **asset** needs to be displayed as clearly as possible, preferably physically, but sometimes, as necessity dictates, digitally. The important thing to remember with **assets** of **games** is to make goals, rules, and progress as visible as possible and then run the fastest possible feedback loop through your daily **rhythm**.

Look at the format of **games** earlier in this chapter to create your **game** plan asset and visit our website for additional templates: *www.bigchange.group/Resources/TLC.*

THE GAME RESET EVENT

Games should be reset on a regular basis. Whether it is monthly or quarterly will depend on your business, **team**, the complexity of the **team's** function and the type of **game** you are playing. The point is, **events** that regularly review, improve, and adjust the **games** to improve their effectiveness, engagement, and your ability to embed new habits into the **culture**. In these **events**, you come together, look at the **games**, and ask your **players** and **teams**:

- What game are we playing here?
- Is this the most effective it can be?
- What do we need to update?
- What do we need to change?
- How does our focus need to shift to keep us moving to **north star**?

Remember, this is not a static process. It is constantly learning, improving, and evolving. Set this as a regular occurrence in your calendar of **events**. You will get better at this over time. Remember the discipline is in running **events**, constantly redesigning and improving your **games** of management and creating the **rhythm** where the **game** is played daily in your **rhythm**.

TAKE IT TO THE RHYTHM

You know by now that we have a **rhythm** where we discuss the agenda. We discuss the **team** ethos, the **games**, and the **players** consistently. In the installation titled **rhythm**, we will go deeper into this practice, but it bears merit to bring it up here.

One of the biggest points of value for this is that in a well-set **game**, we have the opportunity to constantly coach and improve our **players** and **team's** performance. We're able to work very well by receiving small pieces of feedback that we can implement right away.

You know how I feel about long-term retrospective performance reviews. To reiterate, they are way less helpful than continuous support and coaching. This is all about using the **rhythm** to coach **players** and **teams** in the **games**. This means measuring what matters and then daily helping them find where the blockers are.

Look at what's working, what's not working, and calibrate their compass to be able to move towards **north star**. Coaching happens in your daily **rhythm** of stand-up meetings and individual coaching, and the things that need your attention are managed by exception.

The **results** and the actions are on the walls or the screen, and from here, it becomes obvious where you need to focus your coaching attention. The key is to do this consistently every day as coaching becomes part of your **culture**.

Remember, this is about giving people fast, useful feedback, not a list of 500 things to improve every month. One small thing each day they can adjust or develop because, of course, we are able to implement small actions much better than we can implement large-scale change. Many small changes make the BIG change work.

Through the **games** instalment, we can now create simple, complicated, complex, chaotic, and even infinite **games** as systems of management to improve our performance and reduce the need for management of our work. In the next instalment, we decide how we are going to measure our company's **results**. We will learn to develop our strategy to win the war on **VUCA**!

INSTALLATION 12

RESULTS

JOHN'S OLD-WORLD STATUS QUO

The quarterly funeral procession.

John's **leadership team** gathered offsite for their quarterly strategy meeting. The boardroom had an air of pessimism. Executives stroked their chins and spoke of their plans by department to make the next quarter profitable. Before they had even begun their next quarter planning, they conducted their traditional retrospective: what went right and what didn't work last quarter. The **results** were not good.

It seemed like all the targets and goals they had set only three months ago had missed the mark. Why was this happening? It seemed like a quarterly funeral where they would stand up one by one and lay to rest the arbitrary plans of the past quarter.

I looked around as people in suits took turns promising to deliver better **results** next time. The outlook was bleak, operations were ineffective, costs were up, and sales were down. Marketing was still working on that new campaign to save us all. Customer service scores had barely moved an inch.

When it came time for John to present the bottom line, the room breathed a dreary sigh. Everyone was counting on others to execute their next plan and strategy, although it was filled with arbitrary numbers driven by the need to survive.

"Why is this happening again and again?" asked John. "What is the biggest reason we keep falling behind like this?"

Operations executives stated that we need to be more efficient, but the staff just don't get it, they just default to their day-to-day habits. Sales promised higher numbers next time. The market had been rough, and we just can't seem to hire and keep the right people who do the right thing at the right time. Every strategy that was put forward fell flat the moment it was time to put the plans into action.

It seemed that everyone in that room had the desire to come up with the right answer based on the knowledge and experience they had and dreamed up and splurged onto another glossy PowerPoint promising change.

HR, head in hands, looked me in the eye. "We blame all these **results** on our people. It's like they just don't get it, they mean well, but..."

Operations jumped in. "If middle management would just do their jobs, we would not have this problem."

"What problem?" I asked.

We create strategies to improve things, but they just don't seem to play out. The behaviours of our people just don't seem to fall in line with our strategic plans. It's like every time we do this the people resist the change, and we cave in and opt for the easy, fast, and most pressing old way of doing things.

We keep going back to our old ways and the "genius" plans we come up with each time just fall by the wayside of the chaos of business as usual.

"What do you think we should do, Benny?" asked John.

"Have you tried involving the staff in the strategy? Have you asked them what they think and listened to them? Have you empowered them to make it happen?"

Silence.

"Well, no. We tend to come up with our plans in these sessions and then go and hand the goals out to each manager. We tell them to make it happen. What's wrong with that?"

"Plenty," I said. "You are expecting people to change their behaviour based on a memo they have no real involvement with. We could involve the influencers in the business to help you lead and to help you manage the changes we set in place. We could share the data with them, ask for their perspective, and educate them on how to use the data to make better decisions. We could ask them to work with you to shape people's beliefs, choices, and actions, so we are moving in the right direction together."

"Okay," said John. "Let's try that."

JOHN'S NEW NORMAL

At the next quarterly offsite meeting three months later, things had changed.

The room was full of dashboards, useful knowledge, and fresh faces. People from all levels and corners of the company were present as **change agents** brought together to bring in the **new normal**. John's **change agent team** was in full force, an army of the willing had assembled to offer their valuable perspectives and to learn how to use the **results** data to make better decisions. People who had no authority in the traditional sense of the word sat right next to the CEO and the executive **team** to put their heads together to find a new way.

These people had been selected for a reason. They had the right attitude and wanted to make things better. They were humble and ambitious. They were there to get involved in reshaping the **culture** of the company and make their suggestions on what they thought would work best. These were the people on the frontline of the business. They were the ones closest to where the real problems were and where the value was created. What's more, they had access to the right information to help build the strategy. The **results** were clear and shared, and the data was presented in a way that made sense to everyone involved.

In the beginning, some were reluctant and wary of this **event**. Why had they been called into the BIG room? What was all this about? Are we in trouble? In a company with a long history and tradition of top-down decision-making, this was most unusual.

John hired me to facilitate this **event** and to set the scene.

"We are here to work together to make the company better. You are here because we want to work with you to make the change happen, and we think you have insights that we might miss in our usual planning process."

There were smiles all around.

"In this room, we will have some special rules and standards to make this happen. You can be completely honest and transparent about what is going on here. In fact, we are going to celebrate and reward this level of honesty. The truth is, we are beginning the process of changing our **results** through our **culture**. We will be changing the way we work around here, and we want your help, guidance, and input. We are going to make this change happen together. We want you to be involved in an ongoing series of **events** where we dig into our data and discuss your ideas on how we can make this company better.

"We will create these changes together and you, alongside the executives of the business, will work together to make it happen. It's up to you to decide if this is for you. It is not compulsory. Please know you have been selected for a reason. You represent all areas of the business, not from your authority, but from your attitude and influence and natural **leadership** potential."

A long silence followed.

Then, suddenly, Ruby, an operator from the manufacturing department, spoke up. "Count me in," she said.

Then, one by one, the people chosen from all areas of the business jumped on board.

"Great, I have been dreaming of this," said one.

"This is fantastic, I really want to do it," said another.

Six months later, they were working as a unified **team** of true **change agents** informed by the **results** of the company. They worked together at all levels, making data-driven decisions and executing strategy informed by the valuable perspectives of a diverse group of **players**.

Now, strategy was formulated not by the solitary and siloed thinking of clever executives but *with* the people responsible for carrying out the change. They discussed, considered options, raised flags, were involved in the process, and could see all the things the clever **team** of executives could not. Yes, it was a strange group—executive directors sitting with machine operators, sales reps, and even janitors—but they were a true representation of what was really going on in the company.

The group became successful in creating and carrying out improvements throughout the company because they *were* the company. They were the ones who had the answers. We just empowered them to have a voice and championed them to make the changes they knew needed to be made. The company started to create strategy based on successful behaviours and got the constant perspective and feedback required to do it well. Their efficiency increased, sales grew, customer service scores skyrocketed, and the company saw profits that previously were unimaginable. The hierarchy of management was still there, guiding, directing, and making the tough decisions at the end of the day.

No, they did not always take on the requests and suggestions of the change **team**.

What they had now was a network of **change agents** who could help lead the change.

And what was in it for these people? They grew as **leaders**, and they learned how to grow and develop their company and the people around them. They found greater meaning in their work and embraced the responsibility to find better ways to work, to call out the problems, to shape their **culture**.

John and his company had established a true **change agent team** and the **players** in this group would be the catalysts who allowed the transformation to happen. Their knowledge was more powerful because it was shared. Their powerful new strategies emerged through sharing and discussing **results** with the people who were closest to the action all working together to plan the next way forward in the direction of **north star** and towards the **new normal**.

WHAT YOU'LL LEARN AND DO IN THIS INSTALMENT

In the **results** instalment, we will learn to monitor and share our **results** to make better, data-driven decisions. We will look at data visualisation and business intelligence and bring these ideas together in **events** to get a bigger and better perspective on our world. We'll involve our **players** and **change agents** to create powerful strategies in moving towards our **new normal.**

BIG RESULTS—THE BOTTOM LINE AND THE INTEGRATED REPORTING FRAMEWORK

The Triple Bottom line is an accounting framework that takes into account three result areas.[141]

- Economic: cost, growth, and revenue
- Social: employee welfare, fair trade, charity contribution
- Environmental: resource consumption, land use, and waste management

Or as People, Planet, Profit, is it good for all three?

- People: organisational needs, individual needs, community issues

141 Timothy F. Slaper and Tanya J. Hall, "The Triple Bottom Line: What Is It and How Does It Work?" *Indiana Business Review* 86, no. 1 (Spring 2011): 4–8, https://www.ibrc.indiana.edu/ibr/2011/spring/pdfs/article2.pdf.

- Planet: reduce, reuse, recycle
- Profit: sales revenue, new customer acquisition, service, and loyalty.

Traditionally, companies were just looking at profit and loss.

The times over the last fifty years have become increasingly demanding of a model of Full Cost Accounting which is all about tracing direct and indirect costs and a full cost-benefit analysis of whether the business is good for society in general. This has become standard for the public sector and social enterprises and is similar to the UN standards around Natural Capital and Human Capital.

The International Integrated Reporting Council (IIRC)[142] is working towards the global vision of a world in which capital allocation and corporate behaviour are aligned to the wider goals of financial stability and sustainable development through the cycle of integrated reporting and thinking.

The IR or Integrated Reporting framework has been developed to place value creation at the centre of accounting and to track accounting r**esults** using a system that looks beyond immediate short-term profits to take into account the following areas of capital, many of which had previously been thought of as intangible:

- Financial Capital—The pool of funds
- Manufactured Capital—Physical objects available for the production of goods and services

142 Integrated Reporting, http://www.theiirc.org.

- Intellectual Capital—Knowledge-based Intangibles, IP, and systems
- Human Capital—People's competencies, capabilities, experience, motivations
- Social and Relationship Capital—relationships with communities, stakeholders, and networks
- Natural Capital—Renewable and non-renewable environmental resources

It is useful to consider these result areas when evaluating the **results** of your **company**, setting your **north star**, and deciding which **games** you want to play. To go deeper on this, please visit the website in the footnotes.

As you know, it is critical to know our numbers and set the BIG goals in place. To effectively achieve them, we need to consider the role and function of strategy and how to make it work towards our **north star**.

GREAT THINKERS

There seems to be a lot of ambiguity when it comes to **results** and strategy. Let's deepen our understanding of what this means so we can be more effective as **TLC** leaders.

The word "strategy" comes from the Greek *strategia*; art of troop leader, office of general, command or general ship.[143] General strategy is about setting goals, determining actions, and mobilising resources. It is the high-level plan to achieve

143 H. G. Liddell and R. Scott, *Greek-English Lexicon*, 9th ed. (UK: Clarendon Press, 1996).

goals in conditions that are uncertain (if they were certain, we would not need a strategy). Strategic planning is particularly important from a resourcing point of view, knowing what it means and where to invest in order to achieve goals. However, in our **VUCA** world, the meaning of strategy is changing and evolving towards a new paradigm to match the times.

My all-time favourite definition of strategy comes from the Legend Henry Mintzberg where he said:

Strategy is a pattern in a stream of decisions.

Mintzberg was wise to point out that strategy in a **VUCA** world emerges from a series of decisions and not the other way around. Because of this, the best-laid plans are the ones that take into account what is actually going on, from as many perspectives as possible, and create the plan based on observable facts and patterns.[144]

When we are examining our **results** through the **TLC** elements, the behaviours of our **players**, the activity of our **teams**, and the performance in our **games**, we develop a more complete view of what is going on. As such, we can better plan our next moves.

Bruce Henderson in 1981 wrote that "Strategy depends on the ability to foresee future consequences of present initiatives." He shared that it requires the following:[145]

144 Henry Mintzberg. "Patterns in Strategy Formation," *Management Science* 24, no. 9 (May 1978): 934–48, https://doi.org/10.1287/mnsc.24.9.934.

145 Bruce Henderson, "The Concept of Strategy," Boston Consulting Group, January 1, 1981, https://www.bcg.com/en-us/publications/1981/concept-of-strategy.

1. Extensive knowledge about the environment, market, and competitors
2. Ability to examine this knowledge as an interactive dynamic system
3. Imagination and logic to choose between specific alternatives

By collecting our **results** and examining them through the lens of external forces, and the dynamics system of the **TLC** and the decision process of transformational **leadership**, we are well-placed to think beyond the knowledge limits of the executive **team**.

Henry Mintzberg went further in 1998 to layout five definitive types of Strategy in his 5P model:[146] This is useful in broadening our thinking of what strategy means in our company.

- Strategy as a plan: a direct course of action to achieve an intended set of goals: **games**.
- Strategy as a pattern: a consistent pattern of past behaviour realised over time rather than planned or intended, when the pattern of **results** was different to the intent, particularly in **VUCA**. He called it Emergent strategy.
- Strategy as position: a strategy determined by analysing factors outside the company, other **brands**, competitors, consumer analysis.

146 Henry Mintzberg, Bruce Ahlstrand, and Joseph Lampel, *Strategy Safari: A Guided Tour Through the Wilds of Strategic Management* (New York: The Free Press, 1998).

- Strategy as a ploy: a manoeuvre with the intent to outwit the competition.
- Strategy as a perspective: executing strategy based on a theory of business and the extension of the mindset or **culture** of the organisation.

Let's recap the benefits of this:

- Strategy as a plan. We are able to plan with greater perspective.
- Strategy as a pattern. We can observe and replicate what works and what does not.
- Strategy as position. We can determine where we are in relation to our competitors.
- Strategy as a ploy. We can move faster and outplay our rivals.
- Strategy as a perspective. We become a data-driven **culture**, capable of developing strategic change at every level of the company.

In the **TLC**, being able to share data and co-create strategy allows us to build our collective intelligence, to see things from more perspectives and to be a more powerful force as a company. In order to do this, we need to make some of our **results** practical, visual, and sharable. Let's start by considering the concept of data visualisation and business intelligence.

THE POWER OF DATA VISUALISATION AND BUSINESS INTELLIGENCE

This is not a new concept. In fact, it's not even modern. Cave paintings of star locations have been around for about 11,000 years, and charts made of clay, sticks, and string were found in ancient Incan and Mesopotamian **cultures** from way back.[147] In 1160 BC, we had a Turin Papyrus map that indicated the accurate distribution of mining resources. By 200 BC, coordinates from Egyptian surveyors were documented into the early forms of latitude and longitude. Sixteenth-century brought all sorts of techniques of measurement, and René Descartes developed analytic geometry and two-dimensional coordinate systems that allowed old mate, William Playfair to create methods for graphically displaying statistics.[148] In the second half of the twentieth century, Jacques Bertin showed us how to represent information "intuitively, clearly, accurately and efficiently."[149]

Then John Tukey and Edward Tufte rolled on in with a shiny new statistical approach and a book with the riveting title of *The Visual Display of Quantitative Information*. This

---

147 "List of Physical Visualizations and Related Artifacts," http://dataphys.org/list/.

148 Michael Friendly, "A Brief History of Data Visualization," in *Handbook of Data Visualization* (Berlin: Springer-Verlag Berlin Heidelberg, 2008), 15–56, https://doi.org/10.1007/978-3-540-33037-0_2.

149 Stephen Few, "Data Visualization for Human Perception," in *The Encyclopedia of Human–Computer Interaction*, 2nd ed. (Denmark: Interactive Design Foundation, 2014), https://www.interaction-design.org/literature/book/the-encyclopedia-of-human-computer-interaction-2nd-ed/data-visualization-for-human-perception.

paved the way for technology to take this from the hands of statisticians and led into the age of Business Intelligence.[150]

Business intelligence is all about using facts and data about historical, real-time and predictive business information about your operations and **results**. This allows us to be well informed to make better decisions across the whole **TLC**, to make fact-based decisions and to bring clarity to the emerging patterns in this stream of information.

Practicing a range of BI techniques and technologies can enable us to identify and develop a range of new opportunities and, when done well, will allow us to inform your **players** to make and inform better decisions within their roles, responsibilities, and **games**.

Using this thinking, you can combine your internal operational data on **results**, both qualitative and quantitative, and external market data to build a better map of how to make better decisions and put together stronger and more whole and robust strategies that can then run through your **Games**, **Teams**, and **Players**.

Central to this idea is the ability to collect and respond to **results** in a timely and collaborative manner. Howard Dresner in 1989 defined Business Intelligence as "Concepts and methods to improve business decision making by using fact-based support systems," and in the 1990s, this idea became mainstream and widespread.[151]

---

150 Michael Friendly, "A Brief History of Data Visualization," in *Handbook of Data Visualization* (Berlin: Springer-Verlag Berlin Heidelberg, 2008), 15–56, https://doi.org/10.1007/978-3-540-33037-0_2.

151 D. J. Power, "A Brief History of Decision Support Systems," DSS Resources, last modified March 10, 2007, https://dssresources.com/history/dsshistory.html.

Solomon Negash and Paul Gray define BI as systems that combine:[152]

- Data gathering
- Data storage
- Knowledge management

Other neighbouring terms such as competitive intelligence and business analytics all tend to tie into this idea of BI and allow us to essentially make better, fact-based decisions, and help us take the guesswork out as much as possible.

BI in your **results** can help with the following:

- Performance improvement
- Reporting to inform strategy
- Collaboration
- Knowledge management
- Analysing processes for better decision-making

Investing in the right software and digital solutions can be very worthwhile, but it is not always necessary. I'll share a story to illustrate this.

152 Solomon Negash and Paul Gray, "Business Intelligence," in *Handbook on Decision Support Systems 2* (Berlin: Springer Berlin Heidelberg, 2008), 175–93, https://doi.org/10.1007/978-3-540-48716-6_9.

STORY TIME: THE INDONESIAN PASTRY WAR ROOM

It's a hot day in downtown Jakarta.

I'm standing in a windowless room in a large bakery with the directors and heads of department and a group of enthusiastic **change agents**. This company is responsible for supplying all of the hotels, catering companies, and every Starbucks café in the area. Each of the walls of the room is covered with charts. The charts are filled with numbers that reflect the **results** of the day, week, month, and year.

The operations manager begins the meeting. He talks about the goals and the improvement towards the goals for the day. He gestures towards the charts as he updates them in red and green. Earlier in the day, the charts were filled by each department with their progress towards improvements. Every **team** and **player** in the business has a **game** and ethos that exists to improve the numbers noted on the charts.

The operations manager looks pleased. He can see progress in front of him, and he knows exactly where he'll be spending his time today to go coach and support the various departments that need his attention.

They called this room the BIG room, the central nervous system of the operation. All updated by hand, by laminated charts and whiteboard markers scribbled in red and green. Anybody could tell at a glance that this company was heading in the right direction and where the gaps were. The direction they were heading in was obvious, based on the sea of green that was populated upon the charts on every wall within the room. This was their hub of improvement, their war room. This is where they came to see the whole business in a snapshot.

The meeting continued, and they looked at the opportunities to improve and the areas where improvement was stable and could be celebrated. They scribbled on their notepads and plotted out their agendas to be able to go and help the workers on the line improve every section of the business.

Six months ago, this was not the case.

Back then, the operations manager spent his days in constant firefighting mode, moving from one area to the next, to whoever yelled the loudest. Six months ago, the business was in chaos. We now stood in a room where everything that needed to be improved was measured and monitored. Every area and every deliverable had a representation on the scoreboard, and they knew exactly what to do next. They were no longer reacting to the world around them. They were responding to the areas that required their attention. There was a sense of calm in this room, along with subtle celebration.

The Indonesian pastry war room allowed the business to scale three times over the next eighteen months because whenever they invested in growth or development, they knew exactly what needed to be measured, how to spot the patterns and emerging strategy, and how to turn it into a **game** they could win.

Peter Drucker once said, "If you can't measure it, you can't manage it."

Well, the Indonesian pastry war room had managed to measure every element that required their attention and manage it in a way that brought everybody along for the ride. We had created something so simple, a **game** so clear that made all the difference to the improvement of the business. That allowed them to not only grow, but grow profitably, and grow with a strong sense of purpose and improvement.

And they did it all with the **TLC** and some whiteboard markers.

RESULTS

By making the right **results**, data was easily accessible and available throughout the company, and we were able to guide better decisions and get more perspectives of the strategies we had put in place.

By harvesting the data of our **brand**, **culture**, **games**, and **results**, we became well-placed to develop far better strategies. In doing this, we became faster, smarter, and more adaptable in the face of **VUCA**.

In this instalment, we discovered that our facts and data can be used to create better strategies by involving the right people. We know what we need to measure and monitor and have clear and effective systems for collecting, visualising, and collaborating on creating our strategies and tactics for moving forward towards our **new normal**. In the next installation, **player**, we look at the individual and learn how to improve their selection, development, and retention through the **TLC** system.

INSTALLATION 13

PLAYER

JOHN'S OLD-WORLD STATUS QUO

"There are some people here who are never going to change," said John.

"We have quite a few toxic people in this business, and it's going to make this transformation a real challenge. We also have a very high turnover rate of staff. It sometimes seems like a revolving door of our best and brightest going somewhere else, chased out by a nasty employee or manager and only to open the door for someone else who can find a quiet place to get by.

What's more, we need to get better at developing our people and helping them thrive and figure out a way of attracting and selecting the new talent we need to grow. It's not that bad. I'm being a bit dramatic, of course. We do have some great people here; I'm just sick to death of this legacy of people getting away with bullshit. We have made all sorts of excuses in the past: there is a shallow talent pool, it is expensive to fire people in this country, or 'we'll just wait and see if they get better and change.'"

John continued to voice his disappointments. "We just keep on investing and investing in trying to fix people who generally don't want to be here. Sometimes I just feel like it would be better to fire everyone and start again. Dramatic, I know."

I could sense John's sheer frustration about this.

"What do we do?" John asked again, looking for the fast answer.

"Well, we begin with the program and work through the **TLC** system. You will see some of the toxic people leave when they understand that things are not going back to the **status quo**."

"They just leave?" asked John.

"More than you might think," I reassured him from a place of experience. "Also, you may find that many of them actually change their tune. Quite often as the rebels get an opportunity to channel some of that energy into something meaningful, they change."

"And what about the rest?"

"Well, John, once you have set your **north star**, shifted the **leadership** style, run **events** of **team** ethos, **game**, and **players** and given them all an opportunity to come along on the journey, if they are still not on board with your **culture**—then let them go. They were never with you anyway."

JOHN'S NEW NORMAL

My, how things change.

Through the transformation process, major shifts in the **players**' behaviour occurred. In fact, the engagement score **result** at John's company had tripled. Beyond that, we saw the revolving door come to a halt as retention rates went up. We doubled their success rate in selecting new **players** by using some very clever assessments.

We had made coaching and development part of the daily **rhythm**, and people experienced a sense of growth in their work. What's more, their **culture** had become so strong that they began attracting great people who formed an orderly line out the door for a chance to join John's company.

The Attraction, Selection, Development and Retention of **players** at John's company had improved so much that the old world felt like a distant memory.

When we don't have a **north star** to guide them towards, a **team** ethos they believe in, and a **game** they can play and win, we're unlikely to be effective with people. Our **players** need to be aligned to the group, to the organization, and the company in order to be effective and efficient. We need to consider within this how we attract the right people, select these people, and then develop them through the **team** ethos in the **games** and retain them so they stick around and want to be part of our company.

WHAT YOU'LL LEARN AND DO IN THIS INSTALLATION

In this instalment of **player**, we look at the process of attracting, selecting, developing, and retaining the individuals who make up the **teams**, playing the **games**, and producing the **results** in your company as we move towards **north star** and transform our company into the **new normal**.

GREAT THINKERS

Before we dive right in, we will scratch the surface of the field of human development and get a basic understanding of some of the greatest thinkers. Please note that this, like all of these great thinkers' sections, fill volumes and libraries. This summary, although incomplete, is hopefully somewhat useful to you, my dear reader.[153]

Enter James Mark Baldwin, 1861–1934,[154] an American philosopher widely regarded as the father of the field of human development. Baldwin saw human development as a complex applied interdisciplinary science built on understanding not just what is possible, but what is preferable and what makes things better. Baldwin's key ideas were based on principles of the biological sciences and reflected the importance of Darwin and evolutionary theory.

His theory, the Baldwin Effect, views human cognitive development as a process of Assimilation, Accommodation and Organic selection through interactions with the environment (more on what this means in a moment).

He taught us that learning is a natural phenomenon that we are predisposed to learn, and that growth happens in humans, just like in nature, when the environmental conditions are right.

---

153 Again, my apologies to the academics, this section exists to honour and share this thinking, not to reduce or minimise the complexity and density of these breakthroughs in science and philosophy.

154 *Handbook of Psychology* (1890), translation of Ribot's *German Psychology of To-day* (1886); *Elements of Psychology* (1893); *Social and Ethical Interpretations in Mental Development* (1898); *Story of the Mind* (1898).

Baldwin showed us that capabilities arise at the intersection of the individual and their environment as the individual **player** organises their thoughts and actions in relation to the world around them. The structures that are around us bring about our limitations, liberations, our constraints, and possibilities.

Baldwin demonstrated that human development is not one BIG process, but many small interrelated processes, that the individual is a complex profile of strengths and weaknesses that become that way through interacting and socialising as they grow and continue to develop through the lifespan.

Baldwin taught us that logic is the morality of thought, and reasoning is at the heart of learning, that we are biologically built to learn, and that good leaders and teachers consider the individual **players'** patterns of strengths and weaknesses and recognises that we learn who we are through the people around us.

ENTER JEAN PIAGET (1896–1980)

Many people think Piaget was a child psychologist who spent all his time playing with marbles. This couldn't be further from the truth, and the significance of his work in understanding human development is astronomical. In Piaget's time, the academic environment was more interested in small mechanical studies than grand universal theories. As such, he was and often still is misunderstood and misrepresented. In fact, Piaget was a biologist, philosopher, and deep interdisciplinary thinker who was heavily influenced by Baldwin and paved the road for the great developmentalists in the decades that followed.

Piaget saw self-organisation as the centre of life itself and developed the following processes that he would later analyse to create descriptive developmental stages of human cognitive development.

Piaget's process has three major parts.

1. EQUILIBRATION

Basically, we process and balance information through assimilation and accommodation.

- Assimilation is the process of adopting new ideas into the existing way we see ourselves, our **culture**, our world.
- Accommodation is the process of changing the way we see ourselves through the new ideas and information we see.

Put in dangerously simple terms, assimilation occurs when we make the new information fit our view of the world. Accommodation occurs when we change our view of the world to fit the new information.

2. REFLECTIVE ABSTRACTION

This is moving from working on something to working on working on something.

For example, making a sandwich to working on the best way to make a sandwich.

We think about things, and as we grow and develop, we end up thinking about how we thought about things.

As we move through stages of development, we are able to think of how we used to think when we were at an earlier stage.

We can reflect on how we learned to master tasks after we have mastered them, and we transcend and include our growth.

3. INTERNALISATION/SOCIALISATION

The norms of your community, company, **culture**, the **status quo**, held assumptions taken for granted.

We build our inner world, how we think, based on our outer world.

Our logic becomes our morality of thought.

Our norms and rules are shared by what we say and think and are internalised through cooperation and shared problems.

Piaget gave us his stage model of cognitive development:

- Sensorimotor: senses and motor responses
- Preoperational: Recognises Symbols
- Concrete operational: concepts attached to situations
- Formal operational: theories, reasoning, strategies, planning[155]

ENTER LAWRENCE KOHLBERG (1927–1987)

Best known for his theory of moral development, Lawrence Kohlberg was heavily influenced by Baldwin and Piaget and codified Piaget's work. He put moral development into the

155 Piaget's resources for further enquiry. I have not read all of these, and this book barely scratches the surface of the implications of his work. *The Grasp of Consciousness: Action and Concept in the Young Child* (2015). *The Mechanisms of Perception* (2006). *Psychology and Epistemology: Towards a Theory of Knowledge* (1972). *The Child's Conception of Time* (1969). *Logic and Psychology* (1953). *The Origin of the Idea of Chance in Children* (1975).

mainstream conversation and was an enormous influence on society.

He developed hard stages that were far more scientific and empirically robust than anything that came before and almost everything that came after. Working through semi-structured interviews, he created a system of codes and analysis that revealed an underlying structure represented in stages of moral development.

- Pre-Conventional: rules and punishment; the rules are the rules because they are the rules and that is the most important thing. No idea of co-creating the rules of the **games**.
- Conventional: rules are a social contract in a social world that we are part of; we have allegiance to the traditions and can ask where the rules come from.
- Post-Conventional: we see rules and laws as handed down by tradition and created by us; we can norm the norms and create new rules together, and we see universal values and human rights. We create rules by which to create rules—**north star**.

ERIK ERIKSON (1902–1994)

Erikson was an enormously influential developmental psychologist who gave us theory of psychosocial development and along with Harry Stack Sullivan, popularised the ego-development movement. You know the term "identify crisis?" That came from Erikson.

Erikson's work looks at the growth of the personality structure in contrast to the hard biological structures. He examined the soft cultural and emotional elements of human development.

Erikson saw the self as a system of emotional self-regulation in sociocultural and biological contexts. He claimed that growth comes through evolving social relationships and that the dynamics of need and emotion are security, sex, and relationships. In love, death moves and motivates the whole system of self.

Erikson taught us about the balancing and integrating of this system across diverse skills and relationships.

The regulation of self-esteem driven by complex needs and structures in the system built through interaction with the environment are called schemas.

The self-system evolves and transforms, and old schemas shape new ones as we grow and develop.

That crisis forces the personality to reorganise as the self-system navigates a series of difficult **events** through life. Once crises are resolved, it marks a new stage, a more complex mature personality and integrates the self-system.

The stages based on the tensions and virtues in the following table come from a series of developmental crises.

There are some heavy implications of this thinking:

- Personality structures to grow and evolve, mostly younger years
- Motivational systems evolve through the life course
- The past is in the present[156]

156 Resources and further reading from Erik Erikson: *Insight and Responsibility* (1966). *Identity: Youth and Crisis* (1968). *Life History and the Historical...*

Stage	Tension	Question	Virtue
0-2	Trust vs. Mistrust	Are my basic needs met?	Hope
2-4	Autonomy vs. Shame/Doubt	OK to be me?	Will
4-5	Initiative vs. Guilt	Is it OK to play?	Purposefulness
5-12	Industry vs. Inferiority	Can I make it in the world?	Competence
13-19	Identity vs. Role Confusion	Who am I?	Fidelity
20-24	Intimacy vs. Isolation	Can I love/be loved?	Love
25-64	Generativity vs. Stagnation	Can my life count?	Care
65-death	Integrity vs. Despair	Was it OK to have been me?	Wisdom

KURT FISCHER (1943–2020)

Educator, researcher, author, and leading developmentalist, Kurt Fischer built further on Piaget's lineage and gave us Dynamics Skills theory, a neo-piagetian theory of cognitive development. He was working toward the goal of establishing a coherent applied science of development using hard stage empirical. Fischer taught us how knowledge, actions,

---

...*Moment* (1975). *Adulthood* (1978). *Vital Involvement in Old Age* (1986). *The Life Cycle Completed* (1987).

concepts, and neural networks develop through the integrative scientific study of biology, psychology, and sociology.

In dynamic skills theory, skills develop:

- In context to physical and social environment: **culture**
- Through the content received: **events/rhythm**
- In sequential, measurable stage like patterns: **results**
- In clusters of related functionality: **games**
- Through a complex ecology of operations: the **TLC**
- With emotion as a rudder steering the ship: **player/teams/leadership**

This practical science taught us that effective learning and development requires:

- Learning is messy
- Emotion is central to learning
- Learning goals must be co-constructed
- The right support and interventions for the individual
- Trying to boost one skill faster can throw out the whole network

Kurt Fischer and a movement of neo-piagetians were ahead of the curve in understanding that emotion was key to development and learning, the neglected twentieth-century topic of emotion and its effect on learning and development came to the forefront as affective neuroscience demonstrated that admiring virtue in others lights up both the emotional and cognitive centres in the brain. Emotion is inseparable from learning, and the recruitment of emotion is essential to learn and develop effectively.

- Emotion and cognition are two sides of the same coin
- Emotion is framed by cognition, and cognition is guided by the rudder of emotion
- Emotion can either catalyse or short circuit learning based on our learning experience

All cycles of learning include tests and emotions:

- We think we know something
- We try it
- We succeed or fail
- We get feedback
- We try again
- We retool and reshape what we think we know[157]

157 Kurt W. Fischer, "A Theory of Cognitive Development: The Control and Construction of Hierarchies of Skills," *Psychological Review* 87, no. 6 (1980): 477–531, https://doi.org/10.1037/0033-295x.87.6.477. Kurt W. Fischer, and Samuel P. Rose, "Dynamic Development of Coordination of Components in Brain and Behavior: A Framework for Theory and Research," in *Human Behavior and the Developing Brain* (New York: Guilford Press, 1994), 3–66. Kurt W. Fischer and Thomas R. Bidell, "Dynamic Development of Action, Thought, and Emotion," in *Handbook of Child Psychology. Vol 1: Theoretical Models of Human Development*, 6th ed. (New York: Wiley, 2006), 313–399, https://www.gse.harvard.edu/~ddl/articlesCopy/FischerBidellProofsCorrected.0706.pdf. *Mind, Brain, and Education in Reading Disorders*, eds. Kurt W. Fischer, Jane Holmes Bernstein, and Mary Helen Immordino-Yang (Cambridge: Cambridge University Press, 2007). Matthew H.Schneps, L. Todd Rose, and Kurt W. Fischer, "Visual Learning and the Brain: Implications for Dyslexia," *Mind, Brain, and Education* 1, no. 3 (September 2007): 128–39. https://doi.org/10.1111/j.1751-228x.2007.00013. Zachary Stein, Theo Dawson, and Kurt W. Fischer, "Redesigning Testing: Operationalizing the New Science of Learning," in *New Science of Learning* (New York: Springer, 2010), 207–24, https://doi.org/10.1007/978-1-4419-5716-0_10.

This plays out in the living system of **TLC events** and **rhythm**.

Understanding the goldilocks zone, (not too easy or hard, but just right), can help leaders set goals appropriately as we move through cycles of experimentation and learning.

This means creating the right game, within the right environment and **culture** and providing the right support and scaffolding through our **rhythm**.

THE FUTURE OF HUMAN DEVELOPMENT— A RESOURCE RECOMMENDATION

The work of Theo Dawson at Lectica.org is at the leading edge of developmental science and learning. I encourage everyone who has come this far in the book to dive deeper into the work of Lectica and in understanding its applications for transformational **leadership**.[158]

MASLOW'S INFLUENCE ON MANAGEMENT

Abraham Maslow's influence on management completely changed the way we view the work motivation of the individual **players** who make up our company.

Although he copped a lot of criticism for the lack of rigour in his work, he had a profound impact on the way the business world and management thought leaders, such as Peter Drucker, viewed the practice of people management.

Some of Maslow's key messages are as follows:[159]

158 Lectica Live, https://lecticalive.org/.

159 Abraham H. Maslow, *Maslow on Management* (New York: Wiley & Sons, 1998).

- Human beings are capable of extraordinary accomplishment, creativity, and innovation are natural elements in our makeup.
- Long-term relationships with customers are the wisest strategy for long-term growth.
- **Team**work, although imperative to business outcomes, is an overlooked source of community and esteem for people.
- Enlightened management does not only improve products and earnings per share; it improves people and thus improves the world.

The ideas that Maslow put forward so many years ago speak very clearly to the changing landscape of **leadership** today and, although they lack scientific rigour, they have shaped the thinking of the broader cultural ideals of what good management looks like.

Before this thinking came along, the dominant theory of **player** motivation and management came from a guy named Douglas McGregor in his theory X and Theory Y.[160]

Theory X sees **players** as lazy, untrustworthy, unambitious, and only doing what they need to do. Work is based wholly and solely on self-interest. Reward and punishment is the way, and it is management vs. staff.

Theory Y postulates that if you give people responsibilities and freedom, they'll do the right thing, they like to work, they are motivated to do the work to better themselves and when regarded as a valuable asset of the company.

---

160 Institute for Work & Employment Research, https://iwer.mit.edu/.

There has been much debate of this over the years.

In 1969, Maslow broke new ground in the field of management by proposing something called Theory Z.[161]

Using his famous hierarchy of needs, he developed Theory Z.

Let's take a quick look at his hierarchy:

- At the bottom of the pyramid, Maslow identifies physiological needs, the most basic needs.
- The next level is safety; the need to be psychologically safe.
- The next level is social, to be part of a group, to belong.
- The next level is esteem, to contribute to this group, to matter.
- The highest level on Maslow's hierarchy was self-actualisation.

Theory Z proposes that once people reach a certain level of economic security and safety, they would strive for a life of actualisation, a life of striving for better.

Theory Z is when people want to become what Maslow refers to as a transcender:

A transcender is somebody who seeks peak experiences.

They speak normally and naturally in the language of being, the language of ethos in **TLC** terms.

They perceive that the sacredness is in all things.

They're conscious and deliberate.

They value truth, beauty, and goodness.

They seem to recognise each other.

---

161 Abraham Maslow, "Theory Z," 2009, www.maslow.org.

They're more responsive to beauty.

They're more holistic about the world.

These people value innovation, discovery, and growth.

These are the people who want to change.

They want to grow.

They seek and embrace self-actualisation.

Maslow viewed human potential and self-actualisation as the highest need of the human.

Maslow saw it as management's duty to help **players** self-actualize through the company and through the organization.

> *This is the simple way of saying that proper management of the work lives of human beings, the way they earn their living, can improve them and improve the world, and in this sense be a utopian or revolutionary technique.*
>
> —*A.H. Maslow,* Maslow on Management[162]

Maslow saw a necessity for enlightened management policies.

He could see into the future:

> *The more evolved people get, the more psychologically healthy they get, the more enlightened management policy will be necessary in order to survive in competition, and the more handicapped will be an enterprise with an authoritarian policy.*

Maslow saw that the right leader would work with their people to help them self-actualize.

162 Abraham H. Maslow, *Maslow on Management* (New York: Wiley & Sons, Inc., 1998).

What would you rather have: a **culture** of people who just turn up to do the job or a cultural people who are there to make every day a bit better than yesterday, find new ways to grow, and exceed and find meaning and hope in this endeavour? The foundation for this kind of thinking is in the development of a growth mindset in your **players**.

GROWTH VS. FIXED MINDSET

A popular and useful model in positive psychology is the idea of growth mindset versus fixed mindset.[163] I would encourage you to apply this thinking in a thought experiment to yourself and also use this as a simple way of selecting and understanding the development needs of your **players**.

Growth mindsets are underpinned by the following beliefs:

- I can learn anything I want to learn
- When I fail, I'm learning
- I learn when other people succeed, and I'm inspired by that
- I am responsible for the **results** I get
- I want challenges when I get frustrated and feel defeated. I persevere and keep going because I am learning
- My attitude is my choice

Fixed mindsets are underpinned by the following beliefs:

---

163 Carol S. Dweck, *Mindset: The New Psychology of Success*, Updated ed. (New York: Ballantine Books, 2006).

- I don't like challenges
- Failure means I'm bad
- I need to be told that I'm okay, that I'm smart
- When other people succeed, I feel threatened by that, and my internal abilities determine everything
- When I have learning opportunities, I avoid them because it could reveal my lack of skill

Knowing the difference between the growth mindset and the fixed mindset allows us to identify when this comes up for people in a conversation and to ask the right questions to help your **players** uncover this truth themselves.

The truth is, I have observed people going in and out of a fixed and growth mindset, based on the situation. Most people will have a predominant mindset, but all people will, under certain situations, move to a fixed mindset from a growth mindset or a growth mindset from a fixed mindset. The exercise here is to promote change through awareness of the distinction, to celebrate growth, and discourage fixed thinking. This not only provides a stake in the ground for constructive coaching conversations over time, but it helps your **culture** begin to attract the right **players**.

ATTRACTING THE RIGHT PLAYERS

After a while of working through the **TLC** process, you will find the language of your organization changes. You will find that the **assets** of **team** ethos are spoken about so often in the **rhythm** that they become how people talk to each other. You may even start to look like a bit of a cult. That's not a bad thing, because this becomes your **brand**. It becomes who you are as a company in the market. The right **players** want to play with **players** like them.

The best places to work are often the places that have strong **team** ethos, great **games**, and attract the best **players**. Your best attraction strategy for the right talent is being very clear about what people can expect from joining your company. When we are very clear about who we are, what's expected, and how we play, the right people can decide if they would like to join your **culture**, and they tend to hear all about it from the **players** who already work for you.

SELECTION AND FIT

Do not try to teach fish how to ride bicycles. The fish doesn't like it, and it takes a lot of time.

I encourage the majority of my clients to use robust and bespoke psychometric profiling to determine the natural personality traits of the **players** they select for their **teams**.

Personality is incredibly important to get right and measure in the most scientific and considered way possible.

This is dangerous and complex territory and requires careful consideration to use the right tool for the right job. As such, I will not be making general recommendations about what to use in this book. For further guidance, feel free to email me or my **team**: *benny@bigchange.group* with the subject line: Selection.

Beyond personality, we also need to consider their experience, skills, and cultural fit. What have they done before? Do they have the skills to be able to achieve in this **game**? How long will it take them to get up to speed within this **team**?

We also need to determine whether they like our **culture**, whether they believe in the **north star**, and whether the **team** ethos of the **team** is something that resonates with them personally.

We need to look for **culture** fit as well as personality and skills, and we need to build a process to be able to do this well. Whenever we bring somebody new into our **team**, we've taken as much of the guesswork as possible out of the decision to let someone join our **culture**.

STORY TIME: EXPENSIVE GUESSWORK

"We have a profitability problem," the managing director said. "When we look at our numbers, our bottom line is suffering because our people are not performing."

I sat in a dreary boardroom poring over a performance document of their salespeople's performance over the last twelve months. Immediately, a trend was clear. When we looked at the top performers, the Pareto Principle was clear. It was obvious. Eighty percent of the firm's revenue came from 20 percent of the consultants. These consultants were the cream of the crop. But more than that, they provided the revenue to support the vast majority of the business.

I asked the question, "Why do these top 20 percent produce the **results** they produce? What makes them different?"

The managing director paused to think. He said, "Well, it's a certain type of person who succeeds. It's a person with drive and get-up-and-go. They have the right empathy; they know that they need to turn up and do the same things consistently to be able to produce the **result**."

I said, "Okay, why don't we just find more people like that?"

The MD laughed and said, "If only there was a way."

I said, "Perhaps there is."

We went through the process of applying bespoke personality profiling to every single person in the business. We mapped twenty-two traits of innate personality, and the **results** were startling. When we looked at the performance curve, we found that 20 percent were indeed producing 80 percent of the firm's **results**. Of those 20 percent, all shared common traits. In this case, we could tell with startling accuracy what personalities were likely to be in the top 20 percent.

We began refining the selection process. We began profiling everybody who was going to be hired into the business to make sure we took as much of the guesswork out of the process of hiring as possible. When we looked at the numbers, we realised that every single time the wrong person fell into the 80 percent category, it cost the business over $300,000 a year in costs and lost revenue in their high-performance high-salary role.

By using a bespoke blueprint for selection of personality, we were able to double the chances of hiring somebody in the top 20 percent. Not only that, we were able to immediately see the areas for development required for these people to be successful in the role. For a long time, this company had been guessing, by using their instincts and making the wrong selection decisions.

They now had a scientific method for taking as much of the guesswork out of the selection process as possible, and we were able to pinpoint the areas that required development for these people.

We turned selection into a science, and the **results** showed up immediately in the bottom-line **results**.

COACHING YOUR PLAYERS

As I mentioned in the **leadership** installation, we live in a time where all the answers to all the questions you could possibly ask are available on a device that you carry in your pocket. Search engines such as Google have brought information to us at lightning speed. The world's knowledge is available to those who seek it.

In past times, the answers and the information was the most valuable resource. Books were held in secret and private libraries that required levels of privilege to access and were reserved for the lucky few. Now you can be the CEO of a world bank or somebody living on the street with a $100 Android smartphone as your only possession and still access the greatest information the world has to offer.

What is missing?

The value has shifted. The value is no longer about having the answers. The value is found in asking the right questions. When we ask the right questions, we begin a line of inquiry.

Good leaders ask great questions, and great questions inspire us to think differently.

They ask questions because they know that the right question asked at the right time can help shape the thinking of the person who asked. They have to do their own work, their own digging, and their own inquiry to come up with an answer. This is the very heart of coaching.

We see this in the traditions of Zen Buddhism and the schools of yoga. The master asks a question, and the student is required to go away and meditate on this question. It is in the process of inquiry and thinking that the work occurs for that person to discover the answer within themselves through their own contemplation and reflection.

> *To ask the right question is already half the solution of a problem.*
>
> —*Carl Jung*

To be a great coach, we need to be great at asking questions. This is a task that is more difficult than first thought. We need to be able to unearth the opportunities by asking the right question at the right time, because not only does asking a great question provide us with new knowledge and insight about the **player**, it also provides the opportunity for your people to develop their own thinking and make their own decisions, which will develop them greatly as people.

Each day in the **rhythm**, we stand around the board, in person or online. We share stories of **team** ethos. We discuss the **games** and ways forward together. Our development is daily, and our feedback loop fast. Together, we identify these problems before they become raging forest fires and help people through them by asking great coaching questions. It is through this conversation that our development plan forms.

The development process for your **players** exists within the compass, **assets**, **events**, and **rhythms** of the day-to-day. Through the regular **rhythm** and **events**, we are able to learn what to expect from each other. We may even be able to perfect this over time.

PERFECTING OUR EXPECTATIONS

So often we expect perfection with those around us. We often expect our **players** to show up and care as much about the businesses as we do. We expect people to perform consistently, and we expect that everything will work out the way it does in our minds. This expectation of perfection usually leads to disappointment.

Instead of expecting perfection, another idea is for the leader to **perfect their expectations**. Perfecting expectations allows us to negotiate the world around us. It allows us to set expectations and standards with people rather than attempting to force them upon the people. By setting clear expectations with somebody, they become a co-creator of the expectation and are more likely to fulfil it.

Co-defining **team** ethos and what we're expected to remain true to form a belief level is important. Co-designing a **game** and setting expectations together around the rules, boundaries, scores, and time leads to better performance. The invitation here is to spend time working with people to make your expectations of the world around you as perfect as possible, and then, you never know—you may be able to expect perfection.

RETAINING TALENT

When we look at what translates to happiness and what leads to people having fulfilled lives, two of the largest indicators are:

1. Doing meaningful work where they feel they've made a difference.
2. Having relationships that they find full of connection and meaning.

The purpose of this work is to create companies where people can find a home.

When people have a **north star**, they can see and understand a **team** ethos within a group they share and believe in, a **game** they can play, and get better at, and are surrounded by people who share these values, beliefs, motivations, and sense of achievement and progress. Then they tend to stick around. It is the responsibility of the transformational leader to create a **culture** and an environment that looks after these human needs for fulfilment.

> *We have three innate psychological needs—competence, autonomy, and relatedness. When those needs are satisfied, we're motivated, productive, and happy.*
>
> *—Daniel H. Pink*[164]

It is our goal to create environments that satisfy these needs so people can be all they can be and are able to find meaning and satisfaction in the work that they do. If we want to retain the top talent, we need to address the dynamic elements of the **TLC** within this book.

---

164 Daniel H. Pink, *Drive: The Surprising Truth About What Motivates Us* (Edinburgh, UK: Cannongat Books, 2018).

EVENTS OF PLAYERS

The purpose of having **events** of **players** is to develop your individual people.

Events of **players** should be scheduled regularly to be able to provide ongoing feedback, training, and support through coaching and through asking questions, so the **players** have what they need to perform within the **games** and to live by the **teams**, **team** ethos, and company **north star**.

These **events** should be built into your calendar. They should be regular, consistent, and predictable. When you give people a solid schedule of **events** where they know that they're going to come back, bring insights, and improve, you give them the certainty they need to succeed with the **TLC** system.

They're an opportunity to coach, develop, iron out problems, dig deeper into the emotions of people, and work on discovering what their blocker and challenges are. There is a massive problem within the world of organizations of retrospective performance reviews. We look back into history and say, "Here's what you didn't do right!"

What we should be doing instead is regularly checking in with and coaching our **players** within the **TLC** system and looking for small incremental improvements on the path towards our **new normal**. **Events** of **players** should happen consistently. You may run these **events** with your **leadership team** or individually. You may run it monthly or quarterly, but the idea of this is to help align the person's individual compass towards the compass of the group, which points towards the **north star** of the company.

ASSETS FOR PLAYERS

Assets for **players** are the outputs that allow us to choose the right people, develop them in the right way, and keep them around by enabling them to experience ongoing progress.

Assets for **players** are there to create accountability, commitment, and a reference for their development. This includes a one-page development plan that is constantly reviewed, reflected upon, and iterated on, a talent map of performance and potential in a matrix where we look at the **players**, and we decide who we are going to develop.

Assets for **players** can also include development assessments that form the basis for the capabilities required to succeed in each **game**, in each **team**, and a blueprint where we can track data about personality, preferences, and performance that can serve as a reference point for selecting and developing **players** as you go through your improvement journey.

You can visit *www.bigchange.group/Resources/TLC* for regularly updated resources and templates.

When we build **assets** for **players**, we build the simplest, most concise documents that allow us to make better decisions around selecting, developing, and ultimately retaining, the top talent. The **assets** for **players** exist to make sure that every session and every **event** spent with your people has a well-defined, concise, and clear output, so everyone can remain on the same page.

ONBOARDING WITH ASSETS

Once we've made the selection decision to bring a new **player** on board, we want to bring them into the **culture** in a way that helps to set them up for success. A good way to do this is to spend time with them discussing the **assets** that exist within the **team** and the **asset** of **north star**. We need to have a series of great conversations with them about the why, about the bigger picture, and about what the group believes. You may want to document this as part of their journey.

I cannot stress enough when onboarding new **players**, this process of discussion and uncovering of shared beliefs and truths is critical to shaping that person's experience and the employee experience of the **team** they're working in and the company they're part of. We also need to onboard them into **games** and show them how we have a coaching **culture**. We need to explain the purpose of the **games**, how we're going to give them feedback, and how we're going to develop them. When we give people clarity around what to expect, they immediately know how to behave in the new environment. They immediately become part of the **culture** we're creating. They can see right away that this is how we do things around here, and it makes the ongoing **rhythm** stronger and more stable.

In this instalment, we have learned the practices of attracting, selecting, developing, and retaining your individual **players**. In the next and final instalment, we will bring all of this together in the **rhythm** and learn how to use this to create our daily habits that move us in the direction of true north and create our **new normal**.

INSTALLATION 14

RHYTHM

JOHN'S OLD-WORLD STATUS QUO

"Another meeting," John grumbled.

Everyone looked half-awake and half-frustrated before the proceedings had even begun. People stumbled into the meeting room. Some were on time, and some were ten minutes or more late. They took their seats and waited, traded stories of the past weekend, and made jokes about the local football **team** losing again.

"Here we go again," said the sales manager.

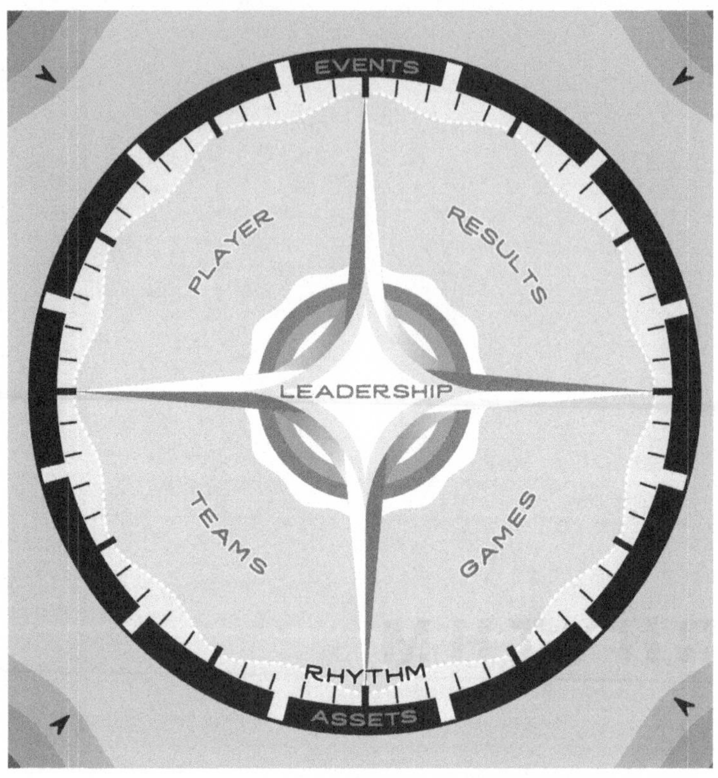

The energy was low and blunted. I sat there as a welcome but strange outsider, observing this Monday ritual and wondering why this was taking place. The agenda was not a surprise. Looking at numbers, people gave their explanations and told stories of how they hoped to fix problems. They were the same old problems they had talked about last week, last month, and last year.

People slumped in their chairs, were checking their phones for a better distraction and for something that would bring good news, or perhaps anything that would help them feel okay about the humdrum routine of this meeting. What a waste of time.

That was how John described most of the meetings happening in the business. "I'm thinking of cancelling all meetings indefinitely," said John.

Curious. I like to sit in meetings for all of my clients and observe. It's a great window into what is going on, and it teaches me volumes about the company's **culture**, **leadership**, and progress.

"John," I asked, "Why are we doing this? If you hate these meetings so much, what purpose do they serve? What would this look like if it was working and was a great use of time?"

"Well," John said, "it would be different from this for a start."

"Go on," I prompted.

"Well, first, we would be organised and well-prepared to make some progress together. We would have some energy and urgency around what we are doing. There would be a clear agenda, and people would feel like it was a great use of their time. We would make new decisions, collaborate, solve problems, and build our **culture** the way we all want."

Wouldn't that be something?

There was work to be done.

JOHN'S NEW NORMAL

Months later, John's world had changed.

Meetings ran through the business at every level and function. Looking from the outside, you would think it was a different company, maybe even from a different planet. People stood up, and everyone was now present and engaged. They started by pointing to the **north star** of the company.

People eagerly shared stories of their **team** ethos and spoke with energy and intent on the way they were shaping the **culture** of the company. They referenced the **assets** of **culture** and **brand** they had created together through their **events.**

They looked at their **games** together. There were clear measures of progress filed in daily, and the group celebrated their day by day movement and improvement towards a clearly set goal. The activities were measured on a clear and visible scoreboard. They shared and stored examples of success and gave each other support and guidance in order to increase performance. **Players** were in flow. A sense of ownership from the individual and responsibility for the **team** were clear and obvious.

It took a while to make it work, but the evidence was clear. Everyone wanted to be there. Everyone gave and received value. Everyone contributed to the **team** and the company through this forum. Ten minutes later in another room, another **rhythm** meeting was going on. This meeting was the daily management **rhythm.** All the **results** from each department meeting cascaded to the measure of the business.

People shared their **team** ethos stories, **results,** and progress scores on a BIG visual board, and there was a distinct sense of purpose, progress, and presence. Problems were not the same for long. They found new solutions for each challenge, and the *deja vu* of challenges past was no longer a headache. Groundhog Day was over.

Although they did have the same basic agenda day in and day out, it was always fresh. It was organised and disciplined, but at the same time, it was always a new story, a new challenge, and a new step forward. John and his company learned that by creating a disciplined **rhythm** of communication, they could find enough consistency, clarity, and eventually certainty and safety to make small steps forward every day.

Their **rhythm** was where they made the **assets** and changes become habits, and the way we work together—the **new normal.** It was the forum to make the changes work, and the proof was in the pudding. We could see the progress inching forward each day in every function of the company. Sometimes, it was two steps forward and one back, but it was always getting better and better—culturally, operationally, and personally.

Through the simple discipline of a short daily meeting, the business began to march together in the same direction. Everyone was headed towards the **north star** and the **new normal.**

WHAT YOU'LL LEARN AND DO IN THIS INSTALLATION

In the instalment of **rhythm,** we learn how to embed consistent communication and practice the **TLC** elements.

Through a simple agenda that addresses each of these elements, we are able to build the discipline and habits of our company. We will learn how to run the **rhythm** and appreciate the **assets** we have created and bring it all together to create our **new normal** through consistent practice and dedication.

WHY WE NEED A RHYTHM OF COMMUNICATION AND PRACTICE

How do we consistently make sure we have the conversations that matter? By running a short daily meeting, we focus, re-centre, find problems before they become fires, and set everyone up for greater performance.

In order to bring our **assets** to life that we've created in our **events**, we need to establish a consistent discipline of coming together for a short period of time each day to discuss and re-centre on what matters most.

The **rhythm** is the calibration and practice of the **TLC**.

The **TLC** is not set and forget. If you want to effect change, the only way to do this sustainably is to do it with consistent practice. Bring everybody back to the same central conversation, align them, and uncover what the next small steps are. The **rhythm** is the practice, the ritual where each group comes together to discuss the **team** ethos, the **game**, and the **players** in a short space of time to set them up for the best day possible.

The power of the **rhythm** is what shapes **culture** over time. What becomes habit becomes the **new normal**.

In the **rhythm**, we realize our commitments and our goals through conversations and provide a consistent opportunity to coach and improve the thinking, talking, and behaviour of our **players**. It's this simple: have a short conversation each day, re-centre, refocus, and bring us back to what matters. This gives the manager an opportunity to clear the path and solve problems before they become BIG problems.

Although this is simple, it is not usually easy. As with any discipline, it takes time, commitment, and consistency to make it work, flow, and be the **new normal**.

THE POWER OF DISCIPLINE AND CONSISTENCY

> *A* **culture** *of discipline is not a principle of business; it is a principle of greatness.*
>
> —*Jim Collins*[165]

Discipline is one of these cultural traits that allows everything else to happen. Discipline is consistent behaviour in a **rhythm**. It's showing up when we don't want to show up.

Instilling a **culture** of discipline takes time, clear conversations, standards, expectations, and consequences. Discipline is a worthy thing to aspire to. In fact, all greatness comes from the discipline of **rhythm**, the constant practice. Discipline means doing your best regardless of being uncomfortable, regardless of whether or not you want to show up, regardless of the cold morning, or the 10,000 other things you have to do. Embed this discipline in your operations, and your **culture** will thrive and your company will transform.

> *When you have disciplined people, you don't need hierarchy. When you have disciplined thought, you don't need bureaucracy. When you have disciplined action, you don't need*

165 Jim Collins, *Good to Great: Why Some Companies Make The Leap...And Others Don't* (New York: HarperBusiness, 2001).

> *excessive controls. When you combine a* **culture** *of discipline with an ethic of entrepreneurship, you get the magical alchemy of great performance.*
>
> —*Jim Collins*

When we agree and hold each other accountable for the things we want most and the actions required to fill our goals, something amazing happens. We become stronger and can set out on a path towards greatness.

> *Our freedom to operate and manoeuvre had increased substantially through disciplined procedures. Discipline equals freedom.*
>
> —*Jocko Willink*[166]

The **rhythm** is very simple.

Show up, work through the **TLC** agenda below, and share what you're learning. What is unusual is the discipline and perseverance required to make this happen every single day without fail. That's the uncommon difference.

> *Without credible communication, and a lot of it, the hearts and minds of people are never captured.*
>
> —*John P. Kotter*

We do mean a lot of communication, indeed. There's a reason why scheduling regular **events** and gatherings of people to discuss what matters most has to support the **rhythm** to

166 Jocko Willink, *Freedom Equals Discipline: Field Manual* (New York: St Martin's Press, 2017).

make the transformation work. We need to drive conversations around it. In fact, overcommunicating these principles to the point where you're blue in the face is one of the most important items in the leader's toolbox.

THE AGENDA

The **TLC rhythm** agenda is one of the elements of the **TLC**. The **team** discusses the **TLC** elements in a short ten- to fifteen-minute regular (ideally daily) meeting.

Quite often, a meeting is held at a management level that consolidates all of the meetings from the other levels.

The **TLC rhythm** agenda:

- **north star**
- **team** ethos
- **results**
- **games**
- **players**
- Challenges and roadblocks
- Next actions

You can also include ***culture*** *and* ***brand*** *in this discussion from time to time.*

THE ELEMENTS OF RHYTHM AND HOW TO FACILITATE THEM

Next, we'll look at what these elements are in more detail, and then we will look at how to effectively facilitate each element.

1. Begin by discussing your **north star** and **team** ethos.

The leader chooses an element or a theme from a **team** ethos **asset** or from the **north star**, and then the **team** discusses it and has a conversation about the identity of the group and the **culture** of the company. This can go on for three to five minutes. The purpose is to share and collect stories and unify the *why*. Why do we exist as a company? As a **team**?

2. Discuss progress **results** and see how we are tracking to the BIG picture.

Look at the BIG goals of the company and the current **results** and progress of how we are tracking as a whole.

3. Now we get into the **games**, we look at the scoreboard, and we check out the **g**oals, **a**ctivities, **m**easures, **e**xpectations, and **s**upport of the whole **team**.

We mark up our scoreboards and discuss our activities, efforts, and challenges.

4. We then run the same process for each individual **player**, their **games**, and we update our scoreboards and support our **players** through coaching in fast feedback cycles of the daily **rhythm**.
5. The next part of the agenda is the twenty-four-hour action board.

The leader facilitates and coaches on what needs to be done to clear a path to create that focus.

For every measure in the **game** that does not show progress towards achieving our goals, we find a way forward. We coach and come up with ONE action to take in the next twenty-four hours to bring us back on track, and we write it up (on a whiteboard or digitally), and we commit to getting this done in the next twenty-four hours.

6. Once we've marked up all of our actions, the **team** comes together and goes around the circle and names one intention for the day, one point of focus of what they need to get done today. They give their most important thing, and we write it down.

Within ten minutes, the whole **team** has re-centred back towards their focus, and they're set up to have a productive day where we track and measure their success within a greater purpose, with a sense of achievement and alignment towards the greater path and movement.

Now, let's look a bit deeper into each of these conversations.

TEAM ETHOS CONVERSATION

Team ethos is the language of **leadership**—it is what unites and aligns us to a common purpose.

We run this with the **team** ethos **asset** and the **north star asset**, and we alternate between them.

The **assets** of **team** ethos are there to inspire and influence a different level of thinking and behaviour. We have a **team** *ethos* conversation at every stand-up meeting, and we are elevating our thinking towards the actions and the behaviour required for the whole company's cultural success.

Some people find it really easy to have a conversation around the **team** ethos. Some people find it very difficult to think of the right questions to stimulate this conversation. For most people I have worked with, **team** ethos conversations are among the hardest conversations to lead, and this can be one of the most difficult things to turn into a habit of how you communicate in your company. The leader of the meeting will point to the **asset**, whether it's a manifesto, a vision statement, or a value system and find questions to ask the group about the **team** ethos.

Remember this is about shaping the thinking of your people, so a great leader is a great facilitator. They'll be able to choose something off that **asset** and ask a challenging question that provokes and promotes good conversation. The most important thing to remember with your **team** ethos **rhythm** is to have conversations that matter to your **culture** every day.

An easy place to start is to come up with twenty preloaded questions you can use to start this conversation each day.

Example: Imagining that an aspirational value the company has in its **north star** is "Be Focused and Present."

Some questions could be:

1. What are we doing to create more focus in our work at the moment?
2. What are we focused on this week?
3. How are we bringing focus and presence to our **team** members?
4. Share a story about a time when you were the most focused you have ever been.

Example: If a values statement is: "Bring honesty even when it's uncomfortable," some questions you can ask are:

1. Where do we recognise honesty in this company?
2. Where have we noticed that we're not being honest?
3. What does honesty mean to you?
4. Who is the most honest person you know?

To do this well, you need to develop your skills as a facilitator. Please understand that this takes practice, and regular practice is required to get good at anything. In the beginning, your **players** may not be used to having these kinds of conversations and this can be uncomfortable—this is okay. It is okay to be uncomfortable at first. That is how we grow. That is how everything grows. As a transformational leader, you need to be comfortable being uncomfortable.

Over time, you will train your **players** to be able to ask a question and then allow space for people to think, reason, and really dig deeper into their own thinking and come up with an answer. Like all practices, this gets better over time. The heart of **rhythm** is about practicing your practices and the truth is that this is the hardest thing for most people to do.

Team ethos is about aligning our beliefs, questioning our beliefs, and remaining in integrity. The only way that can happen to transform a company is when we talk about it all the time, when we make it a priority to start with our purpose, beliefs, values, what we think matters most, and bring stories, examples, and difficult questions into this conversation so people are involved. If you don't involve people in this conversation, it will mean nothing to them, the **assets** will decline in value, your **TLC** will shrink, and getting to your **new normal** will be highly improbable.

The **team** ethos part of the agenda is to stimulate the conversation about the **team** ethos, to bring them back to **north star**, remind them of the identity, and strengthen the bonds. Sure, some people will not want to have the conversation in the beginning. Some people will be more introverted and quiet, and that's okay. When we get the **team** ethos conversation right, we are well on our way to creating one unified **culture**. This is worth three minutes a day. Trust me on this point.

GAMES CONVERSATION

Remember **games.**

- The Goals of the **team** aligned to the goals of **north star**
- The Activities that are the most effective in achieving the goals
- The Measures that make the activities and progress towards the goals Visible
- The Expectations that set the rules of the **Game** and examples that show the way
- The Support to perform in the **games** with the help of the group and the coach

The games rhythm conversation is all about the ongoing support and development, the daily coaching habit that helps us get a bit better each day. **Assets** of **games** are how we manage our improvement in the business, how we create focus around what matters, and how we create a coaching cycle that helps the **players** get a little bit better every single day. When you create an **asset** of **games** through an **event** of **games**, you're going to co-design it with people.

You're going to ask them, "What matters most?" Distil their thinking, and the output will be a clear scoreboard where we're measuring what action towards success looks like.

In the **rhythm**, we work on the performance within the **games** through coaching our **players.**

- Goals—How are we tracking towards our goals?
- Activities—Are we consistent in our efforts?

- Measures—Does the scoreboard reflect our actions and commitment to the goals?
- Expectations—Are we living up to the rules we set for ourselves?
- Support—What do we need help with?

PLAYER CONVERSATION

I said it before: late performance reviews are one of the stupidest problems in business.

We're always reflecting back on last quarter, on what a **player** didn't do or what they did do, and trying to adjust every behaviour in the future. This is not the way of the **TLC. Players'** conversations are about coaching.

They're about really identifying where the gaps are in the person's thinking and where the gaps are in the person's behaviour and doing small interventions for incremental change. It will become obvious in your **rhythm** when somebody requires more help, more assistance, more coaching, and to be able to help them perform at their best. You will know as a manager and a leader where the gaps are, and you'll be able to set time with the **players** in your **team** individually, after the **rhythm** session, to sit down with them and help them calibrate their own **TLC.**

Remember, we all have an internal **TLC.** We all have a direction we're moving towards.

It's a leader and a manager's job to be able to notice where to make the difference and help that person make small, incremental changes. Instead of trying to run your performance reviews by looking in a rearview mirror, perhaps you should invest in creating a coaching **culture** where support, feedback, and guidance happens on a daily basis and is valued by the people who receive it. The only way to do this is to create a consistent **rhythm** where this becomes the new norm.

Your **player**'s conversation will come naturally out of your **rhythm** provided the leader is the right fit. You'll know exactly what conversations need to be had and what interventions you need to take with this person.

EVENTS THAT RESET THE RHYTHM

Keep it growing and fresh.

One of the challenges you will inevitably face in **rhythm** is the repetition that it requires to maintain consistency. The way of the **TLC** is to keep it fresh and always growing. You do this by having regular **events** that reset the **rhythm.**

At each calendar **event**, you will step out of the **rhythm** to work on the **assets** of each **team** in close collaboration. Over the **events** cycle, you will reflect and refine your **team** ethos and the beliefs of each **team**.

In the next event, you'll examine some of the beliefs within the **team** ethos that aren't working, aren't true, aren't really embodied by the **team and then** shape it, shift it, and refine it. The power of the **TLC** is that when we do this process on purpose, it is a feedback and growth system.

Look at the **games**. You'll consider, is this the most important goal to be focused on measuring right now?

Are we doing the right activities to get us there?

Are our measures and scoreboards working?

Are we meeting our expectations to each other?

And you'll redesign the **games**.

You'll reset your scoreboards.

You'll put the new numbers up.

You'll air grievances.

You'll talk about what worked and what didn't.

You'll have some robust and valuable conversations.

And in this process, you'll be ready to come back again, fresh.

You'll be ready to enter the **rhythm** again with a new sense of shared purpose and **team** *ethos*, an improved set of **games** and an aligned group of **players** ready to create the **new normal**.

STORY TIME: THE RHYTHM

It's 6:00 a.m. in Dandenong factory. Fifteen people stand around a whiteboard, stretching, and turning as one lady named Ruth leads the charge for warmup exercises. People are just waking up. They're moving. They're getting into their bodies, and they're getting ready for the day's work. They're standing in a circle, having a joke and a laugh, and moving their joints to be able to perform their daily activities.

A lady named Leanne moves to the front and points to the company's manifesto.

Choosing an item to talk about for the day's meeting, she points to "You will be heard," and says, "Okay. Today we're going to discuss an item from the manifesto. That item is 'you will be heard.' What does this mean?"

The group starts sharing. One person named Joe says, "It means if we have an idea, people will listen to us." The group nods in appreciation to Joe's contribution.

A lady named Sally says, "No idea is a bad idea."

The group produces a small round of applause in recognition of Sally speaking up.

Sam, the supervisor, says, "When we have an idea to make the place better, we put it in the system, and management listens to us."

Everybody nods in agreement with Sam. Everyone is feeling good, appreciated, on the same page with why they are there, and how they can make the place better.

The next item they move into is the **results**.

Sam points to a chart on the wall and says, "We are 85 percent towards our goal for production for the month. Three, two, one, clap," and the whole group claps together in unison.

They look at the visual markers of improvement and feel a sense of satisfaction that they're moving towards their goals together. They go straight into each department, look at charts, and look at the production line's improvements each day marked with red and green. Everybody in the group knows that green is a celebration, which deserves some thunderous applause, and red immediately goes to discussing the next action to make it right.

They look at the **game** charts and someone says, "Did we do safety walks yesterday?"

"Yes," the group responds.

"Three, two, one, clap."

"Did we check the line filters?"

"No," was the response.

"Why didn't we check the line filters?"

"I thought it was Harry's job."

"Harry's away on holiday."

Immediately the task goes up on the board as a twenty-four-hour next action step. Sue is to check for line filters while Harry is on holiday in the Bahamas. The group forms together, and they look at the board for the progress they made yesterday, and they are set up to have a great day today.

Everybody puts their hands into the huddle, and three, two, one, clap. They're off into their workday, except Sam, who takes the information from the board in a quick snapshot on his phone, and he's off to another meeting.

When Sam arrives at the next meeting, there are heads of every single line on-site, scribbling their **results** and their responses onto the dashboards of the management room.

Looking around the room of management, it's updated each day. You can see every line in the factory at the top level as the managers assemble to discuss the bigger problems of the business.

Just as the frontline workers had discussed earlier, the manager, Steve, who is in charge, points to the values poster and says, "Let's talk about safety," and then he leads the **team** in a conversation about the safety procedures.

Everybody contributes. Everybody has a story to tell and something to share about how safety is important to them and how they're making their workplace a safer place.

On to goals: They point up towards the goals and say, "Here's how we're tracking for the month."

Every line on site is on track.

And we're making great headway towards our BIG goal. Then they look at each individual line.

They find two problems out of ten that the managers will spend their time focusing on that day. All hands-in.

The meeting is complete.

In less than two, ten-minute meetings, they have established the **team** ethos.

They've recorded the points of the **games**, and they know exactly where they're heading and where to put their resources in problem-solving.

Everybody is involved, engaged, and knows how to make today just a little bit better than yesterday.

It's by measuring what matters that we're able to focus and communicate on making things better. It is this **rhythm** that plays out every single day in this business, and the noise, distractions, and things that take away our focus become quiet and are replaced by conversations that matter, conversations about **culture**, conversations about productivity and improvement, and conversations involved in a **game** that everybody can play, win, get better at, and contribute to a cause that's bigger than themselves.

We now know what we need to do to embed the **rhythm** in our company.

We meet consistently with every **team** and **player** and work through the agenda. In doing so, we create the practices and habits that become the **culture**, the way we do things around here, our **new normal**.

SUMMATION

We began this book in **VUCA**, surrounded by chaos and complexity.

We needed a system to bring it all together, and we needed a method to help us transform our company.

John was stuck in the old world, looking for a way to:

- Remain profitable as his business grows in size
- Develop **leadership** capability
- Manage his company's performance
- Build a strong **culture** that people feel proud to be a part of
- Build a **brand** people ecognize and trust in the market

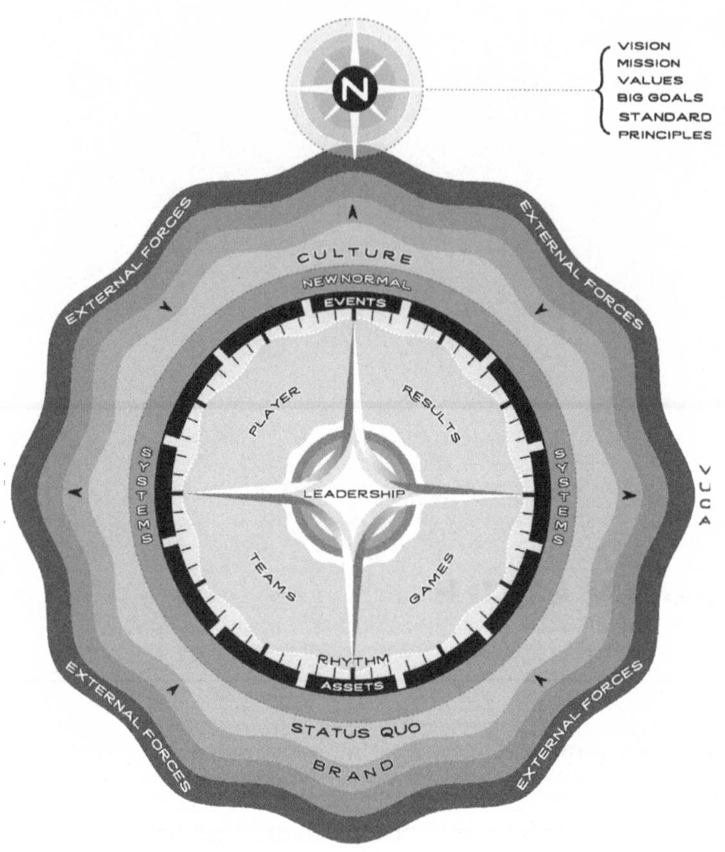

- Develop the foresight and discipline to develop and execute corporate strategy
- Find a better way of collaborating and working together

To move from:

- Volatility
- Uncertainty
- Complexity
- Ambiguity

And move towards:

- Vision
- Understanding
- Clarity
- Agility

We Now Have the Transformational Leadership Compass—The Dynamic Coaching System for creating BIG change.

Through understanding and action, we are able to use the **TLC** to create our **new normal**, our new world. By teaching this language and thinking to those around us, we are able to work together in moving the **status quo** world of **VUCA** to the **new normal** world, which is actually a drastic improvement.

In the **TLC** installation, we learned the language of the **TLC** and the dynamic elements of transformation. By understanding each of the elements, we installed your mental software and provided the foundations for the right discussions to take place and decisions to be made. Because this language is intuitive and simple, we can take others along for the journey and have the clarity required to navigate complexity and change together as one company.

It is with this understanding that we gain a whole picture of the company and can navigate the complex world of change and transformation by using the **TLC**—the transformational **leadership** compass.

In the **status quo** installation, we began mapping our **status quo**, and we learned the process of map-making, documenting our journey, and planning the steps ahead as our transformation unfolds. We use the **TLC** to create a living and evolving maps and plans that allow us to constantly evolve and grow through change and adaptation. As we go about the work of transformation, we take note of our current conditions, consider the elements of the **TLC**, and decide on the next step to move us forward in a deliberate and balanced manner. Over time, as we make these changes stable and constant, we build and document our **new normal** and shape the new world around us using the **TLC** methodology.

In the **leadership** installation, we defined what effective **leadership** means, and we went through the process of self-examination to document our own internal **TLC**. We made our declaration to the world around us and helped our people understand what **leadership** means at our company. Through this process, we were ready to develop leaders around us to take on the work of transforming our company and creating the **new normal**.

In the **north star** installation, we learned how to go about creating our **north star asset**. We now have our vision, mission, values, BIG goals, standards, and principles that will serve as the guiding light in creating our **assets** for our **players**, **teams**, **games**, and **results**. We then began the work of bringing this to life by working through each of the elements of our **TLC** and running **events** that create the **assets** we will use in our **rhythm** to create our **new normal** and direct our company towards our compelling future.

In the **change agents** installation, we gathered our **change agents** as we selected our group from all areas and levels of our company. We developed an understanding of how to go about the process of change based on the best models and practices available. We created the charter that defines the **change agents** group and began the work of developing our transformational leaders through the **TLC** process.

In **the culture** installation, we learned how our deep, taken-for-granted assumptions are at the essence of who we are as a company. Through the **TLC**, we are able to run **events** with our **players** and **teams** to consciously create our **assets** that, when practiced and refined over time in our **rhythm**, become our **new normal** and shape our **culture**.

In the **brand** installation, we learned that an authentic **brand** is an inside job. We shape the **culture** and express our **culture** as our **brand** to the world around us. In doing this, we can grow through matching our promises and messages to the desires and expectations of our customers. We can grow and expand because we are able to invite the world to be part of the value we create through our **culture** and express as our **brand** to the world around us.

In the **events** installation, we learned how to run our own **events** to bring our people together and work on improving our company. We used the best organisational development thinking to create forums where we can build our collective intelligence and make the changes we need to make to keep going and growing. By working through a consistent calendar of **events**, we make constant improvements a part of who we are, and we build our capability of responding to external **events** that require us to change the way we work as a company. We also learned how to create a calendar and bring people together to work *on* the company, improving our **teams**, **players**, **games**, and **results** as we move towards our **new normal.** Now we will use our calendar to practice our facilitation skills and create the **assets** required to transform our company.

In the **assets** installation, we learned how to create our **assets** using design thinking. We brought everyone together and worked on improving the company, and now we are able to create the plans and reference points to practice in our **rhythm.**

In the **teams** installation, we learned how they make up our organisational structure and developed an understanding of how to build different types of **teams** through the language of **team** ethos.

In the **games** installation, with our shared beliefs in heart and mind, we began to build the systems of management—the **games** that allow us to perform at our best and achieve our BIG goals together. We also learned how to design and develop our systems of management using a simple yet powerful process. We examined the evolution of management theory and emerged with a framework that allows us to improve our effectiveness, efficiency, and performance of our work. Perhaps most importantly through this process, we can help our **players** create their **game** plans and reduce the need for management.

In the **results** installation, we learned to monitor and share our **results** and involve our **players** and **change agents** to create better plans and strategies. We leveraged data visualisation and business intelligence and brought these ideas together in **events** to get a bigger and better perspective on our world, which allows us to create much more powerful strategies in moving towards our **new normal.** We know what we need to measure and monitor and have clear and effective systems for collecting, visualising, and collaborating on creating our strategies and tactics for moving forward towards our **new normal.**

In the **player** installation, we looked at the process of attracting, selecting, developing, and retaining the individual **players** who make up the **teams**, play the **games**, and produce the **results** of your company as we move towards **north star** and transform our company into the **new normal.**

Finally, in the installation of **rhythm**, we learned how to embed consistent communication and practice of the **TLC** elements through a simple agenda that addresses each of the **TLC** elements as we build the discipline and habits of our company. By running the **rhythm** and appreciating the **assets** we have created, we will bring it all together to create our **new normal** through consistent practice and dedication. We now know what we need to do to embed the **rhythm** in our company. We meet consistently with every **team** and **player** and work through the agenda. In doing so, we create the practices and habits that become the **culture**, the way we do things around here, our **new normal.**

Now go forth, dear reader, and transform your company with the TLC.

APPENDIX I

TLC INSTALLATION ASSESSMENT QUESTIONS

TLC LEADERSHIP ASSESSMENT QUESTIONS

TLC	Leadership
Leadership	Is the definition of **leadership** clearly defined, declared, and understood throughout the company?
Culture	Does the leader work to shape the **culture**?
Brand	Does the leader's communication match the **brand**'s promise?
Events	Does the leader facilitate **events** that involve the **players** in the change?
Assets	Has the leader created powerful **assets** with their **players**?
Rhythm	Is the leader supporting a consistent **rhythm** of communication and practice?
North Star	Does the leader clearly define and communicate the **north star** consistently?
Games	Is the leader aware of and across the **g**oals, **a**ctivities, **m**easures, **e**xpectations, and **s**upport for management?
Teams	Does the **leadership team** work cohesively together to balance the **TLC**?
Player	Does the leader make time to coach the individuals and consider their uniqueness and value in their development plans?
Results	Does the leader monitor and track **results** and take the full system into account in the decision-making process and strategy development?

TLC CULTURE ASSESSMENT QUESTIONS

TLC	Culture
Leadership	Are the basic assumptions and the **status quo** constantly upgraded through leadership communication?
Culture	Is the concept of **culture** clearly defined and understood at the company?
Brand	Is the **brand**'s promise owned and supported by the **culture**?
Events	Do we run **events** that celebrate our **culture**?
Assets	Do we regularly produce **assets** that document and express our culture?
Rhythm	Can we see our **culture** in our **rhythm** as a window into our way of doing things?
North Star	Does our **culture** embrace the **north star** and make decisions aligned to its direction?
Games	Do we, as a collective group of **players**, co-create, play, and win our **games**?
Teams	Do we share a collective purpose and ethos, and are we a true **team** of **teams**?
Player	Is each **player** the right fit for the **culture**?
Results	Is the **culture** effectively measured with the right tools and instruments?

TLC BRAND ASSESSMENT QUESTIONS

TLC	Brand
Leadership	Is the leader a spokesperson for the **brand**?
Culture	Is the **brand** a true expression of the **culture**?
Brand	Is our **brand** clearly defined and known to all in our company?
Events	Do we have **events** that celebrate, build, and refine our **brand**?
Assets	Do we have a well-designed collection of **brand assets**?
Rhythm	Do we have a regular practice of communicating and sharing our **brand** with the world?
North Star	Does who we claim we are as a **brand** match where we are heading?
Games	Do we play **games** that reflect our **brand** promise?
Teams	Do our **teams** take pride in representing our **brand**?
Player	Does the individual take pride in representing our **brand**?
Results	Do we have a constant stream of new enquiries and leads as a result of our expressed **brand**?

TLC EVENTS ASSESSMENT QUESTIONS

TLC	Events
Leadership	Does the leader facilitate regular **events** with **players** from all areas of the company?
Culture	Do we have internal **events** that celebrate the **culture** we have created?
Brand	Do we celebrate our **brand** publicly?
Events	Do we have a calendar of **events**?
Assets	Do we showcase our work and how we do it?
Rhythm	Do we create tradition through the consistent practice of **events**?
North Star	Do our **events** align and move us towards our **north star**?
Games	Do we regularly co-design, reset, and upgrade our **games** of management in participatory **events**?
Teams	Do we bring **teams** together and across functions to connect, create, and bond?
Player	Do we practice regular individual **player** coaching and development sessions?
Results	Do we analyse, strategise, share, and celebrate our **results** in an event forum?

TLC ASSETS ASSESSMENT QUESTIONS

TLC	Assets
Leadership	Does the leader appreciate and maintain the value of the **assets** through the **rhythm**?
Culture	Do we have **assets** of **culture** beyond **north star**, manifestos, **culture** decks, and live documents?
Brand	Do we have a well-designed collection of **brand assets**?
Events	Do we run a calendar of **events** to step out of the business and work on the business to create **assets** of all forms?
Assets	Does the company know what an asset is and how to use it?
Rhythm	Do the **assets** appreciate in value through the **rhythm**?
North Star	Do we have a clear **north star** asset?
Games	Do we have management asset systems of **g**oals, **a**ctivities, **m**easures, **e**xpectations/**e**xamples, and **s**upport?
Teams	Did the **teams** co-create the **assets**, and do they act like they own them?
Player	Do the **players** have their own **assets** of who they are, what they do, and how to best work with them?
Results	Do we use dashboards to inform data-driven decision-making across the company?

TLC RHYTHM ASSESSMENT QUESTIONS

TLC	Rhythm
Leadership	Does the leader make sure that the consistency of meetings, communications, and practices are improved and maintained?
Culture	Does our **culture** come through in our **rhythm**, and is it a basic assumption that we work to a **rhythm**?
Brand	Do we consistently share and document customer stories in our **rhythm**?
Events	Do we reset and improve our **rhythm** with regular **events**?
Assets	Do we use our **assets** in our **rhythm** to keep us focused on our commitments?
Rhythm	Is our **rhythm** existent, consistent, dynamic, and engaging?
North Star	Do we regularly refer to the **north star** as a guiding point for discussion and decision-making?
Games	Do we track and discuss our **g**oals, **a**ctivities, **m**easures, **e**xamples/**e**xpectations and receive coaching support in the **rhythm**?
Teams	Does the **rhythm** involve functional and cross-functional **teams**?
Player	Does the **player** participate in the **rhythm** to receive regular feedback?
Results	Are our **results** visible and openly discussed in the **rhythm**?

TLC NORTH STAR ASSESSMENT QUESTIONS

TLC	North Star
Leadership	Has **leadership** defined and clearly communicated the **north star**?
Culture	Does the **North star** provide broad guidance on maintaining and shaping the **culture**?
Brand	Does the **north star** appeal and match the **Brand** Avatar's own Vision, Mission, Values and Principles?
Events	Do we have regular **events** to update the **north star** and our progress towards it?
Assets	Is the **north star** displayed and discussed as an asset of direction?
Rhythm	Do we regularly refer to the **north star** as a guiding point for discussion and decision-making?
North Star	Do we have a **north star** defined and does it inform and direct every element of the **TLC**?
Games	Do our BIG goals, values, principles and standards align to our **games goals**, **activities**, **measures**, **expectations/examples**, and support?
Teams	Are the **teams** able to form and articulate their own understanding of the **north star** through their ethos?
Player	Does the **player**'s own purpose, calling, and values align to the **north star**?
Results	Do we measure and monitor both qualitative and quantitative progress towards or away from our **north star**?

TLC GAMES ASSESSMENT QUESTIONS

TLC	Games
Leadership	Is the leader aware of the **g**oals, **a**ctivities, **m**easures, **e**xpectations, and **s**upport for management?
Culture	Do the **games** match the values?
Brand	Do we play **games** that our customers/clients would like?
Events	Do we regularly hold **events** to co-design, reset, and upgrade our **games** of management?
Assets	Do we create clear and visible game plan **assets**, including **g**oals, **a**ctivities, **m**easures, **e**xpectations, and a live scoreboard?
Rhythm	Do we track and discuss our **g**oals, **a**ctivities, **m**easures, **e**xamples/expectations and receive coaching support in the **rhythm**?
North Star	Do the goals of our **games** match the BIG goals of our **north star**?
Games	Do we use **games** to manage our progress and engage our people?
Teams	Do the **games** balance skill level and challenge for the **team**?
Player	Does the **player** have a clear and valuable role to play in the **games**?
Results	Do we record and reflect on the **results** of our **games**?

TLC TEAMS ASSESSMENT QUESTIONS

TLC	Teams
Leadership	Does the leader build effective **teams**?
Culture	Does the **team**'s sub**culture** support the company **culture**?
Brand	Do we show the world how our **teams** make their dreams come true?
Events	Do we bring **teams** together and across functions to connect and bond?
Assets	Did the **teams** co-create the **assets** and do they act like they own them?
Rhythm	Does the **rhythm** involve functional and cross-functional **teams**?
North Star	Are the **teams** able to form and articulate their own understanding of the **north star** through their ethos?
Games	Do the **games** balance skill level and challenge for the **team**?
Teams	Does each **team** have a well-defined purpose?
Player	Does the **player** make a valuable contribution to the **team**?
Results	Does the **team** track, celebrate, and learn from their collective **results**?

TLC PLAYERS ASSESSMENT QUESTIONS

TLC	Player
Leadership	Does the leader make time to coach the individuals and consider their uniqueness and value?
Culture	Is the **culture** the right fit for the **player**?
Brand	Does the individual represent our **brand**?
Events	Do we practice regular individual **player** coaching and **TLC** reviews?
Assets	Do the **players** have their own **assets** of who they are, what they do, and how to best work with them?
Rhythm	Does the **player** participate in the **rhythm** to receive regular feedback?
North Star	Does the individual **player**'s own purpose, calling, and values align to the **north star**?
Games	Does the **player** have a clear and valuable role to play in the **games**?
Teams	Does the **player** make a valuable contribution to the **team**?
Player	Do we consider the individual's own development of hard and soft skills and styles?
Results	Does the **player** produce **results**?

TLC RESULTS ASSESSMENT QUESTIONS

TLC	Results
Leadership	Does the leader monitor and track **results** and take the full system into account in the decision-making process?
Culture	Does the **culture** make data-driven decisions?
Brand	Do we have a constant stream of new enquiries and leads?
Events	Do we analyse, strategise, share, and celebrate our **results**?
Assets	Do we use dashboards to inform better decision-making across the company?
Rhythm	Are our **results** visible and openly discussed in the **rhythm**?
North Star	Do we measure and monitor both qualitative and quantitative progress towards or away from our **north star**?
Games	Do we record and reflect on the **results** of our **games**?
Teams	Does the **team** track, celebrate, and learn from their collective **results**?
Player	Does the **player** produce **results**?
Results	Do we record and monitor the facts, and are we able to make decisions based on these objective measures?

APPENDIX II

EXERCISE

YOUR OWN INTERNAL TLC

Okay, dear reader, time to get to work and create your own internal **TLC**, the compass that guides your own **leadership**. We begin by doing this with your own life. Use yourself as the reference and don't worry about mapping this out for your whole company. We will be doing that later through the whole book. Grab your notebook and get this stuff out of your head and onto a page, so we can see it clearly. Do not try and get this perfect. Just sit for forty-five minutes and work through these questions, writing down what comes to mind.

Here are your questions, and there is a template for this at the back of the book and on the website at *www.bigchange.group/Resources/TLC.*

STEP ONE. WHAT IS MY OWN NORTH STAR?

Think of this as your highest personal vision, your personal mission, values, standards, principles, and your biggest, lifelong goals.

- My Vision: What do I want my life to look like in three years?
- My Mission: What am I working, fighting, standing for?
- My Values: What are the top five values I hold as priorities in my life?
- My BIG Goals: What are my two biggest goals?
- My Standards: What are the nonnegotiable standards that I have for myself?
- My Principles: What are the three biggest guiding principles I live my life by?

STEP TWO. WHAT ARE MY RESULTS?

What **results** are showing up in your life?

Write down all the current results you can think of that inform you about how you are doing in the following areas:

- Business and career
- Finances
- Romance
- Health and fitness
- Family and friends

- Personal growth
- Fun and recreation
- Physical environment

STEP THREE: WHAT GAMES AM I PLAYING?

Create **games** for each result area in your life that you would like to improve.

- Goals
- Activities
- Measures
- Expectations
- Support

STEP FOUR: WHO ARE YOUR MAIN PLAYERS?

- Who are the main individuals in your personal and professional life?
- What is important to them?
- What are their strengths and challenges?

STEP FIVE: WHO ARE MY TEAMS?

- What are the groups of **players** in my life that come together: the groups that are a part of my life, and the collections of people who are working together for the same goals?
- What types of **teams** are they?

- What do they believe?
- What is their ethos?
- What **games** do they play?

STEP SIX: WHAT EVENTS DO YOU NEED TO CREATE?

- What are the **events** that you plan and run?
- What **events** have occurred recently in your life?
- What have some of the greatest **events** in your life been?
- What **events** would you like to create?

STEP SEVEN: HOW DOES YOUR RHYTHM WORK?

- What does the average day look like?
- What are your habits?
- Are they consistent or inconsistent?
- What do you practice consistently?
- What do you communicate consistently?

STEP EIGHT: HOW DOES THIS SHAPE MY CULTURE?

- What is the **culture** I am part of?
- Are there smaller sub**cultures** that I am a part of?
- What role do I play in this **culture**?

STEP NINE: WHAT IS MY OWN BRAND?

- How do I think people see me?
- What do they think of me?
- How do I represent myself in the world?

STEP TEN: SHARE AND DISCUSS.

The final step is for you to take this to someone you know and trust and walk them through what you have written down. You will find it useful to ask them to respectfully challenge you in your thinking and to let them know that you would like them to help you identify any blind spots you might not be aware of.

This process should be a regular activity (aka **event**) scheduled into your calendar where you revisit these words and reflect on your world.

GRATITUDE

Thank you so much to all the people who inspired, participated, guided, and supported the creation of this first edition.

There are so many important people I want to include, so I have decided to create a living document of gratitude that you can find at: *www.bigchange.group/grattitude.*

To my family. My infinitely amazing wife, Fernanda, my mum, Maureen, and father, Nile, my amazing in-laws, Osanan and Ivanyr, my brothers Sam (both of them), sister, Emma, and all the extended fam...thank you, I love you.

To my kids, Tyler and baby Nile, may you share joy in a long life of love and learning.

Thanks to my nearest and dearest friends, you know who you are. Extra special thanks to Matt Lavars and Zulu Flow for always being there whenever I need ya.

Thanks to the Scribe Media Tribe for helping me through the process of writing my first book and supporting me through this journey with your unwavering grace and collective expertise.

Thanks to Jona for the help in designing the **TLC** model artwork and for putting up with my 10,000 change requests and to the genius of MUSUBI **brand** agency for their brilliant work in the **brand** architecture of BIG Change.

Thank you to all of my clients, colleagues, and teachers, past, present, and future.

Thank you to all the great thinkers referenced in this book.

And finally, a BIG thanks to you, my dear reader. I wish you every success.

ABOUT THE AUTHOR

For over a decade, organisational development coach Benny Ausmus has broken the mould of executive coaching and management consulting.

Refusing to limit his methods to a one-size-fits-all formula, he approaches each new project by merging hard data with strategic development initiatives, tailoring bespoke transformation programs for companies, teams, and individuals using his dynamic TLC coaching system.

Benny works seamlessly with each leader's individual strengths, challenges, and style to design, iterate, and execute powerful programs for improvement, growth, and exceptional ROI.

Now, in *The Transformational Leadership Compass*, he lays out this dynamic system of transformation to help leaders create the BIG changes required to adapt, thrive, and shape the future.

Made in the USA
Las Vegas, NV
01 May 2021

22317610R00246